101 DAYS
IN THE
GOSPELS
WITH
OSWALD
CHAMBERS

101 DAYS
IN THE
GOSPELS
WITH
OSWALD
CHAMBERS

including selections from
The Gospels Interwoven in the words
of the *New International Version*
by Kermit Zarley

Compiled by James R. Adair
and Harry Verploegh

VICTOR BOOKS

A DIVISION OF SCRIPTURE PRESS PUBLICATIONS INC.
USA CANADA ENGLAND

Copyediting: Barbara Williams
Jacket Design: Joe DeLeon

Library of Congress Cataloging-in-Publication Data

Chambers, Oswald, 1874-1917.
    101 days in the Gospels with Oswald Chambers : including selections from The Gospels interwoven in the words of the New International Version by Kermit Zarley / compiled by James R. Adair and Harry Verploegh.
    p.   cm.
    ISBN 0-89693-120-X
    1. Bible. N.T. Gospels—Meditations. 2. Devotional calendars. I. Zarley, Kermit. II. James R. Adair, 1923–   . III. Verploegh, Harry. IV. Bible. N.T. Gospels. English. New International. 1992. V. Title.
BS2555.C44   1992   92-17176
242'.5—dc20   CIP

---

1 2 3 4 5 6 7 8 9 10 Printing/Year 96 95 94 93 92

CONTENTS

Preface 9

Introduction: Oswald Chambers: High Climber 11

Key to Sources 16

1. The Beginning 19
2. Births of John the Baptist and Jesus Foretold 23
3. The Birth of John the Baptist and Joseph's Dream 27
4. The Birth of Jesus Christ 31
5. Jesus' Early Years 35
6. John the Baptist Prepares the Way 39
7. The Temptation of Jesus 43
8. Jesus the Lamb of God 47
9. Jesus Reveals His Glory and Authority 49
10. Jesus Teaches Nicodemus 53
11. John the Baptist's Testimony about Jesus 57
12. Jesus Talks with a Samaritan Woman 59
13. Jesus Begins to Preach and Heal 63
14. The Calling of the First Disciples 67
15. Jesus Heals Many and Drives Out Evil Spirits 71
16. Jesus Prays, Preaches, and Heals 75
17. Life Through the Son 79
18. Lord of the Sabbath 83
19. Jesus Begins the Sermon on the Mount 87
20. Salt and Light on to Oaths 91
21. An Eye for an Eye on to Treasures 97
22. The Sermon on the Mount Concluded 103

23. A Servant Healed and a Dead Man Raised **109**

24. Jesus Anointed by a Sinful Woman **113**

25. The Sign of Jonah and Doing God's Will **117**

26. The Parable of the Sower **121**

27. The Parable of the Weeds **125**

28. Jesus Calms a Storm **127**

29. The Healing of a Demon-Possessed Man **129**

30. A Dead Girl and a Sick Woman **133**

31. A Prophet without Honor **137**

32. Jesus Sends Out the Twelve **139**

33. Jesus Feeds Five Thousand **145**

34. Jesus Walks on Water **149**

35. Jesus the Bread of Life **153**

36. Many Disciples Desert Jesus **157**

37. Clean and Unclean **161**

38. Peter's Confession of Christ **165**

39. The Transfiguration **169**

40. A Boy with an Evil Spirit **173**

41. The Greatest in the Kingdom of Heaven **177**

42. When a Brother Sins Against You **181**

43. The Parable of the Unmerciful Servant **183**

44. Jesus at the Feast of Tabernacles **185**

45. The Cost of Following Jesus **191**

46. A Woman Caught in Adultery **195**

47. The Validity of Jesus' Testimony **197**

48. Whose Children? **201**

49. The Claims of Jesus about Himself **205**

50. Jesus Heals a Man Born Blind   **209**

51. The Shepherd and His Flock   **213**

52. Jesus Sends Out the Seventy-Two   **217**

53. The Parable of the Good Samaritan   **221**

54. Jesus' Teaching on Prayer   **225**

55. Six Woes   **229**

56. Warnings and Encouragements   **233**

57. The Parable of the Rich Fool   **235**

58. Do Not Worry   **237**

59. Jesus Teaches Watchfulness   **239**

60. The Unbelief of the Jews   **243**

61. The Narrow Door   **247**

62. Jesus at a Pharisee's House   **249**

63. The Cost of Discipleship   **253**

64. The Parable of the Lost Son   **257**

65. The Death and Resurrection of Lazarus   **261**

66. Ten Healed of Leprosy   **267**

67. The Coming of the Kingdom of God   **269**

68. The Parable of the Pharisee and the Tax Collector   **271**

69. A Rich Young Ruler   **273**

70. The Request of James, John, and Their Mother   **277**

71. Zacchaeus the Tax Collector   **279**

72. The Triumphal Entry   **281**

73. The Parable of the Two Sons   **285**

74. The Greatest Commandment   **287**

75. Warning about Teachers of the Law   **289**

76. A Widow's Offering   **291**

77. Some Greeks Seek Jesus   293

78. Signs of the End of the Age   295

79. The Parable of the Ten Virgins   297

80. The Parable of the Talents   299

81. The Sheep and the Goats   301

82. Mary Anoints Jesus at Bethany   305

83. The Passover Meal Is Prepared   307

84. The Last Supper   311

85. Jesus Predicts Peter's Denial   315

86. Jesus Promises the Holy Spirit   319

87. The Vine and the Branches   323

88. The Work of the Holy Spirit   325

89. Jesus Prays for Himself and All Believers   327

90. Gethsemane   331

91. Jesus Arrested   335

92. Peter's Three Denials   339

93. Jesus Sentenced to Be Crucified   343

94. The Death of Jesus   349

95. The Burial of Jesus   353

96. The Resurrection   357

97. Jesus Appears to Mary Magdalene
    and Other Women   361

98. On the Road to Emmaus   365

99. Jesus Appears to the Disciples   369

100. The Miraculous Catch of Fish   371

101. The Great Commission   375

Advice Given by Oswald Chambers at Age 23
to a Woman Who Had Accepted an Assignment
to Teach a Girl's Sunday School Class   379

PREFACE

This book contains a portion of Scripture for each day that you can comfortably read and assimilate in your devotional time. It is our hope that God's Word combined with enlightening comments by Oswald Chambers, the beloved writer of the classic devotional *My Utmost for His Highest,* will nurture you and help you climb to a new level in your walk with Jesus Christ.

Almost all of Chambers' comments are from a collection of some 10,000 excerpts from the author's books chosen by my long-time friend Harry Verploegh. Some excerpts are from Chambers' articles written for *God's Revivalist and Bible Advocate,* published by God's Bible School, Cincinnati.

It was in the mid-1980s that Harry "discovered" Oswald Chambers. Prior to then he had begun his current collection of some 100,000 quotations from various Christian writers. After he began his Chambers' collection, I vividly recall his raving about Chambers' uncanny knack for expressing Christian truth.

This intense interest resulted in Harry's compiling three topically arranged books of Chambers' quotations published by Oliver-Nelson Books: *Oswald Chambers: The Best From All His Books,* volumes I and II (both awarded Gold Medallions by the Evangelical Christian Publishers Association), and *The Oswald Chambers Devotional Reader.*

Thus Chambers became our logical choice as the inspirational writer for a new devotional book. We decided to draw Scripture from *The Gospels Interwoven,* compiled by Kermit Zarley, a chronological narrative harmony of the Gospels published by Victor Books in 1987. It blends details of accounts of the life of Jesus reported by Matthew, Mark, Luke, and John, all in the words of the *New International Version.* As a senior editor for Victor Books, I had been responsible for editing his excellent work.

Kermit Zarley* graciously gave permission to use selections from his work, and we chose 101 separate readings representing about two-thirds of the book's NIV section. Some portions consist of interwoven details minus repetition from two or more Gospel accounts (italicized words in these sections indicate words added to the NIV text for clarification); other readings are verbatim from the NIV, being accounts in the life of Jesus that appear in only one of the Gospels.

9

Almost all Chambers' comments cast light on one key thought in each of the 101 readings; in some instances excerpts illuminate entire Gospel passages.

We are indebted to Discovery House, Grand Rapids, Michigan, the U.S. representative of the Oswald Chambers Publications Association, South Croydon, Surrey, England, and to the Association itself for permission to include the excerpts from Chambers' writings.

The quotations have been slightly edited and styled from the standpoint of punctuation and spelling. Pronouns referring to Deity in Chambers' quotations are capitalized, whereas in the NIV text they are rendered in lowercase per NIV style. Bible citations in excerpts are from a version of the *King James Bible* in use in the early 1900s.

James R. Adair

*After becoming intensely interested in Bible prophecy in the 1970s, Kermit Zarley became a successful professional golfer on the PGA Tour. In his travels, he spent much time in libraries studying theological books. He became a writer, resulting in the publication in 1990 of *Palestine Is Coming* (Hannibal Books) concerning predicted events to come in the Mideast. He now continues his theological writing between play-for-pay golf tournaments on the Senior PGA Tour.

OSWALD CHAMBERS: HIGH CLIMBER

Even as a child, Oswald Chambers had utmost confidence in God. After he had gone to bed, older members of his family enjoyed listening to him pray as they stood on the stairway near his room. Once he asked God to send him two wild guinea pigs for pets, and morning after morning he inspected the chicken run to see if his visitors had arrived. Certain that God would not disappoint him, he continued to watch until finally, to his great delight, one morning he discovered two of the furry little animals. His childlike faith and simplicity remained throughout life.

Oswald was born July 24, 1874 in Aberdeen, Scotland, the fourth son of Clarence and Hannah Chambers. His father pastored a Baptist church in Aberdeen, and later served Scottish churches in Stoke-on-Trent and Perth; his last pastorate was in London.

Oswald unashamedly gave tribute to his parents for his godly heritage. When he was a student in the University of Edinburgh, he wrote:

"God is the mover, prime and sole, above and through circumstances. I feel traits in my character I knew not of before, and it causes me to bow in deeper gratitude for that home training. . . . Indeed we do not know how deep a debt we owe to our mothers and fathers and their training."

After he entered his teens and was living in Southgate, London, Oswald heard Charles Haddon Spurgeon preach. On the way home Oswald mentioned to his father that had there been an opportunity at the close of the service he would have given himself to the Lord. His father responded, "You can do it now, my boy," and there in the street beneath a gas lamp Oswald opened his heart to Christ. By this time his father had retired from the regular ministry, and Oswald was baptized and joined a Baptist church where his family were members. In time he became a Sunday School teacher and during the week took time to minister the Gospel to men — some of them ex-convicts — in lodging houses and missions.

In his early years Oswald blossomed as a musician and an artist. In Perth, he began his schooling in Sharp's Institute, and here drawing became a marked joy. While in Infants' Class, he drew a large golden eagle in chalks that remained on exhibit for several days.

When he was eighteen, Oswald earned an Art Master's Certificate, enabling him to teach and illustrate for his livelihood. He won a scholarship for study abroad but turned it down, noting that such ventures wrecked some men both morally and physically. Instead, he studied art at the University of Edinburgh; but at the age of twenty-three he decided to study for the ministry, following the counsel of several Scottish men of God. On November 11, 1896 he penned: "It would be playing with the sacred touch of God to neglect or stifle this strange yet deep conviction that sometime I must be a minister."

Oswald entered the Scottish Dunoon Training College in 1897 and here took a dominating position. Within a year he became a tutor in logic, moral philosophy, psychology, and art. In 1900 he prepared and published a book titled *Outlines for the Study of Historical Philosophy*. He also started a Browning Society, encouraging students and townspeople to become enthusiastic readers of the poetry of the Brownings — Robert and his wife, Elizabeth.

He became president of Christian Endeavor, leading special prayer meetings for young people and conducting a young men's enquiry meeting on Sundays at the college, where he would sit with students and talk as one friend to another. One student recalled that "the table-talk [with Chambers] taught us how to cultivate the art of conversation. Ability to change the theme and lift the conversation to a more elevated plane was characteristic of Mr. Chambers. Without monopolizing the conversation, he would regulate it and charm and entertain us all."

In 1902 Chambers began to concentrate more and more on being totally God's man, sharing with others the message of redemption in Christ that, along with sanctification, became so much the theme of his preaching and writings. He began to minimize such side interests as art, poetry, music, and philosophy, giving himself to more preaching. For a time his messages struck terror to the hearts of his hearers instead of confidence and love. However, in time as he supplied pulpits in various parts of Scotland, his intensity and vehemence gradually mellowed.

By this time Chambers was a tall, slender young man with a gaunt face and piercing gray-blue eyes set under a broad cleft of brow; his mouth was firm, his lips thin; and his accent decidedly Scottish. A minister who knew him wrote that "the whole together might have given an impression of austerity, but on the contrary; the countenance was unusually pleasing and inviting. This decided cast of features gave him a look older than his years," though at times "he looked a mere youth" and another time "a man of maturer years."

Without doubt, Chambers passed through definite phases in his spiritual climb. He often said, "Consistency is the hobgoblin of little minds." During a period at Dunoon he often tramped the Scottish hills with feelings of being a wretch far from God. Though God obviously used him to reach others for Christ, Chambers described that period as "four years of hell on earth." A friend observed: "In his own soul there was darkness and misery" and "he had never believed possible what the sinful disposition in him was capable of."

Yet Chambers was pursuaded that there was more to Christianity than he had experienced, prompting him to write:

Let me climb, let me climb, I'm sure I've time,
'Ere the mist comes up from the sea;
Let me climb in time to the height sublime;
Let me reach where I long to be.

Then came the day when Oswald Chambers abandoned himself absolutely to God, advancing to a new plateau of spiritual fullness that set him aflame in his remaining years to be an instrument of blessing to millions. While in Dunoon College as a tutor in philosophy, he heard Dr. F.B. Meyer speak about the Holy Spirit. Later in his room he asked God for the baptism of the Holy Spirit, "whatever that meant," he later wrote. Then followed the four years when God seemed distant and the Bible became "the dullest, most uninteresting book in existence," and Chambers saw the "vileness and bad-motivedness" of his nature.

During these valley years he testified that God spoke to him only three times — and in unusual ways! First, as Chambers sat in his room one night, his collie came in through the window, put his head on his knee, looked into his master's eyes for a few minutes, then went out again. Another time when Chambers was a guest of friends, a small boy, barefoot and in his nightclothes,

13

came up and said, "Mr. Chambers, I loves you," and went off to bed. Again, while Chambers was conducting a Christian Endeavor meeting, a retarded girl laid a bunch of withered flowers on the table for him, with a piece of paper on which was written, "With love from Meg."

Finally, God spoke to him through Luke 11:13 — "If ye then, being evil, know how to give good gifts to your children, how much more shall your Heavenly Father give the Holy Spirit to them that ask Him?" Though he had been born of the Spirit as a teenager, for a time Chambers viewed himself too unworthy to take God at His word to receive the fullness of the Spirit. Days passed until at a mission meeting he "claimed the gift of the Holy Spirit in dogged committal on Luke 11:13." But he still felt "dry and empty as ever, no power or realization of God, no witness of the Holy Spirit," he declared.

Then as he talked with a friend, he realized that he "had been wanting power" in his own hand, so that he could say, "Look what I have by putting my all on the altar." And then and there his heart was "filled to overflowing with the love of God," he wrote.

"On various occasions Chambers warned against the imitation of the experience of some great soul," according to his colleague and biographer D.W. Lambert. "What Paul, Augustine, Luther, and others went through were classic examples of how God could deal with souls in their desperate need, but they are not to be slavishly imitated. So we believe Chambers would not want any seeking soul to go through the long agony that was his until he came out into the glorious sunshine of the redeeming Christ. On the other hand his experience is a challenge to all for whom conversion and even sanctification have been but glib and superficial expressions."

From that time on Oswald Chambers became a mighty messenger of God, not only in the British Isles but to thousands abroad. He made at least two evangelistic trips to the United States to preach in holiness camps from coast to coast, and spent time teaching at God's Bible School in Cincinnati. This resulted in his writing 181 articles for the school's *God's Revivalist and Bible Advocate* from 1907 to 1916. His wife, Gertrude (Biddy), whom he married in 1910 and who in later years used her language skills to publish her husband's manuscripts and sermons, accompanied him in 1911 on a four-month visit to the States.

14

After this trip, Chambers returned to establish the Bible Training College in Battersea, London, to prepare young people for the Gospel ministry. However, in July 1915 the college was closed for the duration of World War I, and in October Chambers sailed for Egypt to join the staff of the Y.M.C.A. to minister to the Mediterranean Expeditionary Force at Zeitoun, seven miles outside Cairo. He was later joined there by Mrs. Chambers and their daughter, Kathleen.

Here, for some two years he extended himself to the limits of his endurance as he ministered faithfully to the troops who were guarding the Suez Canal during the Great War. Then in the fall of 1917 he fell suddenly ill and was rushed to a hospital in Cairo. An operation for appendicitis brought partial recovery. But on November 15, 1917, at the age of forty-three, Oswald Chambers heard God's call to heavenly realms. A prophetic statement he had once written had come true:

"I feel I shall . . . suddenly . . . flame out, do my work, and be gone."

A simple headstone in the military cemetery in Cairo marks his earthly resting place. On it: "A believer in Jesus Christ." Engraved on an open marble Bible at the base of the grave marker is his testimony taken from Luke 11:13—"How much more will your Heavenly Father give the Holy Spirit to them that ask Him?"

James R. Adair
Based on *Oswald Chambers: His Life and Work,* 1933

KEY TO SOURCES

The sources of Oswald Chambers' quotations appearing with daily Gospel readings in this volume are indicated in each instance by the abbreviation of the title of the Chambers' book from which the extract was taken. Page numbers shown relate to editions of Chambers' books published and copyrighted by Marshall, Morgan & Scott, London, England; and/or Christian Literature Crusade, Fort Washington, Pennsylvania.

In the source list, the word *Discovery* following titles and dates indicate Oswald Chambers' titles more recently published and copyrighted by Discovery House Publishers, Grand Rapids, Michigan. *Zondervan* indicates titles now published and copyrighted by Zondervan Publishing House, Grand Rapids. *Chosen* indicates books now published and copyrighted by Chosen Books, Tarrytown, New York. In all cases, rights have been granted by the Oswald Chambers Publication Association.

AUG	*Approved unto God,* 1946, 1948
BFB	*Baffled to Fight Better,* 1931, 1990, Discovery
BE	*Biblical Ethics,* 1947
BP	*Biblical Psychology,* 1962
BSG	*Bringing Sons unto Glory,* 1943, 1990, Discovery (combined with *Making All Things New*)
CD VOL. 1	*Christian Discipline,* Vol. I, 1935, 1936, 1985, Zondervan
CD VOL. 2	*Christian Discipline,* Vol. II, 1935, 1936, 1986, Zondervan
CHI	*Conformed to His Image,* 1950, 1985, Chosen
DDL	*Devotions for a Deeper Life,* edited by Glenn D. Black (Grand Rapids: Frances Asbury Press, © 1986, God's Bible School)
DI	*Disciples Indeed,* 1955
GR	*God's Revivalist and Bible Advocate*
GW	*God's Workmanship,* 1953
HGM	*He Shall Glorify Me,* 1946
HG	*The Highest Good,* 1937, 1938, 1940, 1992, Discovery

HRL	*His Resurrection and Our Life,* 1930, by Oswald Chambers Publication, Assoc. combined with *Bringing Sons Unto Glory, Making All Things New* © 1990, Discovery house
IWP	*If Thou Wilt Be Perfect,* 1941
IYA	*If Ye Shall Ask,* 1958, 1985, Chosen (*If You Will Ask,* revised title, 1989, Discovery)
LG	*The Love of God,* 1973, 1985, Chosen (Discovery, 1988)
MFL	*Moral Foundations of Life,* 1966
MUH	*My Utmost for His Highest,* © 1935, Dodd, Mead & Co., 1935; © renewed by Oswald Chambers Publications Association, 1963 (Discovery, 1989)
NKW	*Not Knowing Whither,* 1934, 1989, Discovery (combined with *Our Portrait in Genesis* under title *Not Knowing Where*)
OBH	*Our Brilliant Heritage,* 1929, 1930, 1931, 1975
OPG	*Our Portrait in Genesis,* 1957, 1989, Discovery (combined with *Not Knowing Where*)
PS	*The Philosophy of Sin,* 1960
PH	*The Place of Help,* 1935, 1989, Discovery
PR	*The Psychology of Redemption,* 1930, 1990, Discovery (under the title *Making All Things New,* combined with *Bringing Sons Unto Glory*)
RTR	*Run Today's Race,* 1968
SHL	*The Servant as His Lord,* 1957
SHH	*The Shade of His Hand,* 1936, 1991, Discovery
SA	*The Shadow of an Agony,* 1934, 1992, Discovery (combined with *The Highest Good*)
SSY	*So Send I You,* 1930
SH	*Still Higher for His Highest* (Grand Rapids: Zondervan Publishing House, by special arrangement with Marshall, Morgan & Scott; © 1970, D.W. Lambert)
SSM	*Studies in the Sermon on the Mount,* 1960
WG	*Workmen of God,* 1937

1

THE BEGINNING

In the beginning was the Word, and the Word was with God, and the Word was God. He was with God in the beginning.

Through him all things were made; without him nothing was made that has been made. In him was life, and that life was the light of men. The light shines in the darkness, but the darkness has not understood[a] it.

He was in the world, and though the world was made through him, the world did not recognize him. He came to that which was his own, but his own did not receive him. Yet to all who received him, to those who believed in his name, he gave the right to become children of God—children born not of natural descent,[b] nor of human decision or a husband's will, but born of God.

The Word became flesh and made his dwelling among us. We have seen his glory, the glory of the One and Only,[c] who came from the Father, full of grace and truth. From the fullness of his grace we have all received one blessing after another. For the law was given through Moses; grace and truth came through Jesus Christ. No one has ever seen God, but God the One and Only,[c, d] who is at the Father's side, has made him known.

JOHN 1:1-5, 10-14, 16-18

"The Word became flesh
and made his dwelling among us."

FROM OSWALD CHAMBERS

⋙ Almighty God is nothing but a mental abstraction unless He becomes concrete and actual, because an ideal has no power unless it can be realized. The doctrine of the Incarnation is that God did become actual; He manifested Himself on the plane of human flesh, and Jesus Christ is the name not only for God and Man in one, but the name of the personal Savior who makes the way back for every man to get into a personal relationship with God. BFB 90

꙾ In the Incarnation we see the amalgam of the Divine and the human. Pure gold cannot be used as coin; it is too soft; in order to make gold serviceable for use, it must be mixed with an alloy. The pure gold of the Divine is of no use in human affairs; there must be an alloy, and the alloy does not stand for sin, but for that which makes the Divine serviceable for use. God Almighty is nothing but a mental abstraction to me unless He can become actual, and the revelation of the New Testament is that God did become actual: "the Word was made flesh." Jesus Christ was not pure Divine. He was unique: Divine and human. BE 51

꙾ Jesus Christ is God-Man. God in essence cannot come anywhere near us. Almighty God does not matter to me; He is in the clouds. To be of any use to me, He must come down to the domain in which I live; and I do not live in the clouds but on the earth. The doctrine of the Incarnation is that God did come down into our domain. The wisdom of God, the Word of God, the exact expression of God, was manifest in the flesh. That is the great doctrine of the New Testament—dust and Deity made one. The pure gold of Deity is of no use to us unless it is amalgamated in the right alloy, viz. the pure Divine working on the basis of the pure human: God and humanity one, as in our Lord Jesus Christ. There is only one God to the Christian, and His name is Jesus Christ, and in Him we see mirrored what the human race will be like on the basis of Redemption—a perfect oneness between God and man. Jesus Christ has the power of reproducing Himself by regeneration, the power of introducing into us His own heredity, so that dust and Deity again become one. SHH 9

꙾ The tremendous revelation of Christianity is not the Fatherhood of God, but the Babyhood of God—God became the weakest thing in His own creation, and in flesh and blood He levered it back to where it was intended to be. No one helped Him; it was done absolutely by God manifest in human flesh. God has undertaken not only to repair the damage, but in Jesus Christ the human race is put in a better condition than when it was originally designed. It is necessary to understand these things if you are to be able to battle for your faith. SA 27

---

a. Or *darkness, and the darkness has not overcome*
b. Greek *of bloods*
c. Or *the Only Begotten*
d. Some manuscripts [of John 1:18] *but the only* (or *only begotten*) *Son*

2

BIRTHS OF JOHN THE BAPTIST
AND JESUS FORETOLD

I n the time of Herod king of Judea there was a priest named Zechariah, who belonged to the priestly division of Abijah; his wife Elizabeth was also a descendant of Aaron. Both of them were upright in the sight of God, observing all the Lord's commandments and regulations blamelessly. But they had no children, because Elizabeth was barren; and they were both well along in years.

Once when Zechariah's division was on duty and he was serving as priest before God, he was chosen by lot, according to the custom of the priesthood, to go into the temple of the Lord and burn incense. And when the time for the burning of incense came, all the assembled worshipers were praying outside.

Then an angel of the Lord appeared to him, standing at the right side of the altar of incense. When Zechariah saw him, he was startled and was gripped with fear. But the angel said to him: "Do not be afraid, Zechariah; your prayer has been heard. Your wife Elizabeth will bear you a son, and you are to give him the name John. He will be a joy and delight to you, and many will rejoice because of his birth, for he will be great in the sight of the Lord. He is never to take wine or other fermented drink, and he will be filled with the Holy Spirit even from birth.[a] Many of the people of Israel will he bring back to the Lord their God. And he will go on before the Lord, in the spirit and power of Elijah, to turn the hearts of the fathers to their children and the disobedient to the wisdom of the righteous—to make ready a people prepared for the Lord."

Zechariah asked the angel, "How can I be sure of this? I am an old man and my wife is well along in years."

The angel answered, "I am Gabriel. I stand in the presence of God, and I have been sent to speak to you and to tell you this good news. And now you will be silent and not able to speak until the day this happens, because you did not believe my words, which will come true at their proper time."

Meanwhile, the people were waiting for Zechariah and wondering why he stayed so long in the temple. When he came out, he could not speak to them. They realized he had seen a vision in the temple, for he kept making signs to them but remained unable to speak.

When his time of service was completed, he returned home. After this his wife Elizabeth became pregnant and for five months remained in seclusion. "The Lord has done this for me," she said. "In these days he has shown his favor and taken away my disgrace among the people." LUKE 1:5-25

THE BIRTH OF JESUS FORETOLD

In the sixth month, God sent the angel Gabriel to Nazareth, a town in Galilee, to a virgin pledged to be married to a man named Joseph, a descendant of David. The virgin's name was Mary. The angel went to her and said, "Greetings, you who are highly favored! The Lord is with you."

Mary was greatly troubled at his words and wondered what kind of greeting this might be. But the angel said to her, "Do not be afraid, Mary; you have found favor with God. You will be with child and give birth to a son, and you are to give him the name Jesus. He will be great and will be called the Son of the Most High. The Lord God will give him the throne of his father David, and he will reign over the house of Jacob forever; his kingdom will never end."

"How will this be," Mary asked the angel, "since I am a virgin?"

The angel answered, "The Holy Spirit will come upon you, and the power of the Most High will overshadow you. So the holy one to be born will be called[b] the Son of God. Even Elizabeth your relative is going to have a child in her old age, and she who was said to be barren is in her sixth month. For nothing is impossible with God."

"I am the Lord's servant," Mary answered. "May it be to me as you have said." Then the angel left her. LUKE 1:26-38

24

Mary Visits Elizabeth

At that time Mary got ready and hurried to a town in the hill country of Judea, where she entered Zechariah's home and greeted Elizabeth. When Elizabeth heard Mary's greeting, the baby leaped in her womb, and Elizabeth was filled with the Holy Spirit. In a loud voice she exclaimed: "Blessed are you among women, and blessed is the child you will bear! But why am I so favored, that the mother of my Lord should come to me? As soon as the sound of your greeting reached my ears, the baby in my womb leaped for joy. Blessed is she who has believed that what the Lord has said to her will be accomplished!" LUKE 1:39-45

Mary's Song

And Mary said:

> "My soul glorifies the Lord
> and my spirit rejoices in God my Savior,
> for he has been mindful
> of the humble state of his servant.
> From now on all generations will call me blessed,
> for the Mighty One has done great things for me —
> holy is his name.
> His mercy extends to those who fear him,
> from generation to generation.
> He has performed mighty deeds with his arm;
> he has scattered those who are proud
> in their inmost thoughts.
> He has brought down rulers from their thrones
> but has lifted up the humble.
> He has filled the hungry with good things
> but has sent the rich away empty.
> He has helped his servant Israel,
> remembering to be merciful
> to Abraham and his descendants forever,
> even as he said to our fathers."

Mary stayed with Elizabeth for about three months and then returned home. LUKE 1:46-56

"The holy one to be born will be called the Son of God."

From Oswald Chambers

❧ Adam is called the son of God. There is only one other "Son of God" in the Bible, and He is Jesus Christ. Yet we are called "sons of God," but how? By being reinstated through the atonement of Jesus Christ. BP 6

❧ On the basis of the Redemption, God expects us to erect characters worthy of the sons of God. He does not expect us to carry on "evangelical capers," but to manifest the life of the Son of God in our mortal flesh. LG 122

❧ We are not made sons of God by magic; we are saved in the great supernatural sense by the sovereign work of God's grace, but sonship is a different matter. I have to become a son of God by deliberate discernment and understanding and chastisement — not by spiritual necromancy, imagining I can ascend to heaven in leaps and bounds. The shortcut would make men mechanisms — not sons, with no discernment of God. If God did not shield His only Begotten Son from any of the requirements of sonship ("Though He was a Son, yet learned obedience by the things which He suffered"), He will not shield us from all the requirements of being His sons and daughters by adoption. PH 101

❧ There is only one beloved Son of God; we are sons of God through His Redemption. PR 52

❧ Jesus Christ was not [merely] a Man who twenty centuries ago lived on this earth for thirty-three years and was crucified; He was God Incarnate, manifested at one point of history. All before looked forward to that point; all since look back to it. The presentation of this fact produces what no other fact in the whole of history ever could produce, viz.: the miracle of God at work in human souls. CHI 33

---

a. Or *from his mother's womb*
b. Or *So the child to be born will be called holy*

3

THE BIRTH OF JOHN THE
BAPTIST AND JOSEPH'S DREAM

When it was time for Elizabeth to have her baby, she gave birth to a son. Her neighbors and relatives heard that the Lord had shown her great mercy, and they shared her joy.

On the eighth day they came to circumcise the child, and they were going to name him after his father Zechariah, but his mother spoke up and said, "No! He is to be called John."

They said to her, "There is no one among your relatives who has that name."

Then they made signs to his father, to find out what he would like to name the child. He asked for a writing tablet, and to everyone's astonishment he wrote, "His name is John." Immediately his mouth was opened and his tongue was loosed, and he began to speak, praising God. The neighbors were all filled with awe, and throughout the hill country of Judea people were talking about all these things. Everyone who heard this wondered about it, asking, "What then is this child going to be?" For the Lord's hand was with him.

His father Zechariah was filled with the Holy Spirit and prophesied:

"Praise be to the Lord, the God of Israel,
because he has come and has redeemed his people.
He has raised up a horn[a] of salvation for us
in the house of his servant David
(as he said through his holy prophets of long ago),
salvation from our enemies
and from the hand of all who hate us —
to show mercy to our fathers

and to remember his holy covenant,
the oath he swore to our father Abraham:
to rescue us from the hand of our enemies,
and to enable us to serve him without fear
in holiness and righteousness before him all our days.
And you, my child, will be called
a prophet of the Most High;
for you will go on before the Lord
to prepare the way for him,
to give his people the knowledge of salvation
through the forgiveness of their sins,
because of the tender mercy of our God,
by which the rising sun
will come to us from heaven
to shine on those living in darkness
and in the shadow of death,
to guide our feet into the path of peace."

And the child grew and became strong in spirit; and he lived in the desert until he appeared publicly to Israel. LUKE 1:57-80

AN ANGEL APPEARS TO JOSEPH IN A DREAM

Mary was pledged to be married to Joseph, but before they came together, she was found to be with child through the Holy Spirit. Because Joseph her husband was a righteous man and did not want to expose her to public disgrace, he had in mind to divorce her quietly.

But after he had considered this, an angel of the Lord appeared to him in a dream and said, "Joseph son of David, do not be afraid to take Mary home as your wife, because what is conceived in her is from the Holy Spirit. She will give birth to a son, and you are to give him the name Jesus,[b] because he will save his people from their sins."

All this took place to fulfill what the Lord had said through the prophet: "The virgin will be with child and will give birth to a son, and they will call him Immanuel"[c]—which means, "God with us."

When Joseph woke up, he did what the angel of the Lord had

28

commanded him and took Mary home as his wife. But he had no union with her until she gave birth to a son. MATTHEW 1:18b-25a.

"She will give birth to a son, and you are to give him the name Jesus, because he will save his people from their sins."

FROM OSWALD CHAMBERS

~ Jesus Christ is not an individual iota of a man; He is the whole of the human race centered before God in one Person. He is God and Man in one. Man is lifted up to God in Christ, and God is brought down to man in Christ. Jesus Christ nowhere said, "He that hath seen *man* hath seen the Father"; but He did say that God was manifest in human flesh in His own Person that He might become the generation center for the same manifestation in every human being, and the place of His travail pangs is the Incarnation, Calvary, and the Resurrection. AUG 70

~ According to the Bible, the Son of God became incarnate in order to bear away the sin of the human race. Before a man can take on him the sin of a family, he must be a member of it; and Jesus Christ took on Him the form of the human family that was cursed with sin, and in that human form He lived a spotlessly holy life, and by means of His death He can introduce the shamed members of the human family into the life He lived. Our Lord made human solidarity His own: He represents the vilest sinner out of hell and the purest saint out of heaven. He stands as the one great Representative of the human race, atoning for its sin. It beggars language to describe what He did—He went into identification with the depths of damnation that the human race might be delivered. BSG 51

~ Jesus Christ is God manifest in the flesh, not a Being with two personalities; He is Son of God (the exact expression of Almighty God) and Son of Man (the presentation of God's normal man). As Son of God, He reveals what God is like; as Son of Man, He mirrors what the human race will be like on the basis of Redemption—a perfect oneness between God and man. SA 35

~ Jesus Christ was born *into* this world, not *from* it. He came into history from the outside of history; He did not evolve out of history.

29

Our Lord's birth was an advent. He did not come from the human race; He came into it from above. Jesus Christ is not the best human being. He is a Being who cannot be accounted for by the human race at all. He is God Incarnate, not man becoming God, but God coming into human flesh, coming into it from the outside. His Life is the highest and the holiest entering in at the lowliest door. Our Lord entered history by the Virgin Mary. PR 29

---

a. *Horn* here symbolizes strength
b. *Jesus* is the Greek form of *Joshua,* which means *the LORD saves*
c. Isaiah 7:14

4

THE BIRTH OF JESUS CHRIST

This is how the birth of Jesus Christ came about. In those days Caesar Augustus issued a decree that a census should be taken of the entire Roman world. (This was the first census that took place while Quirinius was governor of Syria.) And everyone went to his own town to register.

So Joseph also went up from the town of Nazareth in Galilee to Judea, to Bethlehem the town of David, because he belonged to the house and line of David. He went there to register with Mary, who was pledged to be married to him and was expecting a child. While they were there, the time came for the baby to be born, and she gave birth to her firstborn, a son. She wrapped him in cloths and placed him in a manger, because there was no room for them in the inn.

And there were shepherds living out in the fields nearby, keeping watch over their flocks at night. An angel of the Lord appeared to them, and the glory of the Lord shone around them, and they were terrified. But the angel said to them, "Do not be afraid. I bring you good news of great joy that will be for all the people. Today in the town of David a Savior has been born to you; he is Christ the Lord. This will be a sign to you: You will find a baby wrapped in cloths and lying in a manger."

Suddenly a great company of the heavenly host appeared with the angel, praising God and saying,

"Glory to God in the highest,
and on earth peace to men
on whom his favor rests."

When the angels had left them and gone into heaven, the

31

shepherds said to one another, "Let's go to Bethlehem and see this thing that has happened, which the Lord has told us about."

So they hurried off and found Mary and Joseph, and the baby, who was lying in the manger. When they had seen him, they spread the word concerning what had been told them about this child, and all who heard it were amazed at what the shepherds said to them. But Mary treasured up all these things and pondered them in her heart. The shepherds returned, glorifying and praising God for all the things they had heard and seen, which were just as they had been told. MATTHEW 1:18a; LUKE 2:1-20

JESUS PRESENTED IN THE TEMPLE

On the eighth day, when it was time to circumcise him, *Joseph* gave him the name Jesus, the name the angel had given him before he had been conceived.

When the time of their purification according to the Law of Moses had been completed, Joseph and Mary took him to Jerusalem to present him to the Lord (as it is written in the Law of the Lord, "Every firstborn male is to be consecrated to the Lord"ª), and to offer a sacrifice in keeping with what is said in the Law of the Lord: "a pair of doves or two young pigeons."ᵇ

Now there was a man in Jerusalem called Simeon, who was righteous and devout. He was waiting for the consolation of Israel, and the Holy Spirit was upon him. It had been revealed to him by the Holy Spirit that he would not die before he had seen the Lord's Christ. Moved by the Spirit, he went into the temple courts. When the parents brought in the child Jesus to do for him what the custom of the Law required, Simeon took him in his arms and praised God, saying:

> "Sovereign Lord, as you have promised,
> you now dismissᶜ your servant in peace.
> For my eyes have seen your salvation,
> which you have prepared
> in the sight of all people,
> a light for revelation to the Gentiles
> and for glory to your people Israel."

The child's father and mother marveled at what was said about him. Then Simeon blessed them and said to Mary, his mother: "This child is destined to cause the falling and rising of many in Israel, and to be a sign that will be spoken against, so that the thoughts of many hearts will be revealed. And a sword will pierce your own soul too."

There was also a prophetess, Anna, the daughter of Phanuel, of the tribe of Asher. She was very old; she had lived with her husband seven years after her marriage, and then was a widow until she was eighty-four[d]. She never left the temple but worshiped night and day, fasting and praying. Coming up to them at that very moment, she gave thanks to God and spoke about the child to all who were looking forward to the redemption of Jerusalem.

When Joseph and Mary had done everything required by the Law of the Lord, they returned. MATTHEW 1:25b; LUKE 2:21-39a

"Glory to God in the highest and peace to men on whom his favor rests."

FROM OSWALD CHAMBERS

❦ Jesus is the "Prince of Peace" because only in Him can men have God's goodwill and peace on earth. Thank God, through that beloved Son the great peace of God may come to every heart and to every nation under heaven, but it can come in no other way. None of us can ever have goodwill toward God if we won't listen to His Son. HGM 9

❦ If you allow anything to hide the face of Jesus Christ from you, you are either disturbed or you have a false security. "My peace I give unto you" [John 14:27] is a peace which comes from looking into His face and realizing His undisturbedness. RTR 74

❦ In our own spiritual experience some terror comes down the road to meet us and our hearts are seized with a tremendous fear; then we hear our own name called, and the voice of Jesus saying, "It is I, be not afraid" [Matt. 14:27], and the peace of God which passeth all understanding takes possession of our hearts. RTR 54

❦ "My help cometh from the Lord who made heaven and earth" (Ps.

121:2). He will take you up, He will remake you, He will make your soul young and will restore to you the years that the cankerworm hath eaten, and place you higher than the loftiest mountain peak, safe in the arms of the Lord Himself, secure from all alarms, and with an imperturbable peace that the world cannot take away. PH 5

❧ The New Testament does not say that the angels prophesied peace: they proclaimed peace—"on earth peace among men in whom He is well pleased," i.e., peace to men of goodwill toward God (see Luke 2:14). PH 59

❧ The coming of Jesus Christ is not a peaceful thing,ʲ it is a disturbing thing, because it means the destruction of every peace that is not based on a personal relationship to Himself. PH 61

❧ The peace that Jesus gives is never engineered by circumstances on the outside; it is a peace based on a personal relationship that holds all through. "In the world ye shall have tribulation . . . in Me . . . peace" (see John 16:33). PH 63

---

a. Exodus 13:2, 12
b. Leviticus 12:8
c. Or *promised, / now dismiss*
d. Or *widow for eighty-four years*

5

JESUS' EARLY YEARS

fter Jesus was born in Bethlehem in Judea, during the time of King Herod, Magi[a] from the east came to Jerusalem and asked, "Where is the one who has been born king of the Jews? We saw his star in the east[b] and have come to worship him."

When King Herod heard this he was disturbed, and all Jerusalem with him. When he had called together all the people's chief priests and teachers of the law, he asked them where the Christ was to be born. "In Bethlehem in Judea," they replied, "for this is what the prophet has written:

" 'But you, Bethlehem, in the land of Judah,
are by no means least among the rulers of Judah;
for out of you will come a ruler
who will be the shepherd of my people Israel.' "[c]

Then Herod called the Magi secretly and found out from them the exact time the star had appeared. He sent them to Bethlehem and said, "Go and make a careful search for the child. As soon as you find him, report to me, so that I too may go and worship him."

After they had heard the king, they went on their way, and the star they had seen in the east[d] went ahead of them until it stopped over the place where the child was. When they saw the star, they were overjoyed. On coming to the house, they saw the child with his mother Mary, and they bowed down and worshiped him. Then they opened their treasures and presented him with gifts of gold and of incense and of myrrh. And having been warned in a dream not to go back to Herod, they returned to their country by another route. MATTHEW 2:1-12

The Escape to Egypt

When they had gone, an angel of the Lord appeared to Joseph in a dream. "Get up," he said, "take the child and his mother and escape to Egypt. Stay there until I tell you, for Herod is going to search for the child to kill him."

So he got up, took the child and his mother during the night and left for Egypt, where he stayed until the death of Herod. And so was fulfilled what the Lord had said through the prophet: "Out of Egypt I called my son."[e]

When Herod realized that he had been outwitted by the Magi, he was furious, and he gave orders to kill all the boys in Bethlehem and its vicinity who were two years old and under, in accordance with the time he had learned from the Magi. Then what was said through the prophet Jeremiah was fulfilled:

"A voice is heard in Ramah,
weeping and great mourning,
Rachel weeping for her children
and refusing to be comforted,
because they are no more."[f] MATTHEW 2:13-18

The Return to Nazareth

After Herod died, an angel of the Lord appeared in a dream to Joseph in Egypt and said, "Get up, take the child and his mother and go to the land of Israel, for those who were trying to take the child's life are dead."

So he got up, took the child and his mother and went to the land of Israel. But when he heard that Archelaus was reigning in Judea in place of his father Herod, he was afraid to go there. Having been warned in a dream, he withdrew to the district of Galilee, and he went and lived in their own town of Nazareth. So was fulfilled what was said through the prophets: "He will be called a Nazarene."

And the child grew and became strong; he was filled with wisdom, and the grace of God was upon him. MATTHEW 2:19-23; LUKE 2:39b-40

36

THE BOY JESUS AT THE TEMPLE

Every year his parents went to Jerusalem for the Feast of the Passover. When he was twelve years old, they went up to the Feast, according to the custom. After the Feast was over, while his parents were returning home, the boy Jesus stayed behind in Jerusalem, but they were unaware of it. Thinking he was in their company, they traveled on for a day. Then they began looking for him among their relatives and friends. When they did not find him, they went back to Jerusalem to look for him. After three days they found him in the temple courts, sitting among the teachers, listening to them and asking them questions. Everyone who heard him was amazed at his understanding and his answers. When his parents saw him, they were astonished. His mother said to him, "Son, why have you treated us like this? Your father and I have been anxiously searching for you."

"Why were you searching for me?" he asked. "Didn't you know I had to be in my Father's house?" But they did not understand what he was saying to them.

Then he went down to Nazareth with them and was obedient to them. But his mother treasured all these things in her heart. And Jesus grew in wisdom and stature, and in favor with God and men. LUKE 2:41-52

"He was filled with wisdom,
and the grace of God was upon him."

FROM OSWALD CHAMBERS

❧ The presentation of true Christian experience brings us face to face with spiritual beauty, a beauty which can never be forced or imitated, because it is a manifestation from within of a simple relationship to God that is being worked out all the time. There is nothing simple saving a man's relation to God in Christ, and that relationship must never be allowed to be complicated. Our Lord's childhood expresses this spiritual beauty—"And the Child grew, and waxed strong, becoming full of widsom." . . . Jesus Christ developed in the way that God intended human beings to develop, and He exhibited the kind of life we ought to live when we have been born from above. SH 77

~ The whole wisdom of God has come down to the shores of our lives in a flesh and blood Man, and John says we have seen Him and we know Him. PR 23

~ "Grace" means the overflowing nature of God; we see it in nature; we have no words to describe the lavishness of God. "The grace of our Lord Jesus Christ" is the overflowing of God's nature in entire and absolute forgiveness through His own sacrifice. BSG 47

~ The essence of the Gospel of God working through conscience and conduct is that it shows itself at once in action. God can make simple, guileless people out of cunning, crafty people; that is the marvel of the grace of God. It can take the strands of evil and twistedness out of a man's mind and imagination and make him simple toward God, so that his life becomes radiantly beautiful by the miracle of God's grace. BP 206

~ The one great problem in spiritual life is whether we are going to put God's grace into practice. God won't do the mechanical; He created us to do that; but we can only do it while we draw on the mysterious realm of His divine grace. BE 57

~ Jesus Christ came to make the great laws of God incarnate in human life; that is the miracle of God's grace. We are to be written epistles, "known and read of all men" (2 Cor. 3:2). There is no allowance whatever in the New Testament for the man who says he is saved by grace but who does not produce the graceful goods. Jesus Christ by His redemption can make our actual life in keeping with our religious profession. SSM 90

~ The surest sign that God has done a work of grace in my heart is that I love Jesus Christ best, not weakly and faintly, not intellectually, but passionately, personally, and devotedly, overwhelming every other love of my life. BP 134

---

a. Traditionally *Wise Men*
b. Or *star when it rose*
c. Micah 5:2
d. Or *seen when it rose*
e. Hosea 11:1
f. Jeremiah 31:15

6

JOHN THE BAPTIST
PREPARES THE WAY

T he beginning of the gospel about Jesus Christ, the Son of God.[a]

In the fifteenth year of the reign of Tiberius Caesar—when Pontius Pilate was governor of Judea, Herod tetrarch of Galilee, his brother Phillip tetrarch of Iturea and Traconitis, and Lysanias tetrarch of Abilene—during the high priesthood of Annas and Caiaphas, there came a man who was sent from God; his name was John.

The word of God came to John son of Zechariah in the desert. He came as a witness to testify concerning that light, so that through him all men might believe. He himself was not the light; he came only as a witness to the light. The true light that gives light to every man was coming into the world.[b]

In those days John the Baptist went into all the country around the Jordan, baptizing in the Desert of Judea and preaching a baptism of repentance for the forgiveness of sins and saying, "Repent, for the kingdom of heaven is near." This is he who was spoken of through the prophet Isaiah:

"I will send my messenger ahead of you,
who will prepare your way"[c]—
"a voice of one calling in the desert,
'Prepare the way for the Lord,
make straight paths for him.
Every valley shall be filled in,
every mountain and hill made low.
The crooked roads shall become straight,
the rough ways smooth.
And all mankind will see God's salvation.' "[d]

39

John's clothes were made of camel's hair, and he had a leather belt around his waist. His food was locusts and wild honey. People went out to him from Jerusalem and all Judea and the whole region of the Jordan. Confessing their sins, they were baptized by him in the Jordan River.

But when he saw many of the Pharisees and Sadducees coming to where he was baptizing, he said to them: "You brood of vipers! Who warned you to flee from the coming wrath? Produce fruit in keeping with repentance. And do not think you can say to yourselves, 'We have Abraham as our father.' I tell you that out of these stones God can raise up children for Abraham. The ax is already at the root of the trees, and every tree that does not produce good fruit will be cut down and thrown into the fire."

"What should we do then?" the crowd asked.

John answered, "The man with two tunics should share with him who has none, and the one who has food should do the same."

Tax collectors also came to be baptized. "Teacher," they asked, "what should we do?"

"Don't collect any more than you are required to," he told them.

Then some soldiers asked him, "And what should we do?"

He replied, "Don't extort money and don't accuse people falsely—be content with your pay."

The people were waiting expectantly and were all wondering in their hearts if John might possibly be the Christ. John answered them all, "I baptize you with water for repentance. But after me one more powerful than I will come, the thongs of whose sandals I am not worthy to stoop down and untie. He who comes after me has surpassed me because he was before me. He will baptize you with the Holy Spirit and with fire. His winnowing fork is in his hand to clear his threshing floor and to gather his wheat into the barn, but he will burn up the chaff with unquenchable fire." And with many other words John exhorted the people and preached the good news to them. MATTHEW 3:1-12; MARK 1:1-8; LUKE 3:1-18; JOHN 1:6-9, 15

THE BAPTISM OF JESUS

At that time Jesus came from Nazareth in Galilee to the Jordan to be baptized by John.

When all the people were being baptized, Jesus came to be baptized too. John tried to deter him, saying, "I need to be baptized by you, and do you come to me?" Jesus replied, "Let it be so now; it is proper for us to do this to fulfill all righteousness." Then John consented, and Jesus was baptized by John in the Jordan. As Jesus went up out of the water he was praying. At that moment he saw heaven being torn open and the Spirit of God descending in bodily form like a dove and lighting on him. And a voice came from heaven: "You are my Son, whom I love; with you I am well pleased."

Now Jesus himself was about thirty years old when he began his ministry. MATTHEW 3:13-17; MARK 1:9-11; LUKE 3:21-23a

"Jesus came from Nazareth in Galilee
to the Jordan to be baptized by John."

FROM OSWALD CHAMBERS

ᴈ John's baptism was a baptism of repentance from sin, and that was the baptism with which Jesus was baptized. He was baptized into sin—*made to be sin*—and that is why His Father was well pleased with Him. PR 52

ᴈ The baptism of our Lord was an extraordinary spiritual experience to Himself. "And there came a voice from heaven, saying, 'Thou art My beloved Son, in whom I am well pleased.' " We have no experience like that; it stands unique. There is only one beloved Son of God; we are sons of God through His redemption. PR 52

ᴈ Jesus Christ is the true Baptizer; He baptizes with the Holy Ghost. He is the Lamb of God which taketh away the sin of the world—*my* sin. He is the One who can make me like Himself; the baptism of John could not do that. PR 49

ᴈ At His baptism the Son of God as Son of Man, i.e., as the whole human race rightly related to God, took on Himself the sin of the whole world; that is why He was baptized with John's baptism, which was a baptism of repentance from sin. PR 85

ᴈ At His baptism Jesus Christ accepted the vocation of bearing away

41

the sin of the world, and immediately He was put by God's Spirit into the testing machine of the devil. But He did not "tire"; He went through the temptations "without sin" and retained the possessions of His personality intact. PS 56

---

a. Some manuscripts [of Mark 1:1] do not have *the Son of God*
b. Or *This was the true light that gives light to every man who comes into the world*
c. Malachi 3:1
d. Isaiah 40:3-5

7

THE TEMPTATION OF JESUS

t once Jesus, full of the Holy Spirit, returned from the Jordan and was led by the Spirit out into the desert to be tempted by the devil. For forty days he was being tempted by Satan. Fasting forty days and forty nights, he ate nothing, and at the end of those days he was hungry.

The tempter came to him and said, "If you are the Son of God, tell these stones to become bread."

Jesus answered, "It is written: 'Man does not live on bread alone, but on every word that comes from the mouth of God.' "[a]

Then the devil took him to the holy city, Jerusalem, and had him stand on the highest point of the temple. "If you are the Son of God," he said, "throw yourself down from here. For it is written:

" 'He will command his angels concerning you,
to guard you carefully;
they will lift you up in their hands,
so that you will not strike your foot
against a stone.' "[b]

Jesus answered him, "It is also written: 'Do not put the Lord your God to the test.'[c]"

Again, the devil took him to a very high mountain and showed him in an instant all the kingdoms of the world. And he said to him, "All this authority and splendor I will give you, for it has been given to me, and I can give it to anyone I want to. So if you will bow down and worship me, it will all be yours."

Jesus said to him, "Away from me, Satan! For it is written: 'Worship the Lord your God, and serve him only.' "[d]

When the devil had finished all this tempting, he left him until an opportune time. *Jesus* was with the wild animals, and angels came and attended him. MATTHEW 4:1-11; MARK 1:12-13; LUKE 4:1-13

"Jesus . . . was led by the Spirit out into
the desert to be tempted by the devil."

FROM OSWALD CHAMBERS

➣ To say that Jesus Christ could not be tempted flatly contradicts the Word of God—He was "in all points tempted like as we are, yet without sin" (Heb. 4:15). BP 33

➣ Jesus Christ was tempted, and so shall we be tempted when we are rightly related to God. BP 191

➣ We have to get rid of the idea that because Jesus was God He could not be tempted. Almighty God cannot be tempted, but in Jesus Christ we deal with God as man, a unique Being—God-Man. It was as Son of Man that "He fought the battle, and proved the possibility of victory." After His baptism, Satan, by the direct permission of the Holy Ghost, tested the faith of Jesus. ("And straightway the Spirit driveth Him forth into the wilderness." Mark 1:12.) Satan broke what Adam held straight off, but he could not break what Jesus held in His person, though he tested Him in every conceivable way; therefore, having Himself "suffered being tempted, He is able to succor them that are tempted (Heb. 2:18)." CHI 56

➣ Having "suffered being tempted," He knows how terrific are the onslaughts of the devil against human nature unaided; He has been there; therefore, He can be touched with the feeling of our infirmities. God Almighty was never "tempted in all points like as we are"—Jesus Christ was. CHI 99

➣ Satan said to Jesus, "If Thou be the Son of God, cast Thyself down from hence," and to us he says, "If you are saved and sanctified and true to God, everyone you know should be saved too." If that were true, Jesus Christ is wrong in His revelation of God. If by our salvation and right relationship to God, we can be the means of turning our world upside down, what has Jesus Christ been doing all these years? The temptation is to claim that God does some-

44

thing that will prove who we are and what He has done for us. It is a temptation of the devil, and can only be detected as a temptation by the Spirit of God. LG 153

❧ The records of our Lord's temptations are given not that we might fathom Him, but that we might know what to expect when we are regenerated. When we are born again of the Spirit of God and enter into fellowship with Jesus Christ, then the temptations of our Lord are applicable to us. We are apt to imagine that when we are saved and sanctified, we are delivered from temptation; we are not; we are loosened into it. Before we are born again, we are not free enough to be tempted, neither morally nor spiritually. When we are born into the kingdom of God, we get our first introduction into what God calls temptation; viz., the temptations of His Son. God does not shield any man or woman from the requirements of a full-grown man or woman. The Son of God is submitted to temptations in our individual lives, and He expects us to remain loyal to Him. PR 61

❧ Satan tried to put Jesus Christ on the way to becoming King of the world and Savior of men in a way other than that predetermined by God. The devil does not tempt us to do wrong things; he tries to make us lose what God has put into us by regeneration, the possibility of being of value to God. When we are born from above, the central citadel of the devil's attack is the same in us as it was in our Lord: viz., to do God's will in our own way. PR 63

---

a. Deuteronomy 8:3
b. Psalm 91:11-12
c. Deuteronomy 6:16
d. Deuteronomy 6:13

8

JESUS THE LAMB OF GOD

ow this was John's testimony when the Jews of Jerusalem sent priests and Levites to ask him who he was. He did not fail to confess, but confessed freely, "I am not the Christ."

They asked him, "Then who are you? Are you Elijah?"

He said, "I am not."

"Are you the Prophet?"

He answered, "No."

Finally they said, "Who are you? Give us an answer to take back to those who sent us. What do you say about yourself?"

John replied in the words of Isaiah the prophet, "I am the voice of one calling in the desert, 'Make straight the way for the Lord.' "[a]

Now some Pharisees who had been sent questioned him, "Why then do you baptize if you are not the Christ, nor Elijah, nor the Prophet?"

"I baptize with[b] water," John replied, "but among you stands one you do not know. He is the one who comes after me, the thongs of whose sandals I am not worthy to untie."

This all happened at Bethany on the other side of the Jordan, where John was baptizing.

The next day John saw Jesus coming toward him and said, "Look, the Lamb of God, who takes away the sin of the world! This is the one I meant when I said, 'A man who comes after me has surpassed me because he was before me.' I myself did not know him, but the reason I came baptizing with water was that he might be revealed to Israel."

Then John gave this testimony: "I saw the Spirit come down from heaven as a dove and remain on him. I would not have known him, except that the one who sent me to baptize with water told me, 'The man on whom you see the Spirit come down and remain is he who will baptize with the Holy Spirit.' I have seen and I testify that this is the Son of God." JOHN 1:19-34

"Look, the Lamb of God, who takes away the sins of the world!"

FROM OSWALD CHAMBERS

In the days of His flesh, Jesus Christ exhibited this divine paradox of the Lion and the Lamb. He was the Lion in majesty, rebuking the winds and demons; He was the Lamb in meekness, "who when He was reviled, reviled not again" (2 Peter 2:23). He was the Lion in power, raising the dead; He was the Lamb in patience—who was "brought as a lamb to the slaughter, and as a sheep before her shearers is dumb, so He openeth not His mouth" (Isa. 53:7). He was the Lion in authority—"Ye have heard that it hath been said . . . *but I say unto you";* He was the Lamb in gentleness— "Suffer the little children to come unto Me . . . and He took them up in His arms, put His hands upon them, and blessed them" (Mark 10:14).

In our personal lives Jesus Christ proves Himself to be all this— He is the Lamb to expiate our sins, to lift us out of condemnation and plant within us His own heredity of holiness; He is the Lion to rule over us, so that we gladly say, "The government of this life shall be upon His shoulders." And what is true in individual life is to be true also in the universe at large. The time is coming when the Lion of the tribe of Judah shall reign, and when "the kingdoms of this world are become the kingdoms of our Lord, and of His Christ" (Rev. 11:15). CHI 121

He came down to the lowest reach of creation in order to bring back the whole human race to God, and in order to do this He must take upon Him, as representative Man, the whole massed sin of the race. That is why He is called "the Lamb of God." PR 52

---

a. Isaiah 40:3
b. Or *in* [and hereinafter, following *baptize*]

48

9

JESUS REVEALS HIS GLORY
AND AUTHORITY

On the third day a wedding took place at Cana in Galilee. Jesus' mother was there, and Jesus and his disciples had also been invited to the wedding. When the wine was gone, Jesus' mother said to him, "They have no more wine."

"Dear woman, why do you involve me?" Jesus replied. "My time has not yet come."

His mother said to the servants, "Do whatever he tells you."

Nearby stood six stone water jars, the kind used by the Jews for ceremonial washing, each holding from twenty to thirty gallons.[a]

Jesus said to the servants, "Fill the jars with water;" so they filled them to the brim.

Then he told them, "Now draw some out and take it to the master of the banquet."

They did so, and the master of the banquet tasted the water that had been turned into wine. He did not realize where it had come from, though the servants who had drawn the water knew. Then he called the bridegroom aside and said, "Everyone brings out the choice wine first and then the cheaper wine after the guests have had too much to drink; but you have saved the best till now."

This, the first of his miraculous signs, Jesus performed in Cana of Galilee. He thus revealed his glory, and his disciples put their faith in him. JOHN 2:1-11

JESUS CLEARS THE TEMPLE

After this he went down to Capernaum with his mother and brothers and his disciples. There they stayed for a few days.

When it was almost time for the Jewish Passover, Jesus went up to Jerusalem. In the temple courts he found men selling cattle, sheep and doves, and others sitting at tables exchanging money. So he made a whip out of cords, and drove all from the temple area, both sheep and cattle; he scattered the coins of the money changers and overturned their tables. To those who sold doves he said, "Get these out of here! How dare you turn my Father's house into a market!"

His disciples remembered that it is written: "Zeal for your house will consume me."[b]

Then the Jews demanded of him, "What miraculous sign can you show us to prove your authority to do all this?"

Jesus answered them, "Destroy this temple, and I will raise it again in three days."

The Jews replied, "It has taken forty-six years to build this temple, and you are going raise it in three days?" But the temple he had spoken of was his body. After he was raised from the dead, his disciples recalled what he had said. Then they believed the Scripture and the words that Jesus had spoken.

Now while he was in Jerusalem at the Passover Feast, many people saw the miraculous signs he was doing and believed in his name.[c] But Jesus would not entrust himself to them, for he knew all men. He did not need man's testimony about man, for he knew what was in a man. JOHN 2:12-25

"So he made a whip . . .
and drove all from the temple. . . .
'Get these out of here!
How dare you turn my Father's house
into a market!' "

FROM OSWALD CHAMBERS

    When the Lord visits the body of a man, the traffic in the man's soul awakens self-love, self-sympathy, and self-pity; and our Lord, who is the truth, scourges them out of the temple. (He does not scourge the temple.) He scourges the whole defiling crew that have no business there, out of the temple, and He says, "Make not My

50

Father's house a house of merchandise." Note that phrase, "My Father's house." Talk about the dignity of the human body! Would that every one of us could realize, when we think of our own bodies, that Jesus Christ means that our bodies are His Father's house. And what did He accuse them of? He accused them of making "My Father's house a house of merchandise." Let this searching go home in every one of us. What am I doing in my body? Am I using my eyes, my ears, my tongue, my heart, my mind, my imagination for the glory and worship of God; or am I making merchandise for myself? The temple of God must be just and holy. When once the Lord has cleansed the defilement out of a man, there is no phrase that expresses his cleanness so marvelously as the phrase of the psalmist—"whiter than snow." GR 6-10-1910

---

a. Greek *two to three metretes* (probably about 75 to 115 liters)
b. Psalm 69:9
c. Or *and believed in him*

10

JESUS TEACHES NICODEMUS

ow there was a man of the Pharisees named Nicodemus, a member of the Jewish ruling council. He came to Jesus at night and said, "Rabbi, we know you are a teacher who has come from God. For no one could perform the miraculous signs you are doing if God were not with him."

In reply Jesus declared, "I tell you the truth, no one can see the kingdom of God unless he is born again."[a]

"How can a man be born when he is old?" Nicodemus asked. "Surely he cannot enter a second time into his mother's womb to be born!"

Jesus answered, "I tell you the truth, no one can enter the kingdom of God unless he is born of water and the Spirit. Flesh gives birth to flesh, but the Spirit[b] gives birth to spirit. You should not be surprised at my saying, 'You[c] must be born again.' The wind blows wherever it pleases. You hear its sound, but you cannot tell where it comes from or where it is going. So it is with everyone born of the Spirit."

"How can this be?" Nicodemus asked.

"You are Israel's teacher," said Jesus, "and do you not understand these things? I tell you the truth, we speak of what we know, and we testify to what we have seen, but still you people do not accept our testimony. I have spoken to you of earthly things and you do not believe; how then will you believe if I speak of heavenly things? No one has ever gone into heaven except the one who came from heaven—the Son of Man.[d] Just as Moses lifted up the snake in the desert, so the Son of Man must be lifted up, that everyone who believes in him may have eternal life.[e]

"For God so loved the world that he gave his one and only

53

Son,[f] that whoever believes in him shall not perish but have eternal life. For God did not send his Son into the world to condemn the world, but to save the world through him. Whoever believes in him is not condemned, but whoever does not believe stands condemned already because he has not believed in the name of God's one and only Son.[g] This is the verdict: Light has come into the world, but men loved darkness instead of light because their deeds were evil. Everyone who does evil hates the light, and will not come into the light for fear that his deeds will be exposed. But whoever lives by the truth comes into the light, so that it may be seen plainly that what he has done has been done through God."[h] JOHN 3:1-21

"You must be born again."

FROM OSWALD CHAMBERS

❧ Are you quite certain you are incapable of *"seeing"* or *"entering into"* the kingdom of God *yourself?* Are you quite persuaded that your gifts, your morality, your religion, cannot enable you to obey God or please Him? If so, thank God you have come to the initial place for entering the kingdom of heaven. Matthew 5:3: "Blessed are the poor in spirit; for theirs is the kingdom of heaven." That means that you know you are a poor, pauper soul, and must receive something from God and be *remade* if you are ever to be what God wants you to be. Read Luke 11 and 13, for that is the simple, scriptural way of receiving the life which will do *in you* what Jesus Christ did *for you.* Ever remember to honor the Holy Ghost in your regeneration. GR 1911

❧ Human earnestness and vowing cannot make a man a disciple of Jesus Christ any more than it can turn him into an angel; a man must receive something, and that is the meaning of being born again. When once a man is struck by his need of the Holy Spirit, God will put the Holy Spirit into his spirit. In regeneration, a man's personal spirit is energized by the Holy Spirit, and the Son of God is formed in him (Gal. 1:15-16; 4:19). This is the New Testament evangel, and it needs to be restated. New birth refers not only to a man's eternal salvation, but to his being of value to God in this order of things; it means infinitely more than being delivered from sin and from hell. The gift of the essential nature of God is made

54

efficacious in us by the entering in of the Holy Spirit; He imparts to us the quickening life of the Son of God, and we are lifted into the domain where Jesus lives. LG 113

⁊ Some teachers make new birth a simple and natural thing; they say it is necessary, but a necessity along the line of natural development. When Jesus Christ talks about it, He implies that the need to be born again is an indication of something radically wrong—"Marvel not that I said unto thee, Ye must be born again." It is a crisis. HGM 54

⁊ The natural man does not want to be born again. If a man's morality is well within his own grasp and he has enough religion to give the right tone to his natural life, to talk about being born again seems utterly needless. The natural man is not in distress; he is not conscious of conviction of sin, or of any disharmony; he is quite contented and at peace. Conviction of sin is the realization that my natural life is based on a disposition that will not have Jesus Christ. The Gospel does not present what the natural man wants but what he needs, and the Gospel awakens an intense resentment as well as an intense craving. We will take God's blessings and loving-kindnesses and prosperities, but when it comes to the need of having our disposition altered, there is opposition at once. SHL 40

⁊ In new birth God does three impossible things; impossible, that is, from the rational standpoint. The first is to make a man's past as though it had never been; the second, to make a man all over again; and the third, to make a man as certain of God as God is of Himself. New birth does not mean merely salvation from hell, but something more radical, something which tells in a man's actual life. PH 183

⁊ When we are born from above, the realization dawns that we are built for God, not for ourselves: "He hath made me." We are brought, by means of new birth, into the individual realization of God's great purpose for the human race, and all our small, miserable, parochial notions disappear. SSY 103

a. Or *born from above* [and hereinafter]
b. Or *but spirit*
c. The Greek is plural
d. Some manuscripts [of John 3:13] *Man, who is in heaven*
e. Or *believes may have eternal life in him*

f. Or *his only begotten Son*
g. Or *God's only begotten Son*
h. Some interpreters end the quotation after [the previous paragraph]

11

JOHN THE BAPTIST'S TESTIMONY ABOUT JESUS

After this, Jesus and his disciples went out into the Judean countryside, where he spent some time with them, and baptized. Now John also was baptizing at Aenon near Salim, because there was plenty of water, and people were constantly coming to be baptized. (This was before John was put in prison.) An argument developed between some of John's disciples and a certain Jew[a] over the matter of ceremonial washing. They came to John and said to him, "Rabbi, that man who was with you on the other side of the Jordan—the one you testified about—well, he is baptizing, and everyone is going to him."

To this John replied, "A man can receive only what is given him from heaven. You yourselves can testify that I said, 'I am not the Christ but am sent ahead of him.' The bride belongs to the bridegroom. The friend who attends the bridegroom waits and listens for him, and is full of joy when he hears the bridegroom's voice. That joy is mine, and it is now complete. He must become greater; I must become less.

"The one who comes from above is above all; the one who is from the earth belongs to the earth, and speaks as one from the earth. The one who comes from heaven is above all. He testifies to what he has seen and heard, but no one accepts his testimony. The man who has accepted it has certified that God is truthful. For the one whom God has sent speaks the words of God, for God[b] gives the Spirit without limit. The Father loves the Son and has placed everything in his hands. Whoever believes in the Son has eternal life, but whoever rejects the Son will not see life, for God's wrath remains on him."[c] JOHN 3:22-36

"He must become greater;
I must become less."

From Oswald Chambers

> If you become a necessity to a soul, you are out of God's order. As a worker, your great responsibility is to be a friend of the Bridegroom. When once you see a soul in sight of the claims of Jesus Christ, you know that your influence has been in the right direction, and instead of putting out a hand to prevent the throes, pray that they grow ten times stronger until there is no power on earth or in hell that can hold that soul away from Jesus Christ. Over and over again, we become amateur providences; we come in and prevent God, and say—"This and that must not be." Instead of proving friends of the Bridegroom, we put our sympathy in the way, and the soul will one day say—"That one was a thief; he stole my affections from Jesus, and I lost my vision of Him."
>
> Beware of rejoicing with a soul in the wrong thing, but see that you do rejoice in the right thing. "The friend of the Bridegroom . . . rejoiceth greatly because of the Bridegroom's voice: this my joy therefore is fulfilled. He must increase, but I must decrease" (John 3:29-30). This is spoken with joy and not with sadness; at last they are to see the Bridegroom! And John says this is his joy. It is the absolute effacement of the worker; he is never thought of again. MUH 84

> I only decrease as He increases, and He only increases in me as I nourish His life by that which decreases me. Am I willing to feed the life of the Son of God in me? SHH 43

> Humility is the one stamp of a saint. Beware of the complacency of superiority when God's grace has done anything for you. RTR 9

> Humility is not an ideal; it is the unconscious result of the life being rightly related to God. RTR 21

> The great characteristic of the saint is humility. SSM 80

---

a. Some manuscripts [of John 3:25] *and certain Jews*
b. Greek *he*
c. Some interpreters end the quotation after [the previous paragraph]

12

JESUS TALKS WITH A
SAMARITAN WOMAN

 ow he had to go through Samaria. So he came to a town in Samaria called Sychar, near the plot of ground Jacob had given to his son Joseph. Jacob's well was there, and Jesus, tired as he was from the journey, sat down by the well. It was about the sixth hour.

When a Samaritan woman came to draw water, Jesus said to her, "Will you give me a drink?" (His disciples had gone into the town to buy food.)

The Samaritan woman said to him, "You are a Jew and I am a Samaritan woman. How can you ask me for a drink?" (For Jews do not associate with Samaritans.[a])

Jesus answered her, "If you knew the gift of God and who it is that asks you for a drink, you would have asked him and he would have given you living water."

"Sir," the woman said, "you have nothing to draw with and the well is deep. Where can you get this living water? Are you greater than our father Jacob, who gave us the well and drank from it himself, as did also his sons and his flocks and herds?"

Jesus answered, "Everyone who drinks this water will be thirsty again, but whoever drinks the water I give him will never thirst. Indeed, the water I give him will become in him a spring of water welling up to eternal life."

The woman said to him, "Sir, give me this water so that I won't get thirsty and have to keep coming here to draw water."

He told her, "Go, call your husband and come back."

"I have no husband," she replied.

Jesus said to her, "You are right when you say you have no husband. The fact is, you have had five husbands, and the man you now have is not your husband. What you have just said is quite true."

59

"Sir," the woman said, "I can see that you are a prophet. Our fathers worshiped on this mountain, but you Jews claim that the place where we must worship is in Jerusalem."

Jesus declared, "Believe me, woman, a time is coming when you will worship the Father neither on this mountain nor in Jerusalem. You Samaritans worship what you do not know; we worship what we do know, for salvation is from the Jews. Yet a time is coming and has now come when the true worshipers will worship the Father in spirit and truth, for they are the kind of worshipers the Father seeks. God is spirit, and his worshipers must worship in spirit and in truth."

The woman said, "I know that Messiah" (called Christ) "is coming. When he comes, he will explain everything to us."

Then Jesus declared, "I who speak to you am he." JOHN 4:4-26

THE DISCIPLES REJOIN JESUS

Just then his disciples returned and were surprised to find him talking with a woman. But no one asked, "What do you want?" or "Why are you talking with her?"

Then, leaving her water jar, the woman went back to the town and said to the people, "Come, see a man who told me everything I ever did. Could this be the Christ?" They came out of the town and made their way toward him.

Meanwhile his disciples urged him, "Rabbi, eat something."

But he said to them, "I have food to eat that you know nothing about."

Then his disciples said to each other, "Could someone have brought him food?"

"My food," said Jesus, "is to do the will of him who sent me and to finish his work. Do you not say, 'Four months more and then the harvest'? I tell you, open your eyes and look at the fields! They are ripe for harvest. Even now the reaper draws his wages, even now he harvests the crop for eternal life, so that the sower and the reaper may be glad together. Thus the saying 'One sows and another reaps' is true. I sent you to reap what you have not worked for. Others have done the hard work, and you have reaped the benefits of their labor." JOHN 4:27-38

MANY SAMARITANS BELIEVE

Many of the Samaritans from that town believed in him because of the woman's testimony, "He told me everything I ever did." So when the Samaritans came to him, they urged him to stay with them, and he stayed two days. And because of his words many more became believers.

They said to the woman, "We no longer believe just because of what you said; now we have heard for ourselves, and we know that this man really is the Savior of the world." JOHN 4:39-42

"The water I give him will become in him a spring
of water welling up to eternal life."

FROM OSWALD CHAMBERS

➤ We are to be centers through which Jesus can flow as rivers of living water in blessing to everyone. Some of us are like the Dead Sea, always taking in but never giving out, because we are not rightly related to the Lord Jesus. As surely as we receive from Him, He will pour out through us, and in the measure He is not pouring it, there is a defect in our relationship to Him. Is there anything between you and Jesus Christ? Is there anything that hinders your belief in Him? If not, Jesus says, out of you will flow rivers of living water. It is not a blessing passed on, not an experience stated, but a river continually flowing. Keep at the Source; guard well your belief in Jesus Christ and your relationship to Him, and there will be a steady flow for other lives—no dryness and no deadness. MUH 251

➤ Are you in constant contact with frozen natures in your own family, in your business, in your friendships? You have talked with them, prayed with them; you have done everything you know how, but there is not the slightest sign of conviction of sin, no trouble of conscience or heart. They are not "out-and-out" sinners, but you know that they are "in-and-in" sinners; you know they are wrong and twisted and have things that are not clean, but you cannot make them realize it; they always get away, frozen and untouched. Then bring your own soul face to face with Jesus Christ: "Lord do *I* believe that Thou canst thaw that man's nature, that woman's nature, until the Holy Spirit has a chance of saving him or her?" That is the first difficulty to be overcome—what state of faith in Jesus

Christ have I? Then next ask yourself, "Do I believe that the Lord Jesus Christ can take that selfish, sensual, twisted, self-satisfied nature that is all wrong and out of order — do I believe that He can make it perfect in the sight of God?" Oh, do let us get back to this tremendous confidence in the Lord Jesus Christ's power, back to reliance on the Holy Spirit, and to remembering that Jesus came to seek the lost. WG 26

---

a. Or *do not use dishes Samaritans have used*

13

JESUS BEGINS TO PREACH AND HEAL

fter the two days Jesus left for Galilee. (Now Jesus himself had pointed out that a prophet has no honor in his own country.) When he arrived in Galilee, the Galileans welcomed him. They had seen all that he had done in Jerusalem at the Passover Feast, for they also had been there.

From that time on Jesus began to preach, proclaiming the good news of God. News about him spread through the whole countryside. He taught in their synagogues, and everyone praised him. "The time has come," he said. "The kingdom of God is near. Repent and believe the good news!" MATTHEW 4:17; MARK 1:14b-15; LUKE 4:14b-15; JOHN 4:43-45

JESUS HEALS AN OFFICIAL'S SON

Once more he visited Cana in Galilee, where he had turned the water into wine. And there was a certain royal official whose son lay sick at Capernaum. When this man heard that Jesus had arrived in Galilee from Judea, he went to him and begged him to come and heal his son, who was close to death.

"Unless you people see miraculous signs and wonders," Jesus told him, "you will never believe."

The royal official said, "Sir, come down before my child dies."

Jesus replied, "You may go. Your son will live."

The man took Jesus at his word and departed. While he was still on the way, his servants met him with the news that his boy was living. When he inquired as to the time when his son got better, they said to him, "The fever left him yesterday at the seventh hour."

Then the father realized that this was the exact time at which

Jesus had said to him, "Your son will live." So he and all his household believed.

This was the second miraculous sign that Jesus performed, having come from Judea to Galilee. JOHN 4:46-54

JESUS REJECTED AT NAZARETH

He went to Nazareth, where he had been brought up, and on the Sabbath day he went into the synagogue, as was his custom. And he stood up to read. The scroll of the prophet Isaiah was handed to him. Unrolling it, he found the place where it is written:

"The Spirit of the Lord is on me,
because he has anointed me
to preach good news to the poor.
He has sent me to proclaim
freedom for the prisoners
and recovery of sight for the blind,
to release the oppressed,
to proclaim the year of the Lord's favor."[a]

Then he rolled up the scroll, gave it back to the attendant and sat down. The eyes of everyone in the synagogue were fastened on him, and he began by saying to them, "Today this scripture is fulfilled in your hearing."

All spoke well of him and were amazed at the gracious words that came from his lips. "Isn't this Joseph's son?" they asked.

Jesus said to them, "Surely you will quote this proverb to me: 'Physician, heal yourself! Do here in your hometown what we have heard that you did in Capernaum.'

"I tell you the truth," he continued, "no prophet is accepted in his hometown. I assure you that there were many widows in Israel in Elijah's time, when the sky was shut for three and a half years and there was a severe famine throughout the land. Yet Elijah was not sent to any of them, but to a widow in Zarephath in the region of Sidon. And there were many in Israel with leprosy[b] in the time of Elisha the prophet, yet not one of them was cleansed—only Naaman the Syrian."

All the people in the synagogue were furious when they heard this. They got up, drove him out of the town, and took him to the brow of the hill on which the town was built, in order to throw him down the cliff. But he walked right through the crowd and went on his way. LUKE 4:16-30

JESUS SETTLES AT CAPERNAUM

Leaving Nazareth, he went and lived in Capernaum, a town in Galilee, which was by the lake in the area of Zebulun and Naphtali—to fulfill what was said through the prophet Isaiah:

"Land of Zebulun and land of Naphtali,
the way to the sea, along the Jordan,
Galilee of the Gentiles—
the people living in darkness
have seen a great light;
on those living in the land
of the shadow of death
a light has dawned."ᶜ MATTHEW 4:13-16

"The Spirit of the Lord is on me, because he has anointed me to preach good news to the poor."

FROM OSWALD CHAMBERS

❧ To picture Jesus Christ, never so beautifully, as One who sits down beside the brokenhearted and by expression of fellow-feeling and overflowing tenderness, enables him to be resigned and submissive to his lot, is not only thoroughly to misunderstand our Lord, but to prevent Him doing what He came to do. He does come to the brokenhearted, to the captives bound by a cursed hereditary tendency, to the blind who grope for light, to the man bruised and crushed by his surroundings, but He does not come as a sympathizer—He "binds up the brokenhearted, gives release to the captives, recovering of sight to the blind; He sets at liberty them that are bruised" (see Luke 4:18). Jesus Christ is not a mere sympathizer, He is a Savior, and the only One. SH 140

❧ We long for something that is not and shut our eyes to the thing that is. When the Lord Jesus awakens us to reality by new birth and brings us in contact with Himself, He does not give us new fathers

65

and mothers and new friends; He gives us new sight, that is, we focus our eyes on the things that are near. "Put thy distance on the near." This craving to go somewhere else, to see the things that are distant, arises from a refusal to attend to what is near. MFL 62

❧ We *see* for the first time when we do not look. We see actual things, and we say that we see them, but we never really see them until we see God; when we see God, everything becomes different. It is not the external things that are different, but a different disposition looks through the same eyes as the result of the internal surgery that has taken place. We see God, and then we see things actually as we never saw them before. NKW 54

❧ The way to keep our sight fit is by looking at the things which are not seen, and external things become a glorious chance of enabling us to concentrate on the invisible things. Once we realize that God's order comes to us in the passing moments, then nothing is unimportant. Every disagreeable thing is a new way of bringing us to realize the wonderful manifestation of the Son of God in that particular. OBH 77

❧ Jesus Christ says, "Come unto Me, and I will give you rest" (see Matt. 11:28), i.e., I will put you in the place where your eyes are open. And notice what Jesus Christ says we will look at—lilies, and sparrows, and grass. What man in his senses bothers about these things! We consider airplanes, and tanks, and shells, because these demand our attention, the other things do not. SHH 75

❧ The salvation of Jesus Christ enables a man to see for the first time in his life, and it is a wonderful thing. SHH 75

---

a. Isaiah 61:1-2
b. The Greek word was used for various diseases affecting the skin—not necessarily leprosy [and hereinafter]
c. Isaiah 9:1-2

14

THE CALLING OF THE FIRST DISCIPLES

One day as Jesus was walking beside the Sea of Galilee (the Lake of Gennesaret), he saw two brothers, Simon called Peter and his brother Andrew. They were casting a net into the lake, for they were fishermen.

As Jesus was standing by the sea, with the people crowding around him and listening to the word of God, he saw at the water's edge two boats, left there by the fishermen, who were washing their nets. He got into one of the boats, the one belonging to Simon, and asked him to put out a little from shore. Then he sat down and taught the people from the boat.

When he had finished speaking, he said to Simon, "Put out into deep water, and let down the nets for a catch."

Simon answered, "Master, we've worked hard all night and haven't caught anything. But because you say so, I will let down the nets."

When they had done so, they caught such a large number of fish that their nets began to break. So they signaled their partners in the other boat to come and help them, and they came and filled both boats so full that they began to sink.

When Simon Peter saw this, he fell at Jesus' knees and said, "Go away from me, Lord; I am a sinful man!" For he and all his companions were astonished at the catch of fish they had taken.

Then Jesus said to Simon, "Don't be afraid; from now on you will catch men."

"Come, follow me," Jesus said, "and I will make you fishers of men." So they pulled their boats up on shore. At once they left their nets, left everything and followed him.

When he had gone a little farther, he saw two other brothers, James son of Zebedee and his brother John, Simon's partners. They were in a boat with their father Zebedee, preparing their nets. Without delay Jesus called them, and immediately they left their father Zebedee in the boat with the hired men and followed him. MATTHEW 4:18-22; MARK 1:16-20; LUKE 5:1-11

THE CALLING OF LEVI (MATTHEW)

After this, Jesus went on from there. He once again went out beside the lake. A large crowd came to him, and he began to teach them. As he walked along, he saw a tax collector by the name of Levi, son of Alphaeus, sitting at his tax booth. "Follow me," Jesus told him, and Levi got up, left everything and followed him.

Then Levi held a great banquet for Jesus at his house. A large crowd of tax collectors and "sinners" were eating with him and his disciples, for there were many who followed him. But when the Pharisees and the teachers of the law who belonged to their sect saw him eating with the "sinners" and tax collectors, they complained to his disciples: "Why do you *and* your teacher eat and drink with tax collectors and 'sinners'?"

On hearing this, Jesus answered them, "It is not the healthy who need a doctor, but the sick. But go and learn what this means: 'I desire mercy, not sacrifice.'ᵃ I have not come to call the righteous, but sinners to repentance." MATTHEW 9:9-13; MARK 2:13-17; LUKE 5:27-32

"Come, follow me . . .
and I will make you fishers of men."

FROM OSWALD CHAMBERS

➣ Pay attention to the Source, believe in Jesus, and God will look after the outflow. God grant we may let the Holy Ghost work out His passion for souls through us. We have not to imitate Jesus by having a passion for souls like His, but to let the Holy Ghost so identify us with Jesus that His mind is expressed through us as He expressed the mind of God. MFL 118

➣ God grant we may understand that the passion for souls is not a placid, scientifically worked-out thing; it compresses all the energy of heart and brain and body in one consuming drive, day and night from the beginning of life to the end — a consuming, fiery, living passion. WG 82

≈ Oh, the skill, the patience, the gentleness and the endurance that are needed for this passion for souls; a sense that men are perishing doesn't do it; only one thing will do it — a blazing, passionate devotion to the Lord Jesus Christ, an all-consuming passion. Then there is no night so long, no work so hard, and no crowd so difficult, but that love will outlast it all. WG 83

≈ Jesus Christ told the disciples He would make them "fishers of men," catchers of men. Unless we have this divine passion for souls burning in us because of our personal love for Jesus Christ, we will quit the work before we are much older. WG 83

≈ In order to catch men for the Lord Jesus Christ, you must love Jesus Christ absolutely, beyond all others. You must have a consuming passion of love; then He will flow through you in a passion of love and yearning and draw men to Himself. WG 88

≈ The only way to learn how to fish is to fish! WG 84

---

a. Hosea 6:6

15

JESUS HEALS MANY AND DRIVES OUT EVIL SPIRITS

hey went to Capernaum, and when the Sabbath came, Jesus went into the synagogue and began to teach. The people were amazed at his teaching, because he taught them as one who had authority, not as the teachers of the law.

In the synagogue there was a man possessed by a demon, an evil[a] spirit. He cried out at the top of his voice, "Ha! What do you want with us, Jesus of Nazareth? Have you come to destroy us? I know who you are—the Holy One of God!"

"Be quiet!" Jesus said sternly. "Come out of him!" Then the demon threw the man down before them all, shook the man violently and came out of him with a shriek, without injuring him.

The people were all so amazed that they asked each other, "What is this? A new teaching? With authority and power he gives orders to evil spirits and they obey him and come out!" News about him spread quickly throughout the surrounding area, over the whole region of Galilee. MARK 1:21-28; LUKE 4:31-37

JESUS HEALS PETER'S MOTHER-IN-LAW

As soon as they left the synagogue, they went with James and John to the home of Simon and Andrew. Now Simon Peter's mother-in-law was lying in bed suffering from a high fever. They told Jesus about her and asked *him* to help her. When Jesus came into Peter's house, he went to her, rebuked the fever, and it left her. He bent over, took her hand and helped her up. She got up at once and began to wait on them.

That evening, when the sun was setting, the people brought to Jesus all who had various kinds of sickness and diseases and many who were demon-possessed. The whole town gathered at

71

the door. Laying his hands on each one, he healed all the sick. This was to fulfill what was spoken through the prophet Isaiah:

> "He took up our infirmities
> and carried our diseases."[b]

Moreover, he drove out the spirits with a word; demons came out of many people, shouting, "You are the Son of God!" But he rebuked them and would not allow them to speak, because they knew who he was. They knew he was the Christ. MATTHEW 8:14-17; MARK 1:29-34; LUKE 4:38-41

> *"He drove out the spirits with a word;*
> *demons came out of many people,*
> *shouting, 'You are the Son of God!' "*

FROM OSWALD CHAMBERS

≈ If you go on the line of accepting whatever can be experienced, you will find you have to accept the wildest, vaguest, most indeterminate things. For example, a man may come and tell you that he has had communication with departed friends; well, he is no more likely to be untruthful than you are—how are you going to judge whether his experience is right or not? The only guide is your personal relationship to Jesus Christ. Jesus Christ prohibits it, and that shuts the door straight off for you from tampering with spiritualism; therefore, you refuse to have anything to do with what He will not allow. BSG 67

≈ We cannot play the fool with our bodies and souls and hoodwink God. Certain kinds of moral disobedience produce sicknesses which no physical remedy can touch, the only cure is obedience to Jesus Christ. The barriers are placed by a God who is absolutely holy, and he has told us clearly, "Not that way." If we turn to necromancy even in such seemingly ridiculous ways of telling fortunes in teacups or by cards or planchette, we commit a crime against our own souls; we are probing where we have no right to probe. People say, "There's no harm in it." There is all the harm and the backing up of the devil in it. The only One who can open up the profound mysteries of life is God, and He will do it as He sees we can stand it. SHL 56

❧ Soul is the expression of the personal spirit in the body, and it is the expression of soul that is either good or bad. What we *do* tells as much as what we are in the final issue. There are two entrances into the soul, viz., the body and the spirit. The body is within our control; the spirit is not, and if our spirit is not under the control of God there is nothing to prevent other spirits communicating through it to the soul and body. It is impossible to guard our spirit; the only One who can guard its entrances is God. If we hand ourselves over to His keeping, we shall be kept not only from what we understand as dangers, but from dangers we have never even imagined. The conscious ring of our life is a mere phase; Jesus Christ did not die to save that only; it is the whole personality that is included in the Redemption. We are safeguarded from dangers we know nothing about. Thank God if the unseen realm does not impinge on you. SHL 57

---

a. Greek *unclean* [and hereafter]
b. Isaiah 53:4

16

JESUS PRAYS, PREACHES, AND HEALS

Very early in the morning, while it was still dark, Jesus got up. At daybreak Jesus left the house and went out to a solitary place, where He prayed. Simon and his companions went to look for him, and when they found him, they exclaimed: "Everyone is looking for you!"

Jesus replied, "Let us go somewhere else — to the nearby villages — so I can preach there also. That is why I have come."

The people were looking for him and when they came to where he was, they tried to keep him from leaving them. But he said, "I must preach the good news of the kingdom of God to the other towns also, because that is why I was sent." So he traveled throughout Galilee,[a] and he kept on teaching in their synagogues, preaching the good news of the kingdom, healing every disease and sickness among the people, and driving out demons.

MATTHEW 4:23; MARK 1:35-39; LUKE 4:42-44

THE MAN WITH LEPROSY

While Jesus was in one of the towns, a man came along who was covered with leprosy. When he saw Jesus, he fell before him, and with his face to the ground, begged him on his knees, "Lord, if you are willing, you can make me clean."

Filled with compassion, Jesus reached out his hand and touched the man. "I am willing," he said. "Be clean!" Immediately the leprosy left him and he was cured.[b]

Then Jesus sent him away at once *and* ordered him with a strong warning: "See that you don't tell this to anyone. But go, show yourself to the priest and offer the sacrifices that Moses commanded for your cleansing, as a testimony to them." Instead he went out and began to talk freely, spreading the news. As a result, Jesus could no longer enter a town openly but stayed outside in lonely places. Yet the news about him spread all the more, so that crowds of people from everywhere came to hear him and to be healed of their sicknesses. But Jesus often withdrew to lonely places and prayed. MATTHEW 8:2-4; MARK 1:40-45; LUKE 5:12-16

JESUS HEALS A PARALYTIC

A few days later Jesus stepped into a boat, crossed over and again entered his own town, Capernaum. The people heard that he had come home. So many gathered that there was no room left, not even outside the door, and he preached the word to them. As he was teaching, Pharisees and teachers of the law, who had come from every village of Galilee and from Judea and Jerusalem, were sitting there. And the power of the Lord was present for him to heal the sick. Some men came, bringing to him a paralytic lying on a mat carried by four of them. They tried to take him into the house to lay him before Jesus. When they could not find a way to do this because of the crowd, they went up on the roof. They made an opening in the roof above Jesus and, after digging through it, lowered him on his mat through the tiles into the middle of the crowd, right in front of Jesus.

"Take heart, son," Jesus said to the paralytic when he saw their faith. "Friend, your sins are forgiven."

Now the Pharisees and some teachers of the law were sitting there, thinking to themselves, "Who is this fellow? Why does this fellow talk like that? He's blaspheming! Who can forgive sins but God alone?"

Immediately Jesus knew in his spirit that this was what they were thinking in their hearts, and he said to them, "Why are you thinking these things? Why do you entertain evil thoughts in your hearts? Which is easier: to say to the paralytic, 'Your sins are forgiven,' or to say, 'Get up, take your mat and walk'? But so that you may know that the Son of Man has authority on earth to forgive sins. . . ." Then he said to the paralyzed man, "I tell you, get up, take your mat and go home." Immediately the man stood up in full view of them all, took his mat he had been lying on, walked out and went home praising God. When the crowd saw this, everyone was amazed and gave praise to God, who had given such authority to men. They were filled with awe and said, "We have never seen anything like this! We have seen remarkable things today." MATTHEW 9:1-8; MARK 2:1-12; LUKE 5:17-26

THE HEALING AT THE POOL

Some time later, Jesus went up to Jerusalem for a feast of the Jews. Now there is in Jerusalem near the Sheep Gate a pool, which in Aramaic is called Bethesda[c] and which is surrounded by five covered colonnades. Here a great number of disabled people used to lie—the blind, the lame, the paralyzed.[d] One who was there had been an invalid for thirty-eight years. When Jesus saw him lying there and learned that he had been in this condition for a long time, he asked him, "Do you want to get well?"

"Sir," the invalid replied, "I have no one to help me into the pool when the water is stirred. While I am trying to get in, someone else goes down ahead of me."

Then Jesus said to him, "Get up! Pick up your mat and walk." At once the man was cured; he picked up his mat and walked.

The day on which this took place was a Sabbath, and so the Jews said to the man who had been healed, "It is the Sabbath; the law forbids you to carry your mat."

But he replied, "The man who made me well said to me, 'Pick up your mat and walk.' "

So they asked him, "Who is this fellow who told you to pick it up and walk?"

The man who was healed had no idea who it was, for Jesus had slipped away into the crowd that was there. JOHN 5:1-15

"Take heart, son . . .
your sins are forgiven."

FROM OSWALD CHAMBERS

☙ The great miracle of the grace of God is that He forgives sin, and it is the death of Jesus Christ alone that enables the divine nature to forgive and to remain true to itself in doing so. It is shallow nonsense to say that God forgives us because He is love. When we have been convicted of sin, we will never say this again. The love of God means Calvary, and nothing less; the love of God is spelled on the Cross and nowhere else. The only ground on which God can forgive me is through the Cross of my Lord. There, His conscience is satisfied. MUH 324

᙮ Forgiveness is the divine miracle of grace; it cost God the Cross of Jesus Christ before He could forgive sin and remain a holy God. MUH 325

᙮ When God forgives a man He gives him the heredity of His own Son, and there is no man on earth but can be presented "perfect in Christ Jesus." Then on the ground of the Redemption, it is up to me to live as a son of God. HGM 102

᙮ When God forgives, He never casts up at us the mean, miserable things we have done. "I have blotted out, as a thick cloud, thy transgressions, and, as a cloud, thy sins." A cloud cannot be seen when it is gone. PH 224

᙮ Forgiveness is a miracle, because in forgiving a man God imparts to him the power to be exactly the opposite of what he has been: God transmutes the sinner who sinned into the saint who does not sin; consequently, the only true repentant man is the holy man. GW 53

᙮ Forgiveness is the great message of the Gospel, and it satisfies a man's sense of justice completely. The fundamental factor of Christianity is "the forgiveness of sins." HGM 100

᙮ The distinctive thing about Christianity is forgiveness, not sanctification or my holiness, but forgiveness — the greatest miracle God ever performs through the Redemption. HGM 105

᙮ The forgiveness of God is a bigger miracle than we are apt to think. It is impossible for a human being to forgive; and it is because this is not realized that we fail to understand that the forgiveness of God is a miracle of divine grace. PH 183

a. [*Judea* in Luke 4:44] Or *the land of the Jews;* some manuscripts *Galilee*
b. Greek *made clean* [and hereinafter]
c. Some manuscripts [of John 5:2] *Bethzatha;* other manuscripts *Bethsaida*
d. Some less important manuscripts [of John 5:3-4] *paralyzed — and they waited for the moving of the waters. From time to time an angel of the Lord would come down and stir up the waters. The first one into the pool after each such disturbance would be cured of whatever disease he had.*

17

LIFE THROUGH THE SON

S o, because Jesus was doing these things on the Sabbath, the Jews persecuted him. Jesus said to them, "My Father is always at his work to this very day, and I too am working." For this reason the Jews tried all the harder to kill him; not only was he breaking the Sabbath, but he was even calling God his own Father, making himself equal with God.

Jesus gave them this answer: "I tell you the truth, the Son can do nothing by himself; he can do only what he sees his Father doing, because whatever the Father does the Son also does. For the Father loves the Son and shows him all he does. Yes, to your amazement he will show him even greater things than these. For just as the Father raises the dead and gives them life, even so the Son gives life to whom he is pleased to give it. Moreover, the Father judges no one, but has entrusted all judgment to the Son, that all may honor the Son just as they honor the Father. He who does not honor the Son does not honor the Father, who sent him.

"I tell you the truth, whoever hears my word and believes him who sent me has eternal life and will not be condemned; he has crossed over from death to life. I tell you the truth, a time is coming and has now come when the dead will hear the voice of the Son of God and those who hear will live. For as the Father has life in himself, so he has granted the Son to have life in himself. And he has given him authority to judge because he is the Son of Man.

"Do not be amazed at this, for a time is coming when all who are in their graves will hear his voice and come out—those who have done good will rise to live, and those who have done evil will rise to be condemned. By myself I can do nothing; I judge only as I hear, and my judgment is just, for I seek not to please myself but him who sent me." JOHN 5:16-30

TESTIMONIES ABOUT JESUS

"If I testify about myself, my testimony is not valid. There is another who testifies in my favor, and I know that his testimony about me is valid.

"You have sent to John and he has testified to the truth. Not that I accept human testimony; but I mention it that you may be saved. John was a lamp that burned and gave light, and you chose for a time to enjoy his light.

"I have testimony weightier than that of John. For the very work that the Father has given me to finish, and which I am doing, testifies that the Father has sent me. And the Father who sent me has himself testified concerning me. You have never heard his voice nor seen his form, nor does his word dwell in you, for you do not believe the one he sent. You diligently study[a] the Scriptures because you think that by them you possess eternal life. These are the Scriptures that testify about me, yet you refuse to come to me to have life.

"I do not accept praise from men, but I know you. I know that you do not have the love of God in your hearts. I have come in my Father's name, and you do not accept me; but if someone else comes in his own name, you will accept him. How can you believe if you accept praise from one another, yet make no effort to obtain the praise that comes from the only God[b]?

"But do not think I will accuse you before the Father. Your accuser is Moses, on whom your hopes are set. If you believed Moses, you would believe me, for he wrote about me. But since you do not believe what he wrote, how are you going to believe what I say?" JOHN 5:31-47

*"Whoever hears my word and believes him
who sent me has eternal life."*

FROM OSWALD CHAMBERS

❧ The life which Jesus Christ exhibited was eternal life, and He says anyone who believes in Him—i.e., commits himself to Him—has that life. To commit myself to Jesus means there is nothing that is not committed. Belief is a twofold transaction—a deliberate de-

80

stroying of all roads back again, and a complete surrender to our Lord Himself. HG 110

☾ "This is life eternal, that they might know Thee." Eternal life is God and God is eternal life; and the meaning of the Atonement is that Jesus produces that life in us. By sanctification we enter into the kingdom of perfect oneness with Jesus Christ; everything He is, we are by faith. He is "made unto us wisdom and righteousness, and sanctification, and redemption"; we have nothing apart from Him. OBH 88

☾ God and His promises are eternal. "The gift *of God* is eternal life." Jesus Christ came to give us eternal life, a life in which there is neither time nor space, which cannot be marked with suffering or death; it is the life Jesus lived. PH 76

☾ Eternal life is the gift of the Lord Jesus Christ. "He that believeth on Me hath everlasting life" (John 6:47) — i.e., the life He manifested in His human flesh when He was here, and says Jesus, "Ye have not (that) life in yourselves'." His life is not ours by natural birth, and it can only be given to us by means of His Cross. Our Lord's Cross is the gateway into His life; His resurrection means that He has power now to convey that life to us. PR 111

☾ This constitutes eternal life — an increasing knowledge of the unfathomable God and His only begotten Son. This is eternal pleasure — to know Him! How far removed it is from our conceptions of rewards and crowns and heaven. The way of a soul walking alone with God, unless we know this same unspeakable fellowship, seems a way overshadowed with sadness and insane with fanaticism. CD, VOL. 2 119

☾ If the bit we do know about Jesus Christ is so full of light, why cannot we leave the matters of heaven and hell, of life and death, in His hand and stake our confidence in Him? "God is light," and one day everything will be seen in that light. "I am the light of the world; he that followeth Me shall not walk in darkness, but shall have the light of life" (John 8:12). AUG 116

☾ Jesus Christ's first obedience was to the will of His Father, and it is by the obedience of Jesus Christ as Son of Man that the whole human race is swung back again to God. HGM 60

ᔓ A great and glorious fact—to believe in Jesus Christ is to receive God, who is described to the believer as "eternal life." Eternal life is not a gift *from* God, but the gift *of* God—that is, God Himself. AUG 106

ᔓ Never confound eternal life with immortality. Eternal has reference to the quality of life, not to its duration. Eternal life is the life Jesus exhibited when He was here on earth, with neither time nor eternity in it, because it is the life of God Himself. IWP 114

---

a. Or *Study diligently* (the imperative)
b. Some early manuscripts [of John 5:44] *the Only One*

18

LORD OF THE SABBATH

ne Sabbath Jesus was going through the grainfields, and his disciples walked along. They were hungry and began to pick some heads of grain, rub them in their hands and eat the kernels. When the Pharisees saw this, they said to him, "Look! Why are your disciples doing what is unlawful on the Sabbath?"

Jesus answered them, "Have you never read what David did when he and his companions were hungry and in need? In the days of Abiathar the high priest, he entered the house of God, and taking the consecrated bread, he ate what is lawful only for priests to eat. And he also gave some to his companions. Or haven't you read in the Law that on the Sabbath the priests in the temple desecrate the day and yet are innocent? I tell you that one[a] greater than the temple is here. If you had known what these words mean, 'I desire mercy, not sacrifice,'[b] you would not have condemned the innocent."

Then he said to them, "The Sabbath was made for man, not man for the Sabbath. So the Son of Man is Lord even of the Sabbath."

Going on from that place, on another Sabbath he went into their synagogue and was teaching, and a man was there whose right hand was shriveled. The Pharisees and the teachers of the law were looking for a reason to accuse Jesus, so they watched him closely to see if he would heal on the Sabbath. They asked him, "Is it lawful to heal on the Sabbath?"

Jesus knew what they were thinking and said to the man with the shriveled hand, "Get up and stand up in front of everyone." So he got up and stood there.

Then Jesus said to them, "I ask you, which is lawful on the Sabbath: to do good or to do evil, to save life or to destroy it?" But they remained silent.

He said to them, "If any of you has a sheep and it falls into a pit on the Sabbath, will you not take hold of it and lift it out? How much more valuable is a man than a sheep! Therefore it is lawful to do good on the Sabbath."

He looked around at them all in anger and, deeply distressed at their stubborn hearts, said to the man, "Stretch out your hand." He stretched it out, and his hand was completely restored, just as sound as the other. But they were furious. Then the Pharisees went out and began to plot with the Herodians what they might do, how they might kill Jesus. MATTHEW 12:1-14; MARK 2:23–3:6; LUKE 6:1-11

JESUS – GOD'S CHOSEN SERVANT

Aware of this, Jesus withdrew with his disciples from that place to the lake, and a large crowd from Galilee followed. News about him spread all over Syria, and people brought to him all who were ill with various diseases, those suffering severe pain, the demon-possessed, those having seizures, and the paralyzed, and he healed them. Large crowds came to him from Galilee, the Decapolis, Judea, Jerusalem, Idumea, and the regions across the Jordan and around Tyre and Sidon. Many followed him.

Because of the crowd he told his disciples to have a small boat ready for him, to keep the people from crowding him. For he had healed many, so that those with diseases were pushing forward to touch him. He healed all their sick, warning them not to tell who he was. Whenever the evil spirits saw him, they fell down before him and cried out, "You are the Son of God." But he gave them strict orders not to tell who he was. This was to fulfill what was spoken through the prophet Isaiah:

> "Here is my servant whom I have chosen,
> the one I love, in whom I delight;
> I will put my Spirit on him,
> and he will proclaim justice to the nations.
> He will not quarrel or cry out;
> no one will hear his voice in the streets.
> A bruised reed he will not break,
> and a smoldering wick he will not snuff out,
> till he leads justice to victory.
> In his name the nations will put their hope."[c] MATTHEW 4:24-25; 12:15-21; MARK 3:7-12

84

*"Here is my servant whom I have chosen,
the one I love, in whom I delight."*

From Oswald Chambers

⤷ We are here with no right to ourselves, for no spiritual blessing for ourselves; we are here for one purpose only—to be made servants of God as Jesus was. PS 17

⤷ "To serve the living and true God" (1 Thes. 1:9). This means a life laid down for Jesus, a life of narrowed interests, a life that deliberately allows itself to be swamped by a crowd of paltry things. It is not fanaticism; it is the stedfast, flintlike attitude of heart and mind and body for one purpose—spoiled for everything saving as we can be used to win souls for Jesus. PS 22

⤷ We are saved and sanctified not for service, but to be absolutely Jesus Christ's; the consuming passion of the life is for Him. DI 61

⤷ Christian service is not our work; loyalty to Jesus is our work. DI 85

⤷ When you are consciously being used as broken bread and poured-out wine, you are interested in your own martyrdom; it is consciously costing you something. When you are laid on the altar of the Cross, all consciousness of self is gone, all consciousness of what you are doing for God, or of what God is doing through you, is gone. It is no longer possible to talk about "my experience of sanctification"; you are brought to the place where you understand what is meant by our Lord's words, "Ye shall be My witnesses." Wherever a saint goes, everything he or she does becomes a sacrament in God's hands, unconsciously to himself.

You never find a saint being consciously used by God; He uses some casual thing you never thought about, which is the surest evidence that you have got beyond the stage of conscious sanctification. You are beyond all consciousness because God is taking you up into His consciousness; you are His, and life becomes the natural simple life of a child.

To be everlastingly on the lookout to do some work for God means I want to evade sacramental service—"I want to do what I want to do." Maintain the attitude of a child toward God and He will do what He likes with you. If God puts you on the shelf, it is in order to season you. If He is pleased to put you in limited circumstances so that you cannot go out into the highways of service, then enter into sacramental service. Once you enter that service, you can enter no other. CHI 93

๛ Jesus Christ did not become humbled—"He humbled Himself" (see Phil. 2:6-8). He was "in the form of God," yet He took on Him "the form of a servant." LG 71

๛ The ecclesiastical idea of a servant of God is not Jesus Christ's idea. His idea is that we serve Him by being the servants of other men. Jesus Christ out-socialists the socialists. He says that in His kingdom he that is greatest shall be the servant of all. The real test of the saint is not preaching the Gospel but washing disciples' feet—that is, doing the things that do not count in the actual estimate of men but count everything in the estimate of God. MUH 56

๛ The things that Jesus did were of the most menial and commonplace order, and this is an indication that it takes all God's power in me to do the most commonplace things in His way. Can I use a towel as He did? Towels and dishes and sandals, all the ordinary sordid things of our lives, reveal more quickly than anything what we are made of. It takes God Almighty Incarnate in us to do the meanest duty as it ought to be done.

"I have given you an example, that ye should do as I have done to you" (John 13:15). Watch the kind of people God brings around you, and you will be humiliated to find that this is His way of revealing to you the kind of person you have been to Him. Now, He says, exhibit to that one exactly what I have shown to you. MUH 255.

---

a. Or *something*
b. Hosea 6:6
c. Isaiah 42:1-4

19

JESUS BEGINS THE SERMON ON THE MOUNT

Now when he saw the crowds, Jesus went up on a mountainside to pray, and spent the night praying to God. When morning came, he called to him those disciples he wanted, and they came to him. He appointed twelve of them, whom he also designated apostles, that they might be with him and that he might send them out to preach and to have authority to drive out demons. These are the names of the twelve apostles: first, Simon (to whom he gave the name Peter) and his brother Andrew; James son of Zebedee and his brother John (to them he gave the name Boanerges, which means Sons of Thunder); Philip and Bartholomew; Thomas and Matthew the tax collector; James son of Alphaeus, and Thaddaeus (Judas son of James); Simon who was called the Zealot and Judas Iscariot, who became a traitor.
MATTHEW 5:1a; 10:2-4; MARK 3:13-19; LUKE 6:12-16

JESUS DECLARES BLESSINGS AND WOES

He went down with them and stood on a level place. A large crowd of his disciples came to him there, and a great number of people from all over Judea, from Jerusalem, and from the coast of Tyre and Sidon, who had come to hear him and to be healed of their diseases. Those troubled by evil spirits were cured, and the people all tried to touch him, because power was coming from him and healing them all.

Looking at his disciples, he sat down and began to teach them, saying:

"Blessed are the poor in spirit,
for theirs is the kingdom of heaven.

87

Blessed are those who mourn,
for they will be comforted.
Blessed are the meek,
for they will inherit the earth.
Blessed are those who hunger
and thirst for righteousness,
for they will be filled.
Blessed are the merciful,
for they will be shown mercy.
Blessed are the pure in heart,
for they will see God.
Blessed are the peacemakers,
for they will be called sons of God.
Blessed are those who are persecuted
because of righteousness,
for theirs is the kingdom of heaven.

"Blessed are you who are poor,
for yours is the kingdom of God.
Blessed are you who hunger now,
for you will be satisfied.
Blessed are you who weep now,
for you will laugh.

"Blessed are you when people hate you,
when they exclude you and insult you,
persecute you and falsely say all kinds of evil against you
and reject your name as evil,
because of me, the Son of Man.

"Rejoice in that day and leap for joy. Be glad, because great is
your reward in heaven. For in the same way their fathers persecuted the prophets who were before you.

"But woe to you who are rich,
for you have already received your comfort.
Woe to you who are well fed now,
for you will go hungry.
Woe to you who laugh now,
for you will mourn and weep.

Woe to you when all men speak well of you,
for that is how their fathers
treated the false prophets." MATTHEW 5:1b-12; LUKE 6:17-26

"Looking at his disciples,
he sat down and began teaching them."

FROM OSWALD CHAMBERS

ʔ Wherever Christianity has ceased to be vigorous it is because it has become Christian *ethics* instead of the Christian *evangel.* People will listen more readily to an exposition of the Sermon on the Mount than they will to the meaning of the Cross; but they forget that to preach the Sermon on the Mount apart from the Cross is to preach an impossibility. What is the good of telling me to love my enemies—and that "Blessed are the pure in heart"? You may talk like that to further orders, but it does not amount to anything. Jesus Christ did not come to teach men to be or do any of these things: He did not come primarily to teach, He came to make a man the possessor of His own disposition, the disposition portrayed in the Sermon on the Mount. BE 66

ʔ The Sermon on the Mount is not a set of principles to be obeyed apart from identification with Jesus Christ. The Sermon on the Mount is a statement of the life we will live when the Holy Spirit is getting His way with us. PR 34

20

SALT AND LIGHT ON TO OATHS

Y ou are the salt of the earth. But if the salt loses its saltiness, how can it be made salty again? It is no longer good for anything, except to be thrown out and trampled by men.

"You are the light of the world. A city on a hill cannot be hidden. Neither do people light a lamp and put it under a bowl. Instead they put it on its stand, and it gives light to everyone in the house. In the same way, let your light shine before men, that they may see your good deeds and praise your Father in heaven." MATTHEW 5:13-16

"You are the salt of the earth. . . .
You are the light of the world."

FROM OSWALD CHAMBERS

~ A Christian is salt, and salt is the most concentrated thing known. Salt preserves wholesomeness and prevents decay. It is a disadvantage to be salt. Think of the action of salt on a wound, and you will realize this. If you get salt into a wound, it hurts, and when God's children are among those who are "raw" towards God, their presence hurts. The man who is wrong with God is like an open wound, and when "salt" gets in it causes annoyance and distress and he is spiteful and bitter. The disciples of Jesus in the present dispensation preserve society from corruption; the "salt" causes excessive irritation which spells persecution for the saint. SSM 19

~ "Ye are the light of the world." We have the idea that we are going to shine in heaven, but we are to shine down here, "in the midst of

91

a crooked and perverse nation." We are to shine as lights in the world in the squalid places, and it cannot be done by putting on a brazen smile, the light must be there all the time. LG 45

THE FULFILLMENT OF THE LAW

"Do not think that I have come to abolish the Law or the Prophets; I have not come to abolish them but to fulfill them. I tell you the truth, until heaven and earth disappear, not the smallest letter, not the least stroke of a pen, will by any means disappear from the Law until everything is accomplished. Anyone who breaks one of the least of these commandments and teaches others to do the same will be called least in the kingdom of heaven, but whoever practices and teaches these commands will be called great in the kingdom of heaven. For I tell you that unless your righteousness surpasses that of the Pharisees and the teachers of the law, you will certainly not enter the kingdom of heaven." MATTHEW 5:17-20

"Unless your righteousness surpasses that of the Pharisees and the teachers of the law, you will certainly not enter the kingdom of heaven."

FROM OSWALD CHAMBERS

- "Except your righteousness shall exceed" — not be different from but *"exceed"*; that is, we have to be all they are and infinitely more! We have to be right in our external behavior, but we have to be as right, and "righter," in our internal behavior. We have to be right in our words and actions, but we have to be as right in our thoughts and feelings. We have to be right according to the conventions of the society of godly people, but we have also to be right in conscience toward God. HG 59

- God's laws are not watered down to suit anyone; if God did that He would cease to be God. The moral law never alters for the noblest or the weakest; it remains abidingly and eternally the same. BE 8

MURDER

"You have heard that it was said to the people long ago, 'Do not murder,[a] and anyone who murders will be subject to judgment.' But I tell you that anyone who is angry with his brother[b] will be subject to judgment. Again, anyone who says to his brother, 'Raca,'[c] is answerable to the Sanhedrin. But anyone who says, 'You fool!' will be in danger of the fire of hell." MATTHEW 5:21-22

"Anyone who is angry with his brother
will be subject to judgment."

FROM OSWALD CHAMBERS

~ There is no vindictiveness in our Lord's judgments; He passes judgment always out of His personal love. HGM 46

~ We have judged our fellowmen as sinners. If God should judge us like that we would be in hell. God judges us through the marvelous atonement of Jesus Christ. RTR 23

~ We cannot judge ourselves by ourselves or by anyone else; there is always one fact more in everyone's life that we do not know. We cannot put men into types; we are never at the balance of one another's heredity; therefore, the judgment cannot lie with us. SHH 37

RECONCILIATION

"Therefore, if you are offering your gift at the altar and there remember that your brother has something against you, leave your gift there in front of the altar. First go and be reconciled to your brother; then come and offer your gift.

"Settle matters quickly with your adversary who is taking you to court. Do it while you are still with him on the way, or he may hand you over to the judge, and the judge may hand you over to the officer, and you may be thrown into prison. I tell you the truth, you will not get out until you have paid the last penny."[d] MATTHEW 5:23-26

"Settle matters quickly with your adversary."

FROM OSWALD CHAMBERS

❧ "Agree with thine adversary quickly." Have you suddenly turned a corner in any relationship and found that you had anger in your heart? Confess it quickly, quickly put it right before God, be reconciled to that one—*do it now.* MUH 182

ADULTERY AND DIVORCE

"You have heard that it was said, 'Do not commit adultery.'e But I tell you that anyone who looks at a woman lustfully has already committed adultery with her in his heart. If your right eye causes you to sin, gouge it out and throw it away. It is better for you to lose one part of your body than for your whole body to be thrown into hell. And if your right hand causes you to sin, cut it off and throw it away. It is better for you to lose one part of your body than for your whole body to go into hell.

"It has been said, 'Anyone who divorces his wife must give her a certificate of divorce.'f But I tell you that anyone who divorces his wife, except for marital unfaithfulness, causes her to become an adulteress, and anyone who marries the divorced woman commits adultery." MATTHEW 5:27-32

"Anyone who looks at a woman lustfully
has already committed adultery with her in his heart."

FROM OSWALD CHAMBERS

❧ Lust is—I must have it at once. Love can wait. Lust makes me impulsively impatient; I want to take shortcuts, and do things right off. Love can wait endlessly. If I have ever seen God and been touched by Him and the Spirit of God has entered into me, I am willing to wait for Him; I wait in the certainty that He will come. PH 170

❧ If ever a man is going to stand where lust never strikes him, it can only be because Jesus has altered his disposition, it is impossible unless Jesus Christ can do what He says He can. A disciple has to be free from the degradation of lust, and the marvel of the Redemption is that Jesus can free him from it. Jesus Christ's claim is that He can do for a man what he cannot do for himself. Jesus does not alter our human nature; it does not need altering: He alters the mainspring. SSM 34

OATHS

"Again, you have heard that it was said to the people long ago, 'Do not break your oath, but keep the oaths you have made to the Lord.' But I tell you, Do not swear at all: either by heaven, for it is God's throne; or by the earth, for it is his footstool; or by Jerusalem, for it is the city of the Great King. And do not swear by your head, for you cannot make even one hair white or black. Simply let your 'Yes' be 'Yes,' and your 'No,' 'No'; anything beyond this comes from the evil one. MATTHEW 5:33-37

"Do not break your oath."

FROM OSWALD CHAMBERS

✣ The Old Testament Scriptures always regard the oath as a peculiar sacrament. If you read what the Bible says about vowing, you will see how culpably negligent we are in the way we promise. If we do not fulfill a promise, we damage our moral and spiritual life. It is infinitely better to refuse to promise anything, even in the most superficial relationships, than to promise and not perform. Spiritual leakages are accounted for in this way. Always do what you ought to do, but be careful of promising anything, because a promise puts the blood of God on your character. NKW 110

---

a. Exodus 20:13
b. Some manuscripts *brother without cause*
c. An Aramaic term of contempt
d. Greek *kodrantes*
e. Exodus 20:14
f. Deuteronomy 24:1

21

AN EYE FOR AN EYE
ON TO TREASURES

You have heard that it was said, 'Eye for eye, and tooth for tooth.'[a] But I tell you, Do not resist an evil person. If someone strikes you on the right cheek, turn to him the other also. And if someone wants to sue you and take your tunic, let him have your cloak as well. If someone takes your cloak, do not stop him from taking your tunic. If someone forces you to go one mile, go with him two miles. Give to everyone who asks you, and do not turn away from the one who wants to borrow from you. If anyone takes what belongs to you, do not demand it back. Do to others as you would have them do to you." MATTHEW 5:38-42; LUKE 6:29-31

"Do not resist."

FROM OSWALD CHAMBERS

∻ These verses reveal the humiliation of being a Christian. Naturally, if a man does not hit back, it is because he is a coward; but spiritually if a man does not hit back, it is a manifestation of the Son of God in him. When you are insulted, you must not only not resent it, but make it an occasion to exhibit the Son of God. You cannot imitate the disposition of Jesus; it is either there or it is not. To the saint, personal insult becomes the occasion of revealing the incredible sweetness of the Lord Jesus.

The teaching of the Sermon on the Mount is not—Do your duty, but—Do what is not your duty. It is not your duty to go the second mile, to turn the other cheek, but Jesus says if we are His disciples we shall always do these things. MUH 196

LOVE FOR ENEMIES

"You have heard that it was said, 'Love your neighbor[b] and hate your enemy.' But I tell you who hear me: Love your enemies, do good to those who hate you, bless those who curse you, pray for those who mistreat you *and* persecute you, that you may be sons of your Father in heaven. He causes his sun to rise on the evil and the good, and sends rain on the righteous and the unrighteous.

"If you love those who love you, what credit is that to you? What reward will you get? Are not even the tax collectors doing that? Even 'sinners' love those who love them. And if you do good to those who are good to you, what credit is that to you? Even 'sinners' do that. And if you greet only your brothers, what are you doing more than others? Do not even pagans do that? And if you lend to those from whom you expect repayment, what credit is that to you? Even 'sinners' lend to 'sinners,' expecting to be repaid in full. But love your enemies, do good to them, and lend to them without expecting to get anything back. Then your reward will be great, and you will be sons of the Most High, because he is kind to the ungrateful and wicked. Be merciful, just as your Father is merciful.

"Be perfect, therefore, as your heavenly Father is perfect."
MATTHEW 5:43-48; LUKE 6:27-28, 32-36

"Be perfect . . . as your heavenly Father is perfect."

FROM OSWALD CHAMBERS

ꙮ Size yourself up with a good sense of humor—*"me,* perfect!" That is what Jesus Christ has undertaken to do. DI 72

ꙮ When a man says he is sanctified, the charge is often made, and there is no reply to it, "Remember, you are not perfect." A saint is required to be perfect toward God. *"Walk before Me,* and be thou perfect"; the standard of judgment is not man's standard, but God's. HG 42

ꙮ We are to be perfect as our Father in heaven is perfect, not by struggle and effort, but by the impartation of that which is Perfect. IWP 9

~ The Bible reveals that "that which is perfect" is a Being. God is the only Perfect Being; no human being is perfect apart from God. IWP 9

~ "If thou wilt be perfect . . ." — "If you want to be perfect, perfect as I am, perfect as your Father in Heaven is" — then come the conditions. Do we really want to be perfect? Beware of mental quibbling over the word *perfect*. Perfection does not mean the full maturity and consummation of a man's powers, but perfect fitness for doing the will of God. IWP 117

~ God always ignores the present perfection for the ultimate perfection. He is not concerned about making you blessed and happy just now; He is working out His ultimate perfection all the time — "that they may be one even as We are." MUH 118

~ "Walk before Me, and be thou perfect," not faultless, but blameless, undeserving of censure in the eyes of God. NKW 129

~ Christian perfection is not, and never can be, human perfection. Christian perfection is the perfection of a relationship to God which shows itself in the total irrelevancy of human life. NKW 148

GIVING TO THE NEEDY

"Be careful not to do your 'acts of righteousness' before men, to be seen by them. If you do, you will have no reward from your Father in heaven.

"So when you give to the needy, do not announce it with trumpets, as the hypocrites do in the synagogues and on the streets, to be honored by men. I tell you the truth, they have received their reward in full. But when you give to the needy, do not let your left hand know what your right hand is doing, so that your giving may be in secret. Then your Father, who sees what is done in secret, will reward you." MATTHEW 6:1-4

*"Be careful not to do
your acts of righteousness
before men, to be seen by them."*

99

From Oswald Chambers

❧ In our Lord's day the Pharisees made a tremendous show of giving; they gave from a play-acting motive, that they might "have glory of men." They would put their money in the boxes in the women's court of the temple with a great clang which sounded like a trumpet. Jesus tells us not to give in that way, with the motive to be seen of men, to be known as a generous giver, for "Verily I say unto you, They have their reward," that is all there is to it. SSM 56

PRAYER

"And when you pray, do not be like the hypocrites, for they love to pray standing in the synagogues and on the street corners to be seen by men. I tell you the truth, they have received their reward in full. But when you pray, go into your room, close the door and pray to your Father, who is unseen. Then your Father, who sees what is done in secret, will reward you. And when you pray, do not keep on babbling like pagans, for they think they will be heard because of their many words. Do not be like them, for your Father knows what you need before you ask him.

"This, then, is how you should pray:

" 'Our Father in heaven,
hallowed be your name,
your kingdom come,
your will be done
on earth as it is in heaven.
Give us today our daily bread.
Forgive us our debts,
as we also have forgiven our debtors.
And lead us not into temptation,
but deliver us from the evil one.'ᶜ

"For if you forgive men when they sin against you, your heavenly Father will also forgive you. But if you do not forgive men their sins, your Father will not forgive your sins." MATTHEW 6:5-15

"When you pray, go into your room, close the door,
and pray to your Father."

❧ We must have a selected place for prayer and when we get there the plague of flies begins — This must be done, and that. "Shut thy door." A secret silence means to shut the door deliberately on emotions and remember God. God is in secret, and He sees us from the secret place; He does not see us as other people see us, or as we see ourselves. MUH 236

FASTING

"When you fast, do not look somber as the hypocrites do, for they disfigure their faces to show men they are fasting. I tell you the truth, they have received their reward in full. But when you fast, put oil on your head and wash your face, so that it will not be obvious to men that you are fasting, but only to your Father, who is unseen; and your Father, who sees what is done in secret, will reward you." MATTHEW 6:16-18

"When your fast . . . wash your face,
so it will not be obvious . . . that you are fasting."

❧ Fasting from food is an easy business, but fasting in its true nature means to fast from everything that is good until the appointments of God in my soul are accepted. PR 58

❧ When you fast; fast to your Father in secret, not before men. Do not make a cheap martyr of yourself, and never ask for pity. If you are going through a time of discipline, pretend you are not going through it — "appear not unto men to fast." SSM 61

TREASURES

"Do not store up for yourselves treasures on earth, where moth and rust destroy, and where thieves break in and steal. But store up for yourselves treasures in heaven, where moth and rust do not destroy, and where thieves do not break in and steal. For where your treasure is, there your heart will be also.

"The eye is the lamp of the body. If your eyes are good, your whole body will be full of light. But if your eyes are bad, your whole body will be full of darkness. If then the light within you is darkness, how great is that darkness!

"No one can serve two masters. Either he will hate the one and love the other, or he will be devoted to the one and despise the other. You cannot serve both God and Money." MATTHEW 6:19-24

"Store up for yourselves treasures in heaven."

FROM OSWALD CHAMBERS

ᴥ When we lay up treasure on earth it may go at any moment, but when we learn to lay up treasure in heaven, nothing can touch it — "therefore will not we fear, though the earth be removed . . ." it is perfectly secure. MFL 112

---

a. Exodus 21:24; Leviticus 24:20; Deuteronomy 19:21
b. Leviticus 19:18
c. Or *from evil;* some late manuscripts [of Matthew 6:13] *one, / for yours is the kingdom and the power and the glory forever. Amen*

22

THE SERMON ON THE MOUNT CONCLUDED

Therefore I tell you, do not worry about your life, what you will eat or drink; or about your body, what you will wear. Is not life more important than food, and the body more important than clothes? Look at the birds of the air; they do not sow or reap or store away in barns, and yet your heavenly Father feeds them. Are you not much more valuable than they? Who of you by worrying can add a single hour to his life?[a]

"And why do you worry about clothes? See how the lilies of the field grow. They do not labor or spin. Yet I tell you that not even Solomon in all his splendor was dressed like one of these. If that is how God clothes the grass of the field, which is here today and tomorrow is thrown into the fire, will he not much more clothe you, O you of little faith? So do not worry, saying, 'What shall we eat?' or 'What shall we wear?' For the pagans run after all these things, and your heavenly Father knows that you need them. But seek first his kingdom and his righteousness, and all these things will be given to you as well. Therefore do not worry about tomorrow, for tomorrow will worry about itself. Each day has enough trouble of its own." MATTHEW 6:25-34

"Do not worry about your life."

FROM OSWALD CHAMBERS

❧ If all power is given to Jesus Christ, what right have I to insult Him by worrying? If we will let these words of Jesus come into our heart, we shall soon see how contemptible our unbelief is. Jesus Christ

103

will do anything for us in keeping with His own character, the power that comes from Him is stamped with His nature. BSG 57

꙳ "Take no thought . . ." don't take the pressure of forethought upon yourself. It is not only wrong to worry, it is infidelity, because worrying means that we do not think that God can look after the practical details of our lives, and it is never anything else that worries us. Have you ever noticed what Jesus said would choke the word He puts in? The devil? No, the cares of this world. It is the little worries always. I will not trust where I cannot see; that is where infidelity begins. The only cure for infidelity is obedience to the Spirit. MUH 144

JUDGING OTHERS

"Do not judge, or you too will be judged. For in the same way you judge others, you will be judged. Do not condemn, and you will not be condemned. Forgive, and you will be forgiven. Give, and it will be given to you. A good measure, pressed down, shaken together and running over, will be poured into your lap. For with the measure you use, it will be measured to you."

He also told them this parable: "Can a blind man lead a blind man? Will they not both fall into a pit? A student is not above his teacher, but everyone who is fully trained will be like his teacher.

"Why do you look at the speck of sawdust in your brother's eye and pay no attention to the plank in your own eye? How can you say to your brother, 'Brother, let me take the speck out of your eye,' when all the time you yourself fail to see there is a plank in your own eye? You hypocrite, first take the plank out of your own eye, and then you will see clearly to remove the speck from your brother's eye.

"Do not give dogs what is sacred; do not throw your pearls to pigs. If you do, they may trample them under their feet, and then turn and tear you to pieces." MATTHEW 7:1-6; Luke 6:37-42

"Why do you look at the speck
. . . in your brother's eye."

FROM OSWALD CHAMBERS

≈ It is easy to see the specks and the wrong in others, because we see in others that of which we are guilty ourselves. PH 121

≈ It is a great education to try to put yourself into the circumstances of others before passing judgment on them. SHH 113

≈ There is always one fact more in every life of which we know nothing, therefore Jesus says, "Judge not." SSM 79

ASK, SEEK, KNOCK

"Ask and it will be given to you; seek and you will find; knock and the door will be opened to you. For everyone who asks receives; he who seeks finds; and to him who knocks, the door will be opened.

"Which of you, if his son asks for bread, will give him a stone? Or if he asks for a fish, will give him a snake? If you, then, though you are evil, know how to give good gifts to your children, how much more will your Father in heaven give good gifts to those who ask him! So in everything, do to others what you would have them do to you, for this sums up the Law and the Prophets." MATTHEW 7:7-12

"Ask and it will be given to you."

FROM OSWALD CHAMBERS

≈ In prayer have we learned the wonderful power of that phrase " . . . boldness to enter into the holiest by the blood of Jesus?" It means that we can talk to God as Jesus Christ did, but only through the right of His atonement. We must never allow the idea that because we have been obedient, because our need is great, because we long for it, therefore God will hear us. There is only one way into the holiest, and that is by the blood of Jesus. OBH 45

THE NARROW AND WIDE GATES

"Enter through the narrow gate. For wide is the gate and broad is the road that leads to destruction, and many enter through it. But small is the gate and narrow the road that leads to life, and only a few find it." MATTHEW 7:13-14

"Enter the narrow gate."

FROM OSWALD CHAMBERS

 The freedom man has is not that of power but of choice; consequently, he is accountable for choosing the course he takes. For instance, we can choose whether or not we will accept the proposition of salvation which God puts before us; whether or not we will let God rule our lives; but we have not the power to do exactly what we like. MFL 27

A TREE AND ITS FRUIT

"Watch out for false prophets. They come to you in sheep's clothing, but inwardly they are ferocious wolves. By their fruit you will recognize them. Do people pick grapes from thornbushes, or figs from thistles? People do not pick figs from thornbushes, or grapes from briers. Likewise every good tree bears good fruit, but a bad tree bears bad fruit. A good tree cannot bear bad fruit, and a bad tree cannot bear good fruit. Every tree that does not bear good fruit is cut down and thrown into the fire.

"Each tree is recognized by its own fruit. Thus, by their fruit you will recognize them. The good man brings good things out of the good stored up in his heart, and the evil man brings evil things out of the evil stored up in his heart. For out of the overflow of his heart his mouth speaks.

"Why do you call me, 'Lord, Lord,' and do not do what I say? Not everyone who says to me, 'Lord, Lord,' will enter the kingdom of heaven, but only he who does the will of my Father who is in heaven. Many will say to me on that day, 'Lord, Lord, did we not prophesy in your name, and in your name drive out demons and perform many miracles?' Then I will tell them plainly, 'I never knew you. Away from me, you evildoers!' " MATTHEW 7:15-23; LUKE 6:43-46

"Watch out for false prophets."

FROM OSWALD CHAMBERS

❧ Jesus tells His disciples to test preachers and teachers by their fruit. There are two tests—one is the fruit in the life of the preacher, and the other is the fruit of the doctrine. The fruit of a man's own life may be perfectly beautiful, and at the same time he may be teaching a doctrine which, if logically worked out, would produce the devil's fruit in other lives. It is easy to be captivated by a beautiful life and to argue that therefore what the life teaches must be right. Jesus says, "Be careful; test your teacher by his fruit." The other side is just as true, a man may be teaching beautiful truths and have magnificent doctrine while the fruit in his own life is rotten. We say that if a man lives a beautiful life, his doctrine must be right; not necessarily so, says Jesus. Then again we say because a man teaches the right thing, therefore his life must be right; not necessarily so, says Jesus. Test the doctrine by its fruit, and test the teacher by his fruit. SSM 98

THE WISE AND FOOLISH BUILDERS

"Therefore everyone who comes to me and hears these words of mine and puts them into practice is like a wise man building a house, who dug down deep and laid the foundation on rock. The rain came down, the streams rose, and the winds blew and beat against that house. When a flood came, the torrent struck that house but could not shake it, because it was well built. It did not fall, because it had its foundation on the rock. But everyone who hears these words of mine and does not put them into practice is like a foolish man who built his house on sand, on the ground without a foundation. The rain came down, the streams rose, and the winds blew and beat against that house. The moment the torrent struck, it collapsed and fell with a great crash, and its destruction was complete."

When Jesus had finished saying these things, the crowds were amazed at his teaching, because he taught as one who had authority, and not as their teachers of the law. MATTHEW 7:24-29; LUKE 6:47-49

*"The crowds were amazed at his [Jesus'] teaching,
because he taught as one who had authority."*

From Oswald Chambers

❧ The mainspring of the heart of Jesus Christ was the mainspring of the heart of God the Father,ʲ consequently, the words Jesus Christ spoke were the exact expression of God's thought. In our Lord the tongue was in its right place; He never spoke from His head, but always from His heart. BP 126

❧ Can Jesus Christ speak to me today? Certainly He can, through the Holy Spirit; but if I take the words of Jesus without His Spirit, they are of no avail to me. I can conjure with them; I can do all kinds of things with them, but they are not "spirit and life." When the Holy Spirit is in me, He will bring to my remembrance what Jesus has said and make His Words alive. The Spirit within me enables me to assimilate the words of Jesus. BP 231

---

a. Or *single cubit to his height*

23

A SERVANT HEALED AND A DEAD MAN RAISED

When Jesus came down from the mountainside, large crowds followed him. He entered Capernaum. There a centurion's servant, whom his master valued highly, was sick and about to die. The centurion heard of Jesus and sent some elders of the Jews to him, asking him to come and heal his servant: "Lord, my servant lies at home paralyzed and in terrible suffering." When they came to Jesus, they pleaded earnestly with him, "This man deserves to have you do this, because he loves our nation and has built our synagogue."

Jesus said, "I will go and heal him." So Jesus went with them.

He was not far from the house when the centurion sent friends to say to him: "Lord, don't trouble yourself, for I do not deserve to have you come under my roof. That is why I did not even consider myself worthy to come to you. But just say the word, and my servant will be healed. For I myself am a man under authority, with soldiers under me. I tell this one, 'Go,' and he goes; and that one, 'Come,' and he comes. I say to my servant, 'Do this,' and he does it."

When Jesus heard this, he was amazed at him, and turning to the crowd following him, he said, "I tell you the truth, I have not found anyone with such great faith even in Israel. I say to you that many will come from the east and the west, and will take their places at the feast with Abraham, Isaac and Jacob in the kingdom of heaven. But the subjects of the kingdom will be thrown outside, into the darkness, where there will be weeping and gnashing of teeth."

Then Jesus said to the centurion, "Go! It will be done just as you believed it would." And his servant was healed at that very hour. Then the men who had been sent returned to the house and found the servant well.

109

Soon afterward, Jesus went to a town called Nain, and his disciples and a large crowd went along with him. As he approached the town gate, a dead person was being carried out — the only son of his mother, and she was a widow. And a large crowd from the town was with her. When the Lord saw her, his heart went out to her and he said, "Don't cry."

Then he went up and touched the coffin, and those carrying it stood still. He said, "Young man, I say to you, get up!" The dead man sat up and began to talk, and Jesus gave him back to his mother.

They were all filled with awe and praised God. "A great prophet has appeared among us," they said. "God has come to help his people." This news about Jesus spread throughout Judea[a] and the surrounding country. MATTHEW 8:1, 5-13; LUKE 7:1-17

"I tell you the truth,
I have not found anyone with such great faith."

FROM OSWALD CHAMBERS

ૐ If we have faith only in what we experience of salvation, we will get depressed and morbid; but to be a believer in Jesus Christ is to have an irrepressible belief and a life of uncrushable gaiety. AUG 116

ૐ A spiritually minded Christian has to go through the throes of a total mental readjustment; it is a God-glorifying process, if a humbling one. People continually say, "How can I have more faith?" You may ask for faith to further orders, but you will never have faith apart from Jesus Christ. You can't pump up faith out of your own heart. Whenever faith is starved in your soul, it is because you are not in contact with Jesus; get in contact with Him; and lack of faith will go in two seconds. CHI 60

ૐ Whenever Jesus Christ came across people who were free from the ban of finality which comes from religious beliefs, He awakened faith in them at once. The only ones who were without faith in Him were those who were bound up by religious certitude. Faith means that I commit myself to Jesus, project myself absolutely on to Him, sink or swim — and you do both; you sink out of yourself and swim

110

into Him. Faith is implicit confidence in Jesus and in His faith. It is one thing to have faith in Jesus and another thing to have faith about everything for which He has faith. CHI 60

❧ Our Lord did not rebuke His disciples for making mistakes, but for not having faith. The two things that astonished Him were "little faith" and "great faith." Faith is not in what Jesus Christ can do, but in Himself, and anything He can do is less than Himself. LG 150

❧ Faith is our personal confidence in a Being whose character we know, but whose ways we cannot trace by common sense. By the reasonings of faith is meant the practical outworking in our life of implicit, determined confidence in God. Common sense is mathematical; faith is not mathematical, faith works on illogical lines. Jesus Christ places the strongest emphasis on faith, and especially on the faith that has been tried. SSM 66

❧ No power can deceive a child of God who keeps in the light with God. I am perfectly certain that the devil likes to deceive us and limit us in our practical belief as to what Jesus Christ can do. There is no limit to what He can do, absolutely none. "All things are possible to him that believeth" (Mark 9:23). Jesus says that faith in Him is omnipotent. SHL 31

---

a. Or *the land of the Jews*

24

JESUS ANOINTED
BY A SINFUL WOMAN

Now one of the Pharisees invited Jesus to have dinner with him, so he went to the Pharisee's house and reclined at the table. When a woman who had lived a sinful life in that town learned that Jesus was eating at the Pharisee's house, she brought an alabaster jar of perfume, and as she stood behind him at his feet weeping, she began to wet his feet with her tears. Then she wiped them with her hair, kissed them and poured perfume on them.

When the Pharisee who had invited him saw this, he said to himself, "If this man were a prophet, he would know who is touching him and what kind of woman she is—that she is a sinner."

Jesus answered him, "Simon, I have something to tell you."

"Tell me, teacher," he said.

"Two men owed money to a certain moneylender. One owed him five hundred denarii,[a] and the other fifty. Neither of them had the money to pay him back, so he canceled the debts of both. Now which of them will love him more?"

Simon replied, "I suppose the one who had the bigger debt canceled."

"You have judged correctly," Jesus said.

Then he turned toward the woman and said to Simon, "Do you see this woman? I came into your house. You did not give me any water for my feet, but she wet my feet with her tears and wiped them with her hair. You did not give me a kiss, but this woman, from the time I entered, has not stopped kissing my feet. You did not put oil on my head, but she has poured perfume on my feet. Therefore, I tell you, her many sins have been forgiven—for she loved much. But he who has been forgiven little loves little."

Then Jesus said to her, "Your sins are forgiven. Your faith has saved you; go in peace."

The other guests began to say among themselves, "Who is this who even forgives sins?" LUKE 7:36-50

"Your sins are forgiven.
Your faith has saved you; go in peace."

FROM OSWALD CHAMBERS

> Jesus Christ did not come to fling forgiveness broadcast; He did not come to the Pharisees, who withstood Him, and said He was possessed with a devil, and say, "I forgive you": He said, "How can you escape the damnation of hell?" We may talk as much as we like about forgiveness, but it will never make any difference to us unless we realize that we need it. God can never forgive the man who does not want to be forgiven. HGM 101

> Jesus Christ taught His disciples to pray "Forgive us our debts, as we forgive our debtors" (Matt. 6:12); that is, He taught them to recognize that God's method of forgiveness is the same as our own. . . . Jesus Christ did not say *"because* we forgive our debtors," but *"as* we forgive our debtors"; that is, as children of God we are forgiven not on the ground of redemption, but on the ground that we show the same forgiveness to our fellows that God has shown to us. HGM 102

> When we turn to God and say we are sorry, Jesus Christ has pledged His word that we will be forgiven, but the forgiveness is not operative unless we turn, because our turning is the proof that we know we need forgiveness. HGM 104

> By means of the Redemption, God undertakes to deal with a man's past, and He does it in two ways—first, He forgives it, and then He makes it a wonderful culture for the future. When God says, "Don't do that anymore," He instills into me the power that enables me not to do it any more, and the power comes by right of what Jesus Christ did on the cross. That is the unspeakable wonder of the forgiveness of God, and when we become rightly related to God, we are to have the same relationship to our fellowmen that

114

God has to us. "And be ye kind one to another, tenderhearted, forgiving one another, even as God for Christ's sake hath forgiven you" (Eph. 4:32). HGM 105

---

a. A denarius was a coin worth about a day's wages

25

THE SIGN OF JONAH AND DOING GOD'S WILL

S ome of the Pharisees and teachers of the law said to him, "Teacher, we want to see a miraculous sign from you."

He answered, "A wicked and adulterous generation asks for a miraculous sign! But none will be given it except the sign of the prophet Jonah. For as Jonah was three days and three nights in the belly of a huge fish, so the Son of Man will be three days and three nights in the heart of the earth. The men of Nineveh will stand up at the judgment with this generation and condemn it; for they repented at the preaching of Jonah, and now one[a] greater than Jonah is here. The Queen of the South will rise at the judgment with this generation and condemn it; for she came from the ends of the earth to listen to Solomon's wisdom, and now one[a] greater than Solomon is here.

"When an evil spirit comes out of a man, it goes through arid places seeking rest and does not find it. Then it says, 'I will return to the house I left.' When it arrives, it finds the house unoccupied, swept clean and put in order. Then it goes and takes with it seven other spirits more wicked than itself, and they go in and live there. And the final condition of that man is worse than the first. That is how it will be with this wicked generation."
MATTHEW 12:38-45

JESUS' MOTHER AND BROTHERS

Now Jesus' mother and brothers arrived to see him, but they were not able to get near him because of the crowd. While Jesus was still talking to the crowd, his mother and brothers stood outside, wanting to speak to him. They sent someone in to call him. A crowd was sitting around him, and they told him, "Your mother and brothers are standing outside looking for you, wanting to speak to you."[b]

"Who is my mother, and who are my brothers?" he asked.

Then he looked at those seated in a circle around him. Pointing to his disciples, he said, "Here are my mother and my brothers — those who hear God's word and put it into practice. For whoever does the will of my Father in heaven is my brother and sister and mother." MATTHEW 12:46-50; MARK 3:31-35; LUKE 8:19-21

"Whoever does the will of my Father in heaven
is my brother and sister and mother."

FROM OSWALD CHAMBERS

> When the Spirit of God comes into a man, He brings His own generating willpower and causes him to will with God, and we have the amazing revelation that the saint's free choices are the predeterminations of God. That is a most wonderful thing in Christian psychology, viz., that a saint chooses exactly what God predetermined he should choose. If you have never received the Spirit of God, this will be one of the things which is "foolishness" to you; but if you have received the Spirit and are obeying Him, you find He brings your spirit into complete harmony with God and the sound of your goings and the sound of God's goings are one and the same. BP 215

> Will is the whole man active. I cannot *give up* my will; I must exercise it. I must *will* to receive God's Spirit. When God gives a vision of truth, it is never a question of what He will do, but of what we will do. MUH 190

> If I am a child of God, I realize not only that God is the source of my will, but that God is *in* me to will. I do not bring an opposed will to God's will; God's will *is* my will, and my natural choices are along the line of His will. Then I begin to understand that God engineers circumstances for me to do His will in them, not for me to lie down under them and give way to self-pity. OBH 130

> Surrender is not the surrender of the external life, but of the will; when that is done, all is done. There are very few crises in life; the

great crisis is the surrender of the will. God never crushes a man's will into surrender; He never beseeches him; He waits until the man yields up his will to Him. MUH 257

---

a. Or *something*
b. Some manuscripts do not have [this sentence in Matthew 12:47]

26

THE PARABLE OF THE SOWER

On another occasion that same day, Jesus went out of the house, sat by the lake and began to teach. People were coming from town after town. Such large crowds gathered around him that he got into a boat and sat in it out on the lake, while all the people stood along the shore at the water's edge. Then he taught them many things by parables.

In his teaching he told this parable: "Listen! A farmer went out to sow his seed. As he was scattering the seed, some fell along the path; it was trampled on, and the birds of the air came and ate it up. Some fell on rocky places, where it did not have much soil. It sprang up quickly, because the soil was shallow. But when the sun came up, the plants were scorched; they withered because they had no moisture, no root. Other seed fell among thorns, which grew up with it and choked the plants, so that they did not bear grain. Still other seed fell on good soil. It came up, grew and produced a crop, multiplying thirty, sixty or even a hundred times more than what was sown."

When he said this, he called out, "He who has ears to hear, let him hear."

When he was alone, the Twelve and the others around him came and asked him about the parables, *and* what this parable meant. The disciples asked, "Why do you speak to the people in parables?"

He replied, "The knowledge of the secrets of the kingdom of heaven has been given to you, but not to them. Whoever has will be given more, and he will have an abundance. Whoever does not have, even what he has will be taken from him. This is why to those others on the outside I speak everything in parables, so that,

" 'Though seeing, they do not see;
though hearing, they do not
hear or understand.'[a]

In them is fulfilled the prophecy of Isaiah:

" 'You will be ever hearing
but never understanding;
you will be ever seeing but never perceiving.
For this people's heart has become calloused;
they hardly hear with their ears,
and they have closed their eyes.
Otherwise they might see with their eyes,
hear with their ears,
understand with their hearts
and turn, and I would heal them
and they might be forgiven.'[b]

"But blessed are your eyes because they see, and your ears because they hear. For I tell you the truth, many prophets and righteous men longed to see what you see but did not see it, and to hear what you hear but did not hear it."

Then Jesus said to them, "Don't you understand this parable? How then will you understand any parable? Listen then to what the parable of the sower means: The seed is the word of God. The farmer sows the word. Some people are like seed along the path, where the word is sown. As soon as they hear the message about the kingdom and *do* not understand it, Satan comes and snatches away the word that was sown in their hearts, so that they may not believe and be saved. Others, like seed sown on rocky places, are the ones who hear the word and at once receive it with joy. But since they have no root, they last only a short time. They believe for a while, but in the time of testing, when trouble or persecution comes because of the word, they quickly fall away. Still others, like seed sown among thorns, hear the word, but as they go on their way they are choked by the worries of this life, the deceitfulness of wealth, and the desires for pleasures and other things, and they do not mature, making *them* unfruitful. But the seed sown on good soil stands for others who, with a noble and good heart, hear the word, understand, accept and retain it, and by persevering produce a crop—thirty, sixty or even a hundred times what was sown." MATTHEW 13:1-23; MARK 4:1-20; LUKE 8:4-15

"Blessed are your eyes because they see,
and your ears because they hear."

FROM OSWALD CHAMBERS

  ➥   If we want to know what God is like, let us study the Lord Jesus. "He that hath seen Me hath seen the Father" (John 14:9). How did people see Him in the days of His flesh? By their natural eyes? No, after His resurrection they received the Holy Spirit, and their eyes were opened and they knew Him. We do not know Him by the reasoning of our minds, but by the new life. Jesus Christ is to us the faithful Face of God. PR 138

  ➥   The eye in the body records exactly what it looks at. The eye simply records, and the record is according to the light thrown on what it looks at. Conscience is the eye of the soul which looks out on what it is taught is God, and how conscience records depends entirely upon what light is thrown upon God. Our Lord Jesus Christ is the only true light on God. When a man sees Jesus Christ, he does not get a new conscience, but a totally new light is thrown upon God, and conscience records accordingly, with the result that he is absolutely upset by conviction of sin. PS 61

  ➥   Jesus Christ continually referred to hearing: "He that hath ears to hear, let him hear." We say that He means the ears of our heart, but that is very misleading. He means our physical ears which are trained to hear by the disposition of our soul life. God spoke to Jesus once and the people said it thundered, but Jesus did not think it thundered; His ears were trained by the disposition of His soul to know His Father's voice. BP 74

  ➥   If you have had a past history with Jesus Christ, if He has delivered and emancipated you, when He speaks, He speaks with the volume of that intimacy of personal acquaintance, and you know, not by hearing only, but implicitly all through you—"It is the Lord! No one else could speak like that to me." HGM 56

ふ God emphatically states, "This is My beloved Son" (Matt. 3:17):
this Man, known to men as the humble Nazarene Carpenter, is
Almighty God presented in the guise of a human life; "Hear Him."
How many of us do hear Him? We always hear the thing we listen
for, and our disposition determines what we listen for. When Jesus
Christ alters our disposition, He gives us the power to hear as He
hears. PR 83

---

a. Isaiah 6:9
b. Isaiah 6:9-10

27

THE PARABLE OF THE WEEDS

Jesus told them another parable: "The kingdom of heaven is like a man who sowed good seed in his field. But while everyone was sleeping, his enemy came and sowed weeds among the wheat, and went away. When the wheat sprouted and formed heads, then the weeds also appeared.

"The owner's servants came to him and said, 'Sir, didn't you sow good seed in your field? Where then did the weeds come from?'

" 'An enemy did this,' he replied.

"The servants asked him, 'Do you want us to go and pull them up?'

" 'No,' he answered, 'because while you are pulling the weeds, you may root up the wheat with them. Let both grow together until the harvest. At that time I will tell the harvesters: First collect the weeds and tie them in bundles to be burned; then gather the wheat and bring it into my barn.' " MATTHEW 13:24-30

THE PARABLE OF THE WEEDS EXPLAINED

Then he left the crowd and went into the house. His disciples came to him and said, "Explain to us the parable of the weeds in the field."

He answered, "The one who sowed the good seed is the Son of Man. The field is the world, and the good seed stands for the sons of the kingdom. The weeds are the sons of the evil one, and the enemy who sows them is the devil. The harvest is the end of the age, and the harvesters are angels.

"As the weeds are pulled up and burned in the fire, so it will be at the end of the age. The Son of Man will send out his angels, and they will weed out of his kingdom everything that causes sin and all who do evil. They will throw them into the fiery furnace, where there will be weeping and gnashing of teeth. Then the righteous will shine like the sun in the kingdom of their Father. He who has ears, let him hear." MATTHEW 13:36-43

"The Son of Man will send out his angels,
and they will weed out of his kingdom
everything that causes sin and all who do evil."

FROM OSWALD CHAMBERS

> ❧ The judgments of God are a consuming fire whereby He destroys in order to deliver; the time to be alarmed in life is when all things are undisturbed. CHI 66

> ❧ The judgments of God leave scars, and the scars remain until I humbly and joyfully recognize that the judgments are deserved and that God is justified in them. CHI 70

> ❧ There are dark and mysterious and perplexing things in life, but the prevailing authority at the back of all is a righteous authority, and a man does not need to be unduly concerned. When we do find out the judgment of God, we shall be absolutely satisfied with it to the last degree; we won't have another word to say—"that Thou mightest be justified when Thou speakest, and be clear when Thou judgest." SHH 37

> ❧ The pronouncement of coming doom is a combining of judgment and deliverance. When God's limit is reached He destroys the unsaveable and liberates the saveable; consequently judgment days are the great mercy of God because they separate between good and evil, between right and wrong. OPG 19

> ❧ There is no problem, no personal grief, no agony or distress [and God knows there are some fathomless agonies just now—awful injustices and wrongs and evils and nobility all mixed up together] but will have an overwhelming explanation one day. If we will hang on to the fact that God is true and loving and just, every judgment He passes will find us in agreement with it finally. SHH 38

126

28

JESUS CALMS A STORM

T hat day when evening came *and* Jesus saw the crowd around him, he gave orders to his disciples: "Let us cross over to the other side of the lake." Then he got into the boat and his disciples followed him. Leaving the crowd behind, they took him along, just as he was, in the boat. There were also other boats with him. They set out. As they sailed, he fell asleep. Without warning, a furious squall came up on the lake, so that the waves swept over the boat. The boat was being swamped, and they were in great danger.

Jesus was in the stern, sleeping on a cushion. The disciples went and woke him, saying, "Master, Master, save us! We're going to drown! Teacher, don't you care if we drown?"

He replied, "You of little faith, why are you so afraid?" Then he got up, rebuked the wind and said to the raging waters, "Quiet! Be still!" Then the storm subsided, the wind died down, and all was completely calm.

"Where is your faith?" he asked his disciples. "Do you still have no faith?"

They were terrified. In fear and amazement they asked one another, "Who is this? What kind of man is this? He commands even the winds and the waves, and they obey him." MATTHEW 8:18, 23-27; MARK 4:35-41; LUKE 8:22-25

"You of little faith,
why are you so afraid?"

127

From Oswald Chambers

❧ The majority of us believe in Jesus Christ only as far as we can see by our own wits. If we really believed Him, what a mighty difference there would be in us! We would trust His mind instead of our own; we would stop being "amateur providences" over other lives, and we would be fit to do our twenty-four hours work like no else. "Except ye become as little children" (see Matt. 18:3) — simple-hearted, trusting, and not being afraid. BE 49

❧ To have faith tests a man for all he is worth. He has to stand in the commonsense universe in the midst of things which conflict with his faith, and place his confidence in the Word whose character is revealed in Jesus Christ. SSM 66

❧ Think what faith in Jesus Christ claims — that He can present us faultless before the throne of God, unutterably pure, absolutely rectified, and profoundly justified. Stand in implicit adoring faith in Him; *He* is made unto us "wisdom, and righteousness, and sanctification, and redemption" (1 Cor. 1:30). How can we talk of making a sacrifice for the Son of God! Our salvation is from hell and perdition, and then we talk about making sacrifices! MUH 318

❧ Faith must be tried or it is not faith; faith is not mathematics nor reason. Scriptural faith is not to be illustrated by the faith we exhibit in our commonsense life; it is trust in the character of One we have never seen, in the integrity of Jesus Christ, and it must be tried. PH 204

❧ Faith is implicit confidence in Jesus and in His faith. It is one thing to have faith in Jesus and another thing to have faith about everything for which He has faith. CHI 61

❧ The thing that is precious in the sight of God is faith that has been tried. Tried faith is spendable; it is so much wealth stored up in heaven, and the more we go through the trial of our faith, the wealthier we become in the heavenly regions. PH 83

29

THE HEALING OF A
DEMON-POSSESSED MAN

They sailed to the region of the Gerasenes (Gadarenes),[a] which is across the lake from Galilee. When he arrived at the other side, Jesus got out of the boat. When Jesus stepped ashore, he was met by a demon-possessed man from the town, who for a long time had not worn clothes or lived in a house, but had lived in the tombs. No one could bind him any more, not even with a chain. Many times an evil spirit had seized him, and though he was chained hand and foot and kept under guard, he tore the chains apart and broke the irons on his feet. No one was strong enough to subdue him. He had been driven by the demon into solitary places. Night and day among the tombs and in the hills he would cry out and cut himself with stones.

When he saw Jesus from a distance, he ran and fell on his knees at his feet. He cried out, shouting at the top of his voice, "What do you want with me, Jesus, Son of the Most High God? Have you come here to torture us before the appointed time? I beg you, don't torture me! Swear to God that you won't torture me!" For Jesus had commanded him, "Come out of this man, you evil spirit!"

Then Jesus asked him, "What is your name?"

"My name is Legion," he replied, "for we are many," because many demons had gone into him. And he begged Jesus again and again not to send them out of the area, not to order them to go into the Abyss.

Some distance from them a large herd of pigs was feeding on the nearby hillside. The demons begged Jesus, "If you drive us out, send us into the herd of pigs; allow us to go into them." He gave them permission. He said to them, "Go!" When the demons came out, they went into the pigs. The whole herd, about two thousand in number, rushed down the steep bank into the lake and were drowned.

When those tending the pigs saw what had happened, they ran off and reported all this, including what had happened to the demon-possessed [man], in the town and countryside. Then the whole town went out to see what had happened. When they came to Jesus, they saw the man who had been possessed by the legion of demons, sitting there at Jesus' feet, dressed and in his right mind; and they were afraid. Those who had seen it told the people how the demon-possessed man had been cured—and told about the pigs as well. Then all the people of the region of the Gerasenes began to plead with Jesus to leave their region, because they were overcome with fear. So he got into the boat and left.

As Jesus was getting into the boat, the man from whom the demons had gone out begged to go with him. Jesus did not let him, but sent him away, saying, "Return home to your family and tell them how much God has done for you, and how the Lord has had mercy on you." So the man went away and told all over town, and began to tell in the Decapolis[b] how much Jesus had done for him. And all the people were amazed. MATTHEW 8:28-34; MARK 5:1-20; LUKE 8:26-39

"Come out of this man,
you evil spirit!"

FROM OSWALD CHAMBERS

∂ You can always tell whether Christians are spiritually minded by their attitude to the supernatural. The modern attitude to demon possession is very instructive; so many take the attitude that there is no such thing as demon possession, and infer that Jesus Christ Himself knew quite well that there was no such thing, not seeing that by such an attitude they put themselves in the place of the superior person, and claim to know all the private opinions of the Almighty about iniquity. BP 91

∂ The New Testament is full of the supernatural; Jesus Christ continually looked on scenery we do not see and saw supernatural forces at work. "Try the spirits whether they are of God" (1 John 4:1). The soul of man may be vastly complicated by interference from the supernatural, but Jesus Christ can guard us there. BP 91

    Just as man may become identified with Jesus Christ, so he can be identified with the devil. Just as a man can be born again into the kingdom where Jesus Christ lives and moves and has His being and can become identified with Him in entire sanctification, so he can be born again, so to speak, into the devil's kingdom and be entirely consecrated to the devil. BP 92

    Our Lord continually saw things and beings we do not see. He talked about Satan and demons and angels. We don't see Satan or demons or angels, but Jesus Christ unquestionably did, and He sees their influence upon us. The man who criticizes Jesus Christ's statements about demon possession does not realize what he is doing. BP 156

    Having "suffered being tempted," He [Jesus] knows how terrific are the onslaughts of the devil against human nature unaided; He has been there; therefore, He can be touched with the feeling of our infirmities. CHI 99

    The devil is a bully, but he cannot stand for a second before God. IYA 32

---

a. Some manuscripts *Gadarenes;* other manuscripts *Gergesenes* [and hereinafter]
b. That is, the Ten Cities [and hereinafter]

30

A DEAD GIRL AND A SICK WOMAN

N ow when Jesus had again crossed over by boat to the other side of the lake, a large crowd gathered around while he was by the lake *and* welcomed him, for they were all expecting him. Just then one of the synagogue rulers, a man named Jairus, came there because his only daughter, a girl of about twelve, was dying. Seeing Jesus, he knelt at his feet and pleaded earnestly with him to come to his house, and said, "My little daughter is dying. Please come and put your hands on her so that she will be healed and live." So Jesus got up and went with him, and so did his disciples.

As Jesus was on his way, a large crowd followed and pressed around him. The crowds almost crushed him. And a woman was there who had been subject to bleeding for twelve years,[a] but no one could heal her. She had suffered a great deal under the care of many doctors and had spent all she had, yet instead of getting better she grew worse. When she heard about Jesus, she said to herself, "If I only touch his cloak, I will be healed." She came up behind him in the crowd and touched the edge of his cloak. Immediately her bleeding stopped, and the woman was healed from that moment. She felt in her body that she was freed from her suffering.

At once Jesus realized that power had gone out from him. He turned around in the crowd and asked, "Who touched my clothes?"

When they all denied it, Peter said, "Master, you see the people are crowding and pressing against you, and yet you can ask, 'Who touched me?' "

But Jesus said, "Someone touched me; I know that power has gone out from me."

Looking around to see who had done it, Jesus turned and saw

her. Then the woman, knowing what had happened to her *and* seeing that she could not go unnoticed, came trembling with fear and fell at his feet. In the presence of all the people, she told him the whole truth: why she had touched him and how she had been instantly healed. Then he said to her, "Take heart, daughter, your faith has healed you. Go in peace and be freed from your suffering."

While Jesus was still speaking, some men came from the house of Jairus, the synagogue ruler. "Your daughter is dead," they said. "Why bother the teacher any more?"

Hearing this *but* ignoring what they said, Jesus told Jairus, "Don't be afraid; just believe, and she will be healed."

Jesus did not let anyone follow him except Peter, James and John the brother of James. They entered the ruler's house and saw the flute players and the noisy commotion with all the people crying and wailing loudly, mourning for her. "Why all this commotion and wailing?" Jesus said. "Stop wailing. Go away. The girl is not dead but asleep." But they laughed at him, knowing that she was dead.

After he put all the crowd outside, he took the child's father and mother and the disciples who were with him, and went in where the child was. He took her by the hand and said to her, "Talitha koum!" (which means, "Little girl, I say to you, get up!"). Immediately her spirit returned, and the girl stood up and walked around. Then he told them to give her something to eat. Her parents were completely astonished, but he gave them strict orders not to tell anyone about what had happened.

News of this spread through all that region. MATTHEW 9:18-26; MARK 5:21-43; LUKE 8:40-56

> *" 'Little girl, I say to you, get up!'*
> *Immediately her spirit returned."*

FROM OSWALD CHAMBERS

⤳ Jesus Christ has destroyed the dominion of death, and He can make us fit to face every problem of life, more than conqueror all along the line. RTR 54

❧ The Bible reveals that death is inevitable—"and so death passed upon all men" (Rom 5:12). "It is appointed unto men once to die" (Heb. 9:27). Repeat that over to yourself. It is appointed to everyone of us that we are going to cease to be as we are now, and the place that knows us now shall know us no more. We may shirk it, we may ignore it, we may be so full of robust health and spirits that the thought of death never enters, but it is inevitable.

Another thing—the Bible says that a certain class of man is totally indifferent to death, "for there are no bands [pangs] in their death" (Ps. 73:4). Over and over again the Bible points out that the wicked man, the Esau-type of man who is perfectly satisfied with life as it is, has not the slightest concern about death—because he is so brave and strong? No, because he is incapable of realizing what death means. The powers that press from the natural world have one tendency, and one only, to deaden all communication with God.

One other thing—the Bible says there are those who are intimidated by death. . . . "That through death He might destroy him that had the power of death, that is, the devil; and deliver them, who through fear of death were all their lifetime subject to bondage" (Heb. 2:14-15). The thought of death is never away from them; it terrorizes their days, it alarms their nights. Now read very reverently Hebrews 5:7: "Who . . . having offered up prayers and supplications with strong crying and tears unto Him that was able to save Him from death." Who is that? The Lord Jesus Christ. We cannot begin to fathom this passage; after years of meditation on it, we come only to the threshold of realizing what Gethsemane represents. Jesus Christ can deliver from the dread of death—"that through death He might destroy him that had the power of death, that is, the devil." SHL 25

---

a. Many manuscripts [of Luke 8:43] *years, and she had spent all she had on doctors*

31

A Prophet without Honor

s Jesus went on from there, two blind men followed him, calling out, "Have mercy on us, Son of David!"

When he had gone indoors, the blind men came to him, and he asked them, "Do you believe that I am able to do this?"

"Yes, Lord," they replied.

Then he touched their eyes and said, "According to your faith will it be done to you"; and their sight was restored. Jesus warned them sternly, "See that no one knows about this." But they went out and spread the news about him all over that region.

While they were going out, a man who was demon-possessed and could not talk was brought to Jesus. And when the demon was driven out, the man who had been mute spoke. The crowd was amazed and said, "Nothing like this has ever been seen in Israel."

But the Pharisees said, "It is by the prince of demons that he drives out demons."

Jesus left there and went to his hometown, accompanied by his disciples. When the Sabbath came, he began to teach the people in the synagogue, and many who heard him were amazed.

"Where did this man get this wisdom and these miraculous powers?" they asked. "Isn't this the carpenter? Isn't this the carpenter's son? Isn't his mother's name Mary, and aren't his brothers James, Joseph,[a] Simon and Judas? Aren't all his sisters here with us? Where then did this man get all these things?" And they took offense at him.

But Jesus said to them, "Only in his hometown, among his relatives and in his own house is a prophet without honor." Because of their lack of faith, he could not do any miracles there,

137

except lay his hands on a few sick people and heal them. And he was amazed at their lack of faith. MATTHEW 9:27-34; 13:54-58; MARK 6:1-6a

"Only in his hometown,
among his relatives and in his own house
is a prophet without honor."

FROM OSWALD CHAMBERS

    How continually the prophets break out with some arresting statement that seems fit only in the mouth of our Lord! How often the psalmist bursts out with utterances of an unaccountable touch, the full meaning of which is found for us in Jesus Christ alone. These prophets, these workmen of God, foreshadowed Jesus Christ in their measure, and experienced the awful loneliness of a servant of God. CD 112

    Before the Holy Spirit can materialize in the saints of this present age as He did in the prophets of old, a perfect holiness—physical, moral, and spiritual—is necessary. This is what Jesus Christ has wrought for us in the Atonement, and this is what is meant by entire sanctification. On that foundation the true elements of prophecy are built. A prophet is not a sanctified gypsy telling fortunes, but one who speaks as he is moved by the Holy Spirit within. CD 113, VOL 2

    The outstanding characteristic of the ancient people of God, of our Lord Jesus Christ and of the missionary, is the "prophet," or preaching, characteristic. In the Old Testament the prophet's calling is placed above that of king and of priest. It is the lives of the prophets that prefigure the Lord Jesus Christ. The character of the prophet is essential to his work. The characteristic of God's elective purpose in the finished condition of His servant is that of preaching. "It pleased God by the foolishness of preaching to save them that believe" (1 Cor. 1:21). SSY 107

a. Greek *Joses,* a variant of *Joseph*

138

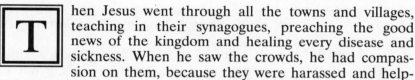

JESUS SENDS OUT THE TWELVE

Then Jesus went through all the towns and villages, teaching in their synagogues, preaching the good news of the kingdom and healing every disease and sickness. When he saw the crowds, he had compassion on them, because they were harassed and helpless, like sheep without a shepherd. Then he said to his disciples, "The harvest is plentiful but the workers are few. Ask the Lord of the harvest, therefore, to send out workers into his harvest field." MATTHEW 9:35-38; MARK 6:6b

DISCIPLES RECEIVE POWER AND AUTHORITY

When Jesus had called the Twelve together to him, he gave them power and authority to drive out all demons and to heal every disease and sickness. He sent them out two by two to preach the kingdom of God and to heal the sick.

These were his instructions: "Do not go among the Gentiles or enter any town of the Samaritans. Go rather to the lost sheep of Israel. As you go, preach this message: 'The kingdom of heaven is near.' Heal the sick, raise the dead, cleanse those who have leprosy, drive out demons. Freely you have received, freely give. Take nothing for the journey except a staff. Wear sandals. Do not take along any gold or silver or copper money in your belts; take no bag for the journey, no bread, no extra tunic or sandals or staff; for the worker is worth his keep.

"Whatever town or village you enter, search for some worthy person there and stay at his house until you leave that town. As you enter the home, give it your greeting. If the home is deserving, let your peace rest on it; if it is not, let your peace return to you. If anyone will not welcome you or listen to your words, shake the dust off your feet when you leave that home or town, as a testimony against them. I tell you the truth, it will be more bearable for Sodom and Gomorrah on the day of judgment than for that town. I am sending you out like sheep among wolves. Therefore be as shrewd as snakes and as innocent as doves.

"Be on your guard against men; they will hand you over to the local councils and flog you in their synagogues. On my account you will be brought before governors and kings as witnesses to them and to the Gentiles. But when they arrest you, do not worry about what to say or how to say it. At that time you will be given what to say, for it will not be you speaking, but the Spirit of your Father speaking through you.

"Brother will betray brother to death, and a father his child; children will rebel against their parents and have them put to death. All men will hate you because of me, but he who stands firm to the end will be saved. When you are persecuted in one place, flee to another. I tell you the truth, you will not finish going through the cities of Israel before the Son of Man comes.

"A student is not above his teacher, nor a servant above his master. It is enough for the student to be like his teacher, and the servant like his master. If the head of the house has been called Beelzebub, how much more the members of his household!

"So do not be afraid of them. There is nothing concealed that will not be disclosed, or hidden that will not be made known. What I tell you in the dark, speak in the daylight; what is whispered in your ear, proclaim from the roofs. Do not be afraid of those who kill the body but cannot kill the soul. Rather, be afraid of the One who can destroy both soul and body in hell. Are not two sparrows sold for a penny[a]? Yet not one of them will fall to the ground apart from the will of your Father. And even the very hairs of your head are all numbered. So don't be afraid; you are worth more than many sparrows.

"Whoever acknowledges me before men, I will also acknowledge him before my Father in heaven. But whoever disowns me before men, I will disown him before my Father in heaven.

"Do not suppose that I have come to bring peace to the earth. I did not come to bring peace, but a sword. For I have come to turn

140

" 'a man against his father,
a daughter against her mother,
a daughter-in-law against her mother-in-law —
a man's enemies will be
the members of his own household.'[b]

"Anyone who loves his father or mother more than me is not worthy of me; anyone who loves his son or daughter more than me is not worthy of me; and anyone who does not take his cross and follow me is not worthy of me. Whoever finds his life will lose it, and whoever loses his life for my sake will find it.

"He who receives you receives me, and he who receives me receives the one who sent me. Anyone who receives a prophet because he is a prophet will receive a prophet's reward, and anyone who receives a righteous man because he is a righteous man will receive a righteous man's reward. And if anyone gives even a cup of cold water to one of these little ones because he is my disciple, I tell you the truth, he will certainly not lose his reward."

So they set out and went from village to village, preaching the gospel, and that people should repent. Everywhere they went they drove out many demons and anointed many sick people with oil and healed them.

After Jesus had finished instructing his twelve disciples, he went on from there to teach and preach in the towns of Galilee.[c]
MATTHEW 10:1, 5–11:1; MARK 6:7-13; LUKE 9:1-6

*"Anyone who does not take his cross
and follow me is not worthy of me."*

From Oswald Chambers

֍ The aspect of the Cross in discipleship is lost altogether in the present-day view of following Jesus. The Cross is looked upon as something beautiful and simple instead of a stern heroism. Our Lord never said it was easy to be a Christian; He warned men that they would have to face a variety of hardships, which He termed "bearing the cross." AUG 49

141

≈ Our cross is something that comes only with the peculiar relationship of a disciple to Jesus. It is the sign that we have denied our right to ourselves and are determined to manifest that we are no longer our own, we have given away forever our right to ourselves to Jesus Christ. AUG 97

≈ What the cross was to our Lord such also in measure was it to be to those who followed Him. The cross is the pain involved in doing the will of God. AUG 51

≈ The cross is the gift of Jesus to His disciples, and it can only bear one aspect: "I am not my own." HG 99

≈ Restate to yourself what you believe. Then do away with as much of it as possible, and get back to the bedrock of the cross of Christ. In external history the cross is an infinitesimal thing; from the Bible point of view it is of more importance than all the empires of the world. MUH 330

≈ The great privilege of discipleship is that I can sign on under His cross, and that means death to sin. Get alone with Jesus and either tell Him that you do not want sin to die out in you; or else tell Him that at all costs you want to be identified with His death. Immediately you transact in confident faith in what our Lord did on the cross, a supernatural identification with His death takes place, and you will know with a knowledge that passeth knowledge that your "old man" is crucified with Christ. MUH 358

≈ If you want a good time in this world, do not become a disciple of Jesus. OBH 61

≈ Our cross is the steady exhibition of the fact that we are not our own but Christ's, and we know it, and are determined not to be enticed from living a life of dedication to Him. This is the beginning of the emergence of the real life of faith. PS 38

≈ The cross is the deliberate recognition of what my personal life is for, viz., to be given to Jesus Christ; I have to take up that cross daily and prove that I am no longer my own. Individual independence has gone, and all that is left is personal passionate devotion to Jesus Christ through identification with His cross. SHL 79

---

a. Greek *an assarion*

142

b. Micah 7:6
c. Greek *in their towns*

33

JESUS FEEDS FIVE THOUSAND

When the apostles returned, they gathered around Jesus and reported to him all they had done and taught. When Jesus heard what had happened *to John, and* because so many people were coming and going that they did not even have a chance to eat, he said to them, "Come with me by yourselves to a quiet place and get some rest."

So he took them with him. They withdrew by themselves in a boat *and* crossed to the far shore of the Sea of Galilee (that is, the Sea of Tiberias) to a town called Bethsaida. But many who saw them leaving recognized them and ran on foot from all the towns and got there ahead of them. A great crowd of people learned about it and followed him on foot from the towns because they saw the miraculous signs he had performed on the sick.

When Jesus landed, he went up on a mountainside to a solitary place and sat down with his disciples. When Jesus looked up and saw a great crowd coming toward him, he had compassion on them, because they were like sheep without a shepherd. He welcomed them and began teaching them many things about the kingdom of God, and he healed those who needed healing. The Jewish Passover Feast was near.

By this time it was late in the afternoon, so the Twelve came to him and said, "This is a remote place, and it's already getting very late. Send the people away so they can go to the surrounding countryside and villages and buy themselves something to eat and find lodging."

Jesus replied, "They do not need to go away. You give them something to eat." He said to Philip, "Where shall we buy bread for these people to eat?" He asked this only to test him, for he already had in mind what he was going to do.

Philip answered him, "Eight months' wages[a] would not buy enough bread for each one to have a bite!" They said to him, "Are we to go and spend that much on bread and give it to them to eat?"

"How many loaves do you have?" he asked. "Go and see."

When they found out, Andrew, Simon Peter's brother, spoke up, "Here is a boy with five small barley loaves and two small fish, but how far will they go among so many?"

"Bring them here to me," he said. Then Jesus directed them to have all the people sit down on the green grass in groups of about fifty each. The disciples did so. There was plenty of grass in that place, and everybody sat down in groups of hundreds and fifties. Taking the five loaves and the two fish and looking up to heaven, Jesus gave thanks and broke the loaves. Then he gave them to the disciples, and the disciples distributed to those who were seated as much as they wanted. He also divided the two fish among them all. They all ate and were satisfied.

When they had all had enough to eat, he said to his disciples, "Gather the pieces that are left over. Let nothing be wasted." So they gathered them up and filled twelve baskets of broken pieces of the five barley loaves of bread and fish that were left over. The number of those who ate was about five thousand men, besides women and children.

After the people saw the miraculous sign that Jesus did, they began to say, "Surely this is the Prophet who is to come into the world." MATTHEW 14:13-21; MARK 6:30-44; LUKE 9:10-17; JOHN 6:1-14

"You give them something to eat."

FROM OSWALD CHAMBERS

∻ Jesus Christ represents the Bread of God broken to feed the world, and the saints are to be broken bread in His hands to satisfy Jesus Christ and His saints. . . . When by the sanctifying power of the grace of God we have been made into bread, our lives are to be offered first of all to Jesus Christ. SHL 122

∻ The consummation of self-sacrifice is that just as our Lord was made broken bread and poured-out wine for us, so He can make us

146

broken bread and poured-out wine for others; but He cannot do it if there is anything in us that would make us give way to self-pity when He begins to break us. The one mainspring of the life is personal, passionate devotion to Jesus Christ. SHL 123

❧ Paul's conception of the altar of sacrifice is "spending and being spent" for the sake of the elementary children of God. He has no other end and aim than that—to be broken bread and poured-out wine in the hands of God that others might be nourished and fed (cf. Col. 1:24). The great Savior and His great apostle go hand-in-hand—the Son of God sacrificed Himself that men might be redeemed; Paul, the bondslave of Jesus, sacrificed himself that men might accept the great salvation. SH 164

❧ Discipling is our work. When God's great redemptive work has issued in lives in salvation and sanctification, then the work of the worker begins. It is then that we find the meaning of being "workers together with Him" (2 Cor. 6:1). LG 91

❧ When a worker has led a soul to Christ, his work has only just begun. Our attitude is apt to be—So many saved; so many sanctified, and then we shout, " 'Hallelujah'." But it is only then that the true work of the worker begins. It is then that we have to be held in God's hand and let the word of God be driven through us. It is then that we have to be put under the millstone and ground, put into the kneading trough and be mixed properly, and then baked—all in order to be made broken bread to feed God's children. "Go ye therefore, and make disciples." LG 91

❧ As disciples of Jesus, we are to identify ourselves with God's interests in other people, to show to the other man what God has shown us, and God will give us ample opportunity in our actual lives to prove that we are perfect as our Father in heaven is perfect. SSM 51

---

a. Greek *two hundred denarii*

34

JESUS WALKS ON WATER

Knowing that they intended to come and make him king by force, immediately Jesus made his disciples get into the boat and go on ahead of him to Bethsaida, while he dismissed the crowd. After he had dismissed them, he withdrew again. He went up on a mountainside by himself to pray. When evening came, he was there alone.

His disciples went down to the lake, where they got into a boat and set off across the lake for Capernaum.

By now it was dark, and Jesus had not yet joined them. A strong wind was blowing and the waters grew rough. The boat was already a considerable distance[a] from land, in the middle of the lake, buffeted by the waves because the wind was against it. Alone on land, he saw the disciples straining at the oars.

About the fourth watch of the night, when they had rowed three or three and a half miles,[b] Jesus went out to them, walking on the lake. He was about to pass by them when they saw Jesus approaching the boat, walking on the water. They all saw him and were terrified. "It's a ghost," they said, and cried out in fear.

But Jesus immediately spoke to them and said, "Take courage! It is I. Don't be afraid."

"Lord, if it's you," Peter replied, "tell me to come to you on the water."

"Come," he said.

Then Peter got down out of the boat, walked on the water and came toward Jesus. But when he saw the wind, he was afraid and, beginning to sink, cried out, "Lord, save me!"

Immediately Jesus reached out his hand and caught him. "You of little faith," he said, "why did you doubt?"

Then they were willing to take him into the boat. And when

they climbed into the boat with them, the wind died down. Then those who were in the boat worshiped him, saying, "Truly you are the Son of God." They were completely amazed, for they had not understood about the loaves; their hearts were hardened.

Immediately the boat reached the shore where they were heading. They landed at Gennesaret and anchored there. As soon as they got out of the boat, the people of that place recognized Jesus. They sent word to all the surrounding country. They ran throughout that whole region and carried the sick on mats to wherever they heard he was. And wherever he went — into villages, towns or countryside — they placed the sick in the marketplaces. They begged him to let the sick just touch even the edge of his cloak, and all who touched him were healed.

The next day the crowd that had stayed on the opposite shore of the lake realized that only one boat had been there, and that Jesus had not entered it with his disciples, but that they had gone away alone. Then some boats from Tiberias landed near the place where the people had eaten the bread after the Lord had given thanks. Once the crowd realized that neither Jesus nor his disciples were there, they got into the boats and went to Capernaum in search of Jesus. MATTHEW 14:22-36; MARK 6:45-56; JOHN 6:15-24

"Take courage! It is I.
Don't be afraid."

FROM OSWALD CHAMBERS

➤ Our Lord rebuked the disciples for fearing when apparently they had good reason for being alarmed. The problem is — if Jesus Christ is only the Carpenter of Nazareth, then the disciples were foolish to put Him at the tiller; but if He is the Son of God, what are they alarmed about? HGM 91

➤ If Jesus Christ is God, where is my trust in Him? If He is not God, why am I so foolish as to pretend to worship Him? HGM 91

➤ Jesus Christ teaches us to build our confidence in the abiding reality of Himself in the midst of everything. If a man puts his confidence in the things which must go, imagine his incomprehensible

150

perplexity when they do go. No wonder Jesus said "men's hearts failing them for fear" (Luke 21:26). These words describe the time we are in now. HGM 93

☙ We step right out on God over some things, then self-consideration enters in and down we go. If you are recognizing your Lord, you have no business with where He engineers your circumstances. The actual things *are,* but immediately you look at them you are over-whelmed; you cannot recognize Jesus, and the rebuke comes: "Wherefore did thou doubt?" Let actual circumstances be what they may; keep recognizing Jesus [and] maintain complete reliance on Him. MUH 170

---

a. Greek *many stadia*
b. Greek *rowed twenty-five or thirty stadia* (about 5 or 6 kilometers)

35

JESUS THE BREAD OF LIFE

hen they found him on the other side of the lake, they asked him, "Rabbi, when did you get here?"

Jesus answered, "I tell you the truth, you are looking for me, not because you saw miraculous signs but because you ate the loaves and had your fill. Do not work for food that spoils, but for food that endures to eternal life, which the Son of Man will give you. On him God the Father has placed his seal of approval."

Then they asked him, "What must we do to do the works God requires?"

Jesus answered, "The work of God is this: to believe in the one he has sent."

So they asked him, "What miraculous sign then will you give that we may see it and believe you? What will you do? Our forefathers ate the manna in the desert; as it is written: 'He gave them bread from heaven to eat.' "[a]

Jesus said to them, "I tell you the truth, it is not Moses who has given you the bread from heaven, but it is my Father who gives you the true bread from heaven. For the bread of God is he who comes down from heaven and gives life to the world."

"Sir," they said, "from now on give us this bread."

Then Jesus declared, "I am the bread of life. He who comes to me will never go hungry, and he who believes in me will never be thirsty. But as I told you, you have seen me and still you do not believe. All that the Father gives me will come to me, and whoever comes to me I will never drive away. For I have come down from heaven not to do my will but to do the will of him who sent me. And this is the will of him who sent me, that I shall lose none of all that he has given me, but raise them up at the last day. For my Father's will is that everyone who looks to the Son and believes in him shall have eternal life, and I will raise him up at the last day."

At this the Jews began to grumble about him because he said, "I am the bread that came down from heaven." They said, "Is this not Jesus, the son of Joseph, whose father and mother we know? How can he now say, 'I came down from heaven'?"

"Stop grumbling among yourselves," Jesus answered. "No one can come to me unless the Father who sent me draws him, and I will raise him up at the last day. It is written in the Prophets: 'They will all be taught by God.'[b] Everyone who listens to the Father and learns from him comes to me. No one has seen the Father except the one who is from God; only he has seen the Father. I tell you the truth, he who believes has everlasting life. I am the bread of life. Your forefathers ate the manna in the desert, yet they died. But here is the bread that comes down from heaven, which a man may eat and not die. I am the living bread that came down from heaven. If anyone eats of this bread, he will live forever. This bread is my flesh, which I will give for the life of the world."

Then the Jews began to argue sharply among themselves, "How can this man give us his flesh to eat?"

Jesus said to them, "I tell you the truth, unless you eat the flesh of the Son of Man and drink his blood, you have no life in you. Whoever eats my flesh and drinks my blood has eternal life, and I will raise him up at the last day. For my flesh is real food and my blood is real drink. Whoever eats my flesh and drinks my blood remains in me, and I in him. Just as the living Father sent me and I live because of the Father, so the one who feeds on me will live because of me. This is the bread that came down from heaven. Your forefathers ate manna and died, but he who feeds on this bread will live forever." He said this while teaching in the synagogue in Capernaum. JOHN 6:25-59

"If anyone eats of this bread,
he will live forever."

FROM OSWALD CHAMBERS

꙳ Whenever we think we can get the life of God by obedience or prayer or some kind of discipline, we are wrong. We must realize the frontiers of death, that there is no more chance of our entering into the life of God than a mineral has of entering the vegetable kingdom; we can only enter into the kingdom of God if God will stoop down and lift us up. That is exactly what Jesus Christ promises to do. The bedrock of spiritual life as our Lord taught is poverty—"Blessed are the poor in spirit" (Matt. 5:3), not, "Blessed are the strong-willed, or the prayerful or the consecrated," but, "Blessed is the man who knows he is weak." When we get there the surprise of God's life may come at any time. SHH 69

Ƽ We say that Jesus Christ came to reveal the fatherhood of God, the loving-kindness of God; the New Testament says He came to bear away the sin of the world. The revelation of His Father is to those to whom He has been introduced as Savior. MUH 303

Ƽ We know nothing about God the Father saving as Jesus Christ has revealed Him. BP 216

Ƽ What is needed is the life of the Father, which is ours in Jesus Christ. CD, VOL. 1 140

Ƽ We may talk about God as the Almighty, the All-powerful, but He means nothing to us unless He has become incarnated and touched human life where we touch it; and the revelation of redemption is that God's thought did express itself in Jesus Christ, that God became manifest on the plane on which we live. HGM 95

Ƽ The Christian revelation is not that Jesus Christ stands to us as the representative of God, but that He *is* God. If He is not, then we have no God. "God *was in Christ,* reconciling the world unto Himself" (2 Cor. 5:19). We do not worship an austere, remote God; He is here in the thick of it. BE 61

Ƽ We can get to God as Creator apart from Jesus Christ (Rom. 1:20), but never to God as our Father saving through Him. Let us receive this inspired idea of our Lord's right into our inmost willing heart, believe it, and pray in the confidence of it. CD, VOL. 2 25

Ƽ I know no other God in time or eternity than Jesus Christ; I have accepted all I know of God on the authority of the revelation He gave of Him. "He that hath seen Me hath seen the Father" (John 14:9). CHI 46

a. Exodus 16:4; Nehemiah 9:15; Psalm 78:24-25
b. Isaiah 54:13

36

MANY DISCIPLES DESERT JESUS

O n hearing it [see last paragraph of previous Gospel portion], many of his disciples said, "This is a hard teaching. Who can accept it?"

Aware that his disciples were grumbling about this, Jesus said to them, "Does this offend you? What if you see the Son of Man ascend to where he was before! The Spirit gives life; the flesh counts for nothing. The words I have spoken to you are spirit[a] and they are life. Yet there are some of you who do not believe." For Jesus had known from the beginning which of them did not believe and who would betray him. He went on to say, "This is why I told you that no one can come to me unless the Father has enabled him."

From this time many of his disciples turned back and no longer followed him.

"You do not want to leave too, do you?" Jesus asked the Twelve.

Simon Peter answered him, "Lord, to whom shall we go? You have the words of eternal life. We believe and know that you are the Holy One of God."

Then Jesus replied, "Have I not chosen you, the Twelve? Yet one of you is a devil!" (He meant Judas, the son of Simon Iscariot, who, though one of the Twelve, was later to betray him.) JOHN 6:60-71

"Lord, to whom shall we go?
You have the words of eternal life."

157

From Oswald Chambers

❧ The teaching of Jesus Christ applies only to the life He puts in, and the marvel of His redemption is that He gives the power of His own disposition to carry any man through who is willing to obey Him. AUG 63

❧ The teachings of Jesus Christ must produce despair, because if He means what He says, where are we in regard to it? "Blessed are the pure in heart"—blessed is the man who has nothing in him for God to censure. Can I come up to that standard? Yet Jesus says only the pure in heart can stand before God. BFB 19

❧ If all Jesus came to do was to tell me I must have an unsullied career, when my past has been blasted by sin and wickedness on my own part, then He but tantalizes me. If He is simply a teacher, He only increases our capacity for misery, for He sets up standards that stagger us. But the teaching of Jesus Christ is not an ideal; it is the statement of the life we will live when we are readjusted to God by the Atonement. BE 119

❧ The teaching of Jesus Christ is very fine and delightful, but it is all up in the clouds; how are we to come up to it with our heredity, with what we are with our past, with our present, and with the outlook we have? How are we going to begin to do it, if all He came to do was to teach? All attempts at imitation will end in despair, in fanaticism, and in all kinds of religious nonsense. But when once we see that the New Testament emphasizes Jesus Christ's death, not His life, that it is by virtue of His death we enter into His life, then we find that His teaching is for the life He puts in. SA 40

❧ The teaching of Jesus Christ comes with astonishing discomfort to begin with, because it is out of all proportion to our natural way of looking at things; but Jesus puts in a new sense of proportion, and slowly we form our way of walking and our conversation on the line of His precepts. Remember that our Lord's teaching applies only to those who are His disciples. SSM 15

❧ A man who has not been born of the Spirit of God will tell you that the teachings of Jesus are simple. But when you are baptized with

158

the Holy Ghost, you find "clouds and darkness are round about Him." When we come into close contact with the teachings of Jesus Christ, we have our first insight into this aspect of things. The only possibility of understanding the teaching of Jesus is by the light of the Spirit of God on the inside. MUH 3

≈ The summing up of our Lord's teaching is that the relationship which He demands is an impossible one unless He has done a supernatural work in us. Jesus Christ demands that there be not the slightest trace of resentment even suppressed in the heart of a disciple when he meets with tyranny and injustice. No enthusiasm will ever stand the strain that Jesus Christ will put upon His worker; only one thing will, and that is a personal relationship to Himself which has gone through the mill of His spring-cleaning until there is only one purpose left—I am here for God to send me where He will. Every other thing may get fogged, but this relationship to Jesus Christ must never be. MUH 269

---

a. Or *Spirit*

37

CLEAN AND UNCLEAN

After this, Jesus went around in Galilee, purposely staying away from Judea because the Jews there were waiting to take his life.

Then some Pharisees and teachers of the law who had come from Jerusalem gathered around Jesus and saw some of his disciples eating food with hands that were "unclean," that is, unwashed. (The Pharisees and all the Jews do not eat unless they give their hands a ceremonial washing, holding to the tradition of the elders. When they come from the marketplace they do not eat unless they wash. And they observe many other traditions, such as the washing of cups, pitchers and kettles.[a])

So the Pharisees and teachers of the law asked Jesus, "Why do your disciples break the tradition of the elders, eating their food with 'unclean' hands? They don't wash their hands before they eat."

He replied, "Isaiah was right when he prophesied about you hypocrites; as it is written:

" 'These people honor me with their lips,
but their hearts are far from me.
They worship me in vain;
their teachings are but rules taught by men.'[b]

You have let go of the commands of God and are holding on to the traditions of men."

And he said to them: "And why do you break the command of God? You have a fine way of setting aside the commands of God in order to observe[c] your own traditions! For God *through* Moses said, 'Honor your father and mother,'[d] and, 'Anyone who curses

161

his father or mother must be put to death.'[e] But you say that if a man says to his father or mother: 'Whatever help you might otherwise have received from me is Corban' (that is, a gift devoted to God), then he is not to 'honor his father'[f] with it. You no longer let him do anything for his father or mother. Thus you nullify the word of God for the sake of your tradition that you have handed down. And you do many things like that."

Again Jesus called the crowd to him and said, "Listen to me, everyone, and understand this. Nothing outside a man can make him 'unclean' by going into him. What goes into a man's mouth does not make him 'unclean.' Rather, it is what comes out of a man, out of his mouth, that makes him 'unclean.' "[g]

After he had left the crowd and entered the house, his disciples came to him and asked, "Do you know that the Pharisees were offended when they heard this?"

He replied, "Every plant that my heavenly Father has not planted will be pulled up by the roots. Leave them; they are blind guides.[h] If a blind man leads a blind man, both will fall into a pit."

Peter said, "Explain the parable to us."

"Are you still so dull?" Jesus asked them. "Don't you see that nothing that enters a man from the outside can make him 'unclean'? For it doesn't go into his heart. Whatever enters his mouth goes into his stomach and then out of his body." (In saying this, Jesus declared all foods "clean.")

He went on: "What comes out of a man is what makes him 'unclean.' The things that come out of the mouth come from the heart, and these make a man 'unclean.' For from within, out of men's hearts, come evil thoughts, murder, adultery, sexual immorality, theft, false testimony, greed, malice, deceit, lewdness, envy, slander, arrogance and folly. All these evils come from inside and are what make a man 'unclean'; but eating with unwashed hands does not make him 'unclean.' " MATTHEW 15:1-20; MARK 7:1-23; JOHN 7:1

"From within, out of men's hearts,
come . . . all these evils."

FROM OSWALD CHAMBERS

❧ Jesus Christ is either the supreme Authority on the human heart or He is not worth listening to, and He said: "For from within, out of the heart of men, proceed" (Mark 7:21) and then comes that very ugly catalog. Jesus did not say, "Into the human heart these things are injected, but "from within, out of the heart of men" all these evil things proceed. If we trust our innocent ignorance to secure us, it is likely that as life goes on there will come a burst-up from underneath into our conscious life which will reveal to us that we are uncommonly like what Jesus Christ said. SHL 63

❧ The honor of Jesus Christ is at stake in my bodily life, and if I walk in the Spirit I will be ruthless to the things that won't submit to Him. To "crucify the flesh with the affections and lusts" (see Gal. 5:24) is not God's business; it is man's. CHI 42

❧ When God has put His Spirit in you and identified you with Jesus Christ, what is to be your attitude to your bodily life? You have the same body, the same appetites, and the same nature as before, your members used to be servants of sin, but Jesus Christ is your example now. He sacrificed Himself to His Father's will; see that you do the same as a saint. He submitted His intelligence to His Father's will, see that you do the same as a saint. He submitted His will to His Father; see that you as a saint do the same. PS 16

❧ One of the first big moral lessons a man has to learn is that he cannot destroy *sin* by neglect; sin has to be handled by the Redemption of Jesus Christ; it cannot be handled by me. Heredity is a bigger problem than I can cope with; but if I will receive the gift of the Holy Spirit on the basis of Christ's redemption, He enables me to work out that redemption in my experience. With regard to sensuality, that is my business; I have to mortify it, and if I don't it will never be mortified. If I take any part of my natural life and use it to satisfy myself, that is sensuality. A Christian has to learn that his body is not his own. "What! know ye not that your body is the temple of the Holy Ghost . . . and ye are not your own?" (1 Cor. 6:19) Watch that you learn to mortify. SA 70

❧ If you have been laid hold of by the Spirit of God, don't think it strange concerning the spring cleaning God is giving you, and don't clamor for anything because it will have to go. The setting apart of my body by the Holy Ghost for a temple of God is a terror to everything in me that is not of God. Sensuality and sordidness lurk about the bodily temple until Jesus Christ cleanses it. SHL 70

ও The heart is the exchange and mart; our words and expressions are simply the coins we use, but the "shop" resides in the heart, the emporium where all the goods are, and that is what God sees but no man can see. BP 102

ও We have not the remotest conception that what Jesus says about the human heart is true until we come up against something further on in our lives. We are apt to be indignant and say—"I don't believe those things are in my heart," and we refuse the diagnosis of the only Master there is of the human heart. We need never know the plague of our own heart and the terrible possibilities in human life if we will hand ourselves over to Jesus Christ; but if we stand on our own right and wisdom at any second, an eruption may occur in our personal lives, and we may discover to our unutterable horror that we can be murderers, etc. SHH 104

---

a. Some early manuscripts [of Mark 7:4] *pitchers, kettles and dining couches*
b. Isaiah 29:13
c. Some manuscripts [of Mark 7:9] *set up*
d. Exodus 20:12; Deuteronomy 5:16
e. Exodus 21:17; Leviticus 20:9
f. Some manuscripts [of Matthew 15:6] *father or his mother*
g. Some early manuscripts [of Mark 7:15] *'unclean.' If anyone has ears to hear, let him hear.*
h. Some manuscripts [of Matthew 15:14] *guides of the blind*

38

PETER'S CONFESSION OF CHRIST

Jesus and his disciples went on to the villages around Caesarea Philippi. On the way, when Jesus was praying in private and his disciples were with him, he asked them, "Who do people say I, the Son of Man, am?"

They replied, "Some say John the Baptist; others say Elijah; and still others, that Jeremiah or one of the prophets of long ago has come back to life."

"But what about you?" he asked. "Who do you say I am?"

Simon Peter answered, "You are the Christ, the Son of the living God."

Jesus replied, "Blessed are you, Simon son of Jonah, for this was not revealed to you by man, but by my Father in heaven. And I tell you that you are Peter,[a] and on this rock I will build my church, and the gates of Hades[b] will not overcome it.[c] I will give you the keys of the kingdom of heaven; whatever you bind on earth will be[d] bound in heaven, and whatever you loose on earth will be[d] loosed in heaven." Then Jesus strictly warned his disciples not to tell anyone that he was the Christ. MATTHEW 16:13-20; MARK 8:27-30; LUKE 9:18-21

JESUS PREDICTS HIS DEATH

From that time on Jesus began to explain to his disciples that he must go to Jerusalem. And he said, "The Son of Man must be rejected and suffer many things at the hands of the elders, chief priests and teachers of the law, and he must be killed and on the third day be raised to life." He spoke plainly about this.

Peter took him aside and began to rebuke him. "Never, Lord!" he said. "This shall never happen to you!"

But when Jesus turned and looked at his disciples, he rebuked Peter. "Get behind me, Satan!" he said to Peter. "You are a stumbling block to me; you do not have in mind the things of God, but the things of men."

Then he called the crowd to him along with his disciples and said to them all: "If anyone would come after me, he must deny himself and take up his cross daily and follow me. For whoever wants to save his life[e] will lose it, but whoever loses his life for me and for the gospel will save it. What good is it for a man to gain the whole world, and yet lose or forfeit his soul, his very self? Or what can a man give in exchange for his soul? If anyone is ashamed of me and my words in this adulterous and sinful generation, the Son of Man will be ashamed of him when he comes in his glory and in the glory of the Father and of the holy angels. And then he will reward each person according to what he has done."

And he said to them, "I tell you the truth, some who are standing here will not taste death before they see the Son of Man coming in his kingdom, the kingdom of God, with power." MATTHEW 16:21-28; Mark 8:3–9:1; LUKE 9:22-27

"You are the Christ,
the Son of the Living God."

FROM OSWALD CHAMBERS

⮞ "If any man will come after Me," said Jesus, "the condition is that he must leave something behind," viz., his right to himself. Is Jesus Christ worth it, or am I one of those who accept His salvation but thoroughly object to giving up my right to myself to Him? AUG 97

⮞ Our cross is something that comes only with the peculiar relationship of a disciple to Jesus. It is the sign that we have denied our right to ourselves and are determined to manifest that we are no longer our own; we have given away forever our right to ourselves to Jesus Christ. AUG 97

⮞ Some folks are so mixed up nervously that they cannot help sacrificing themselves, but unless Jesus Christ is the lodestar there is no benefit in the sacrifice. Self-denial must have its spring in personal outflowing love to our Lord; we are no longer our own; we are spoiled for every other interest in life saving as we can win men to Jesus Christ. AUG 53

꙯ The cross is the gift of Jesus to His disciples and it can only bear one aspect: "I am not my own." The whole attitude of the life is that I have given up my right to myself. I live like a crucified man. Unless that crisis is reached, it is perilously possible for my religious life to end as a sentimental fiasco. "I don't mind being saved from hell and receiving the Holy Spirit, but it is too much to expect me to give up my right to myself to Jesus Christ, to give up my manhood, my womanhood, all my ambitions." Jesus said [that] if any man [would be His] disciple, those are the conditions. It is that kind of thing that offended the historic disciples, and it will offend you and me. It is a slander to the Cross of Christ to say we believe in Jesus and please ourselves all the time, choosing our own way. HG 99

꙯ "If any man would come after Me." "If" means, "You don't need to unless you like, but you won't be of any account to Me in this life unless you do." Wherever Christian experience is proving unsatisfactory, it is because the Holy Spirit is still battling around this one point—my right to myself—and until that is deliberately given over by me to Jesus Christ, I will never have the relationship to Him He asks for. HGM 140

꙯ We are apt to imagine that the cross we have to carry means the ordinary troubles and trials of life, but we must have these whether we are Christians or not. Neither is our cross suffering for conscience's sake. Our cross is something that comes only with the peculiar relationship of a disciple to Jesus Christ; it is the evidence that we have denied our right to ourselves. PR 102

---

a. Peter means *rock*
b. Or *hell*
c. Or *not prove stronger than it*
d. Or *have been*
e. The Greek word means either *life* or *soul* [and hereinafter]

39

THE TRANSFIGURATION

After six days Jesus took with him Peter, James and John the brother of James, and led them up onto a high mountain by themselves, where they were all alone to pray. As he was praying there, he was transfigured before them. The appearance of his face changed and shone like the sun. His clothes became dazzling white, whiter than anyone in the world could bleach them, as white as the light, bright as a flash of lightning. Just then there appeared before them two men in glorious splendor, Moses and Elijah, who were talking with Jesus. They spoke about his departure, which he was about to bring to fulfillment at Jerusalem. Peter and his companions were very sleepy, but when they became fully awake, they saw his glory and the two men standing with him. As the men were leaving Jesus, Peter said to him, "Rabbi, it is good for us to be here. Let us put up three shelters—one for you, one for Moses and one for Elijah." (He did not know what he was saying, they were so frightened.)

While he was still speaking, a bright cloud appeared and enveloped them, and they were afraid as they entered the cloud. A voice came from the cloud, saying, "This is my Son, whom I love, whom I have chosen; with him I am well pleased. Listen to him!"

When the disciples heard this, they fell facedown to the ground, terrified. But Jesus came and touched them. "Get up," he said. "Don't be afraid." Suddenly, when they looked up, they no longer saw anyone with them except Jesus.

As they were coming down the mountain, Jesus instructed them, "Don't tell anyone what you have seen, until the Son of Man has been raised from the dead." They kept the matter to themselves, discussing what "rising from the dead" meant.

The disciples asked him, "Why then do the teachers of the law

169

say that Elijah must come first?"

Jesus replied, "To be sure, Elijah does come first, and restores all things. Why then is it written that the Son of Man must suffer much and be rejected? But I tell you, Elijah has already come, and they did not recognize him, but have done to him everything they wished, just as it is written about him. In the same way the Son of Man is going to suffer at their hands." Then the disciples understood that he was talking to them about John the Baptist.

The disciples told no one at that time what they had seen.

MATTHEW 17:1-13; MARK 9:2-13; LUKE 9:28-36

"This is my Son, whom I love,
whom I have chosen; with him
I am well pleased. Listen to him!"

FROM OSWALD CHAMBERS

❧ We say, "No cross, no crown"; in the life of our Lord the crown of the glory of the Transfiguration came before the cross. You never know Jesus Christ, and Him crucified, unless you have seen Him transfigured in all His transcendent majesty and glory; the cross to you is nothing but the cross of a martyr. If you have seen Jesus glorified, you know that the cross is the revelation of God's judgment on sin, that on the cross our Lord bore the whole massed sin of the human race. "Him who knew no sin He made to be sin on our behalf" (2 Cor. 5:21). BSG 38

❧ If Jesus Christ had gone to heaven from the Mount of Transfiguration, He would have gone alone. He would have been to us a glorious Figure, One who manifested the life of God's normal man and how wonderful it is for God and man to live as one, but what good would that have been to us? We can never live in the power of an ideal put before us. What is the use of Jesus Christ telling us we must be as pure in heart as He is when we know we are impure? But Jesus Christ did not go to heaven from the Mount. Moses and Elijah talked with Him, not of His glory, nor of His deity, but of His *death,* the issue which He was about to accomplish at Jerusalem. By His death on the cross Jesus Christ made the way for every son of man to get into communion with God. PR 119

170

🙲 Jesus Christ, the second Adam, the second federal Head of the race, entered into this order of things as Adam did, straight from the hand of God; and He took part in His own development until it reached its climax, and He was transfigured. Earth lost its hold on Him, and He was back in the glory which He had with the Father before the world was. But He did not go to heaven from the Mount of Transfiguration because He had Redemption to fulfill. He emptied Himself of His glory a second time, and came down into the world again to identify Himself with the sin of man. SA 46

40

A Boy with an Evil Spirit

he next day, when they came down from the mountain to the other disciples, they saw a large crowd around them and the teachers of the law arguing with them. As soon as all the people saw Jesus, they were overwhelmed with wonder and ran to greet him.

"What are you arguing with them about?" he asked.

A man in the crowd called out, "Teacher, I beg you to look at my son, for he is my only child." He approached Jesus and knelt before him. "Lord, have mercy on my son, who is possessed by a spirit that has robbed him of speech," he said. "He has seizures and is suffering greatly. Whenever *the* spirit seizes him, he suddenly screams; it throws him to the ground into convulsions. He foams at the mouth, gnashes his teeth and becomes rigid. It scarcely ever leaves him and is destroying him. I brought him *and* begged your disciples to drive out the spirit, but they could not."

"O unbelieving and perverse generation," Jesus replied, "how long shall I stay with you? How long shall I put up with you? Bring the boy here to me."

So they brought him. Even while the boy was coming, the spirit saw Jesus. The demon immediately threw the boy into a convulsion. He fell to the ground and rolled around, foaming at the mouth.

Jesus asked the boy's father, "How long has he been like this?"

"From childhood," he answered. "It has often thrown him into fire or water to kill him. But if you can do anything, take pity on us and help us."

" 'If you can'?" said Jesus. "Everything is possible for him who believes."

Immediately the boy's father exclaimed, "I do believe; help me overcome my unbelief!"

When Jesus saw that a crowd was running to the scene, he rebuked the evil spirit. "You deaf and mute spirit," he said, "I command you, come out of him and never enter him again."

The spirit shrieked, convulsed him violently and came out. The boy looked so much like a corpse that many said, "He's dead." But Jesus took him by the hand and lifted him to his feet, and he stood up. He was healed from that moment. Jesus gave him back to his father. And they were all amazed at the greatness of God.

After Jesus had gone indoors, his disciples asked him privately, "Why couldn't we drive it out?"

He replied, "Because you have so little faith. I tell you the truth, if you have faith as small as a mustard seed, you can say to this mountain, 'Move from here to there' and it will move. Nothing will be impossible for you. *But* this kind can come out only by prayer.[a]

While everyone was marveling at all that Jesus did, they left that place and passed through Galilee. Jesus did not want anyone to know where they were, because he was teaching his disciples. He said to them, "Listen carefully to what I am about to tell you: The Son of Man is going to be betrayed into the hands of men. They will kill him, and on the third day he will be raised to life." And the disciples were filled with grief. But they did not understand what he meant. It was hidden from them, so that they did not grasp it, and they were afraid to ask him about it. MATTHEW 17:14-23; MARK 9:14-32; LUKE 9:37-45

"Everything is possible for him who believes."

FROM OSWALD CHAMBERS

≈ Mediumship, whereby unseen spirits talk to men and women, will destroy the basis of moral sanity because it introduces a man into domains he had better leave alone. Drunkenness and debauchery are child's play compared with the peril of spiritualism. There is something uncannily awful about tampering with these supernatural powers, and in the speeding up of these days the necromantic element is increasing. Be on the lookout for the manifestations that are not of God; all have the one sign—they ignore Jesus Christ. SHL 55

꙳ It is a great thing to be a believer, but easy to misunderstand what the New Testament means by it. It is not that we believe Jesus Christ can *do* things, or that we believe in a plan of salvation; it is that we believe *Him;* whatever happens we will hang on to the fact that He is true. AUG 114

꙳ Every abortion and wrongdoing in spiritual life begins when we cease believing in Jesus Christ. If we believe in a state of mind He produces in us, we will be disappointed, because circumstances will come in our lives when these works of Jesus Christ are shadowed over; but if we believe in Him, no matter how dark the passage is we shall be carried right through, and when the crisis is passed, our souls will have been built up into a stronger attitude toward Him. AUG 115

꙳ All the fuss and energy and work that goes on if we are not believing in Jesus Christ and His redemption, has not a touch of the almighty power of God about it; it is a panic of unbelief veneered over with Christian phrases. As long as we pretend to be believers in Jesus Christ and are not, we produce humbugs, and people say, "Do you call that Christianity?" There is nothing in it; or what is worse, we produce frauds, and the worst type of fraud is the religious fraud. The greatest type of reality is the Christian believer — one who has been totally readjusted on the basis of his belief. When you come across a believer in Jesus, his very presence alters your outlook. It is not that you have come to someone with amazing intelligence, but that you have come into a sanctuary which is based on a real knowledge of the redemption. HG 104

---

a. Some manuscripts [of Mark 9:29] *prayer and fasting;* some manuscripts [of Matthew 17:21] *you. But this kind does not go out except by prayer and fasting*

41

THE GREATEST IN THE KINGDOM OF HEAVEN

On the way, an argument started among the disciples as to which of them would be the greatest. When he was in the house, the disciples came to Jesus and asked, "Who is the greatest in the kingdom of heaven?"

Jesus, knowing their thoughts, asked them, "What were you arguing about on the road?" But they kept quiet.

Sitting down, Jesus called the Twelve and said, "If anyone wants to be first, he must be the very last, and the servant of all."

He called a little child and had him stand beside him. Taking him in his arms, he said to them, "I tell you the truth, unless you change and become like little children, you will never enter the kingdom of heaven. Therefore, whoever humbles himself like this child is the greatest in the kingdom of heaven. And whoever welcomes a little child like this in my name welcomes me; and whoever welcomes me does not welcome me but the one who sent me. For he who is least among you all—he is the greatest."

MATTHEW 18:1-5; MARK 9:33b-37; LUKE 9:46-48

CAUSING TO SIN

"But if anyone causes one of these little ones who believe in me to sin, it would be better for him to have a large millstone hung around his neck and to be thrown into the sea to be drowned in the depths.

"Woe to the world because of the things that cause people to sin! Such things must come, but woe to the man through whom they come! If your hand causes you to sin, cut it off and throw it away. It is better for you to enter life maimed than with two hands to go into eternal hell, where the fire never goes out.[a] And if your foot causes you to sin, cut it off. It is better for you to enter life crippled than to have two feet and be thrown into hell.[b] And if your eye causes you to sin, gouge it out and throw it away. It is better for you to enter the kingdom of God with one eye than to have two eyes and be thrown into the fire of hell, where

> " 'their worm does not die,
> and the fire is not quenched.'[c]

Everyone will be salted with fire.

"Salt is good, but if it loses its saltiness, how can you make it salty again? Have salt in yourselves, and be at peace with each other." MATTHEW 18:6-9; MARK 9:42-50

THE PARABLE OF THE LOST SHEEP

"See that you do not look down on one of these little ones. For I tell you that their angels in heaven always see the face of my Father in heaven.[d]

"What do you think? If a man owns a hundred sheep, and one of them wanders away, will he not leave the ninety-nine on the hills and go to look for the one that wandered off? And if he finds it, I tell you the truth, he is happier about that one sheep than about the ninety-nine that did not wander off. In the same way your Father in heaven is not willing that any of these little ones should be lost." MATTHEW 18:10-14

"I tell you the truth, unless you change
and become like little children,
you will never enter the kingdom of heaven."

FROM OSWALD CHAMBERS

ཀ We all know what a child is until we are asked, and then we find we do not know. We can mention his extra goodness or his extra badness, but none of this is the child himself. We know implicitly what a child is, and we know implicitly what Jesus Christ means, but as soon as we try to put it into words it escapes. A child works from an unconscious principle within, and if we are born again and are obeying the Holy Spirit, we shall unconsciously manifest humility all along the line. We shall easily be the servant of all men, not be-

178

cause it is our ideal, but because we cannot help it. Our eye is not consciously on our service, but on our Savior. BP 186

▸ Jesus Christ uses the child-spirit as a touchstone for the character of a disciple. He did not put up a child before His disciples as an ideal, but as an expression of the simple-hearted life they would live when they were born again. The life of a little child is expectant, full of wonder, and free from self-consciousness, and Jesus said, "Except ye turn, and become as little children, ye shall in no wise enter into the kingdom of heaven." We cannot enter into the kingdom of heaven head first. How many of us thought about how we should live before we were born? Why, none. But numbers of people try to think of how to live as Christians before they are born again. "Marvel not that I said unto thee, Ye must be born anew" — that is, become as little children, with openhearted, unprejudiced minds in relation to God. There is a marvelous rejuvenescence once we let God have His way. The most seriously minded Christian is the one who has just become a Christian; the mature saint is just like a young child, absolutely simple and joyful. PH 185

▸ With a child the element of wonder is always there, a freshness and spontaneity, and the same is true of those who follow Jesus Christ's teaching and become as little children. HG 34

▸ The Lord Jesus spoke and worked from the great big child-heart of God. God Almighty became incarnate as a little child, and Jesus Christ's message is you must become as that, little children. IYA 43

▸ The religion of Jesus Christ is the religion of a little child. There is no affectation about a disciple of Jesus; he is as a little child, amazingly simple but unfathomably deep. Many of us are not childlike enough; we are childish. Jesus said — "Except ye become *as little children.*" OBH 97

---

a. Some manuscripts [of Mark 9:44] *out, where* / " *'their worm does not die,* / *and the fire is not quenched'* "
b. Some manuscripts [of Mark 9:46] *hell, where* / " *'their worm does not die,* / *and the fire is not quenched'* "
c. Isaiah 66:24
d. Some manuscripts [of Matthew 18:11] *heaven. The Son of Man came to save what was lost*

42

WHEN A BROTHER SINS AGAINST YOU

If your brother sins against you,[a] go and show him his fault, just between the two of you. If he listens to you, you have won your brother over. But if he will not listen, take one or two others along, so that 'every matter may be established by the testimony of two or three witnesses.'[b] If he refuses to listen to them, tell it to the church; and if he refuses to listen even to the church, treat him as you would a pagan or a tax collector.

"I tell you the truth, whatever you bind on earth will be[c] bound in heaven, and whatever you loose on earth will be[c] loosed in heaven.

"Again, I tell you that if two of you on earth agree about anything you ask for, it will be done for you by my Father in heaven. For where two or three come together in my name, there am I with them." MATTHEW 18:15-20

"If two of you on earth agree about anything you ask for,
it will be done for you by my Father in heaven."

FROM OSWALD CHAMBERS

✍ The revelation of our spiritual standing is what we ask in prayer; sometimes what we ask is an insult to God; we ask with our eyes on the possibilities or on ourselves, not on Jesus Christ. Get on to the supernatural line; remember that Jesus Christ is omniscient, and He says, "If ye shall ask anything in My name, *I will do it.*" BSG 58

✍ Remember that Jesus Christ's silences are always signs that He knows we can stand a bigger revelation than we think we can. If He gives you the exact answer, He cannot trust you yet. IYA 51

181

ᔌ God has one prayer He must answer, and that is the prayer of Jesus Christ. It does not matter how imperfect or immature a disciple may be, if he will hang in, that prayer will be answered. IYA 55

ᔌ Because Jesus Christ keeps silence it does not mean that He is displeased, but exactly the opposite. He is bringing us into the great run of His purpose, and the answer will be an amazing revelation. No wonder our Lord said, "Greater works than these shall he do. . . . And whatsoever ye shall ask in My name, that will I do." IYA 52

ᔌ It is always a wonder when God answers prayer. We hear people say, "We must not say it is wonderful that God answers prayer"; but it is wonderful. It is so wonderful that a great many people believe it impossible. Listen! — "Whatsoever ye shall ask in My name, that will I do." Isn't that wonderful? It is so wonderful that I do not suppose more than half of us really believe it. "Everyone that asketh receiveth." Isn't that wonderful? It is so wonderful that many of us have never even asked God to give us the Holy Spirit because we don't believe He will. "If two of you shall agree on earth as touching anything that they shall ask, it shall be done for them of My Father which is in heaven." Isn't that wonderful? It is tremendously wonderful. "The effectual fervent prayer of a righteous man availeth much." Isn't that wonderful? IYA 40

a. Some manuscripts [of Matthew 18:15] do not have *against you*
b. Deuteronomy 19:15
c. Or *have been*

43

THE PARABLE OF THE UNMERCIFUL SERVANT

hen Peter came to Jesus and asked, "Lord, how many times shall I forgive my brother when he sins against me? Up to seven times?"

Jesus answered, "I tell you, not seven times, but seventy-seven times.[a]

"Therefore, the kingdom of heaven is like a king who wanted to settle accounts with his servants. As he began the settlement, a man who owed him ten thousand talents[b] was brought to him. Since he was not able to pay, the master ordered that he and his wife and his children and all that he had be sold to repay the debt.

"The servant fell on his knees before him. 'Be patient with me,' he begged, 'and I will pay back everything.' The servant's master took pity on him, canceled the debt and let him go.

"But when that servant went out, he found one of his fellow servants who owed him a hundred denarii.[c] He grabbed him and began to choke him. 'Pay back what you owe me!' he demanded.

"His fellow servant fell to his knees and begged him, 'Be patient with me, and I will pay you back.'

"But he refused. Instead, he went off and had the man thrown into prison until he could pay the debt. When the other servants saw what had happened, they were greatly distressed and went and told their master everything that had happened.

"Then the master called the servant in. 'You wicked servant,' he said, 'I canceled all that debt of yours because you begged me to. Shouldn't you have had mercy on your fellow servant just as I had on you?' In anger his master turned him over to the jailers to be tortured, until he should pay back all he owed.

"This is how my heavenly Father will treat each of you unless you forgive your brother from your heart." MATTHEW 18:21-35

"Lord, how many times shall I forgive my brother when he sins against me?"

From Oswald Chambers

- I have no right to say that I believe in forgiveness as an attribute of God if in my own heart I cherish an unforgiving temper. The forgiveness of God is the test by which I myself am judged. DI 1

- When we have experienced the unfathomable forgiveness of God for all our wrong, we must exhibit that same forgiveness to others. HGM 47

- Forgiveness is the divine miracle of grace. Have we ever contemplated the amazing fact that God through the death of Jesus Christ forgives us for every wrong we have ever done, not because we are sorry, but out of His sheer mercy? AUG 47

- Jesus Christ did not say "Because we forgive our debtors," but, "As we forgive our debtors," that is, as children of God we are forgiven not on the ground of redemption, but on the ground that we show the same forgiveness to our fellows that God has shown to us. "For if ye forgive men their trespasses, your Heavenly Father will also forgive you; but if ye forgive not men their trespasses, neither will your Father forgive your trespasses" (Matt. 6:14-15). HGM 102

- The love of God is based on justice and holiness, and I must forgive on the same basis. HGM 104

- When God says, "Don't do that anymore," He instills into me the power that enables me not to do it anymore, and the power comes by right of what Jesus Christ did on the cross. That is the unspeakable wonder of the forgiveness of God, and when we become rightly related to God, we are to have the same relationship to our fellowmen that God has to us. "And be ye kind one to another, tenderhearted, forgiving one another, even as God for Christ's sake hath forgiven you" (Eph. 4:32). HGM 105

---

a. Or *seventy times seven*
b. That is, millions of dollars
c. That is, a few dollars

44

JESUS AT THE FEAST OF TABERNACLES

When the Jewish Feast of Tabernacles was near, Jesus' brothers said to him, "You ought to leave here and go to Judea, so that your disciples may see the miracles you do. No one who wants to become a public figure acts in secret. Since you are doing these things, show yourself to the world." For even his own brothers did not believe in him.

Therefore Jesus told them, "The right time for me has not yet come; for you any time is right. The world cannot hate you, but it hates me because I testify that what it does is evil. You go to the Feast. I am not yet[a] going up to this Feast, because for me the right time has not yet come." Having said this, he stayed in Galilee.

After his brothers had left for the Feast, *Jesus* went also, not publicly, but in secret. Now at the Feast the Jews were watching for him and asking, "Where is that man?"

Among the crowds there was widespread whispering about him. Some said, "He is a good man."

Others replied, "No, he deceives the people." But no one would say anything publicly about him for fear of the Jews.

Not until halfway through the Feast did Jesus go up to the temple courts and begin to teach. The Jews were amazed and asked, "How did this man get such learning without having studied?"

Jesus answered, "My teaching is not my own. It comes from him who sent me. If anyone chooses to do God's will, he will find out whether my teaching comes from God or whether I speak on my own. He who speaks on his own does so to gain honor for himself, but he who works for the honor of the one who sent him is a man of truth; there is nothing false about him. Has not

Moses given you the law? Yet not one of you keeps the law. Why are you trying to kill me?"

"You are demon-possessed," the crowd answered. "Who is trying to kill you?"

Jesus said to them, "I did one miracle, and you are all astonished. Yet, because Moses gave you circumcision (though actual-ly it did not come from Moses, but from the patriarchs), you circumcise a child on the Sabbath. Now if a child can be circumcised on the Sabbath so that the law of Moses may not be broken, why are you angry with me for healing the whole man on the Sabbath? Stop judging by mere appearances, and make a right judgment." JOHN 7:2-24

IS JESUS THE CHRIST?

At that point some of the people of Jerusalem began to ask, "Isn't this the man they are trying to kill? Here he is, speaking publicly, and they are not saying a word to him. Have the authorities really concluded that he is the Christ? But we know where this man is from; when the Christ comes, no one will know where he is from."

Then Jesus, still teaching in the temple courts, cried out, "Yes, you know me, and you know where I am from. I am not here on my own, but he who sent me is true. You do not know him, but I know him because I am from him and he sent me."

At this they tried to seize him, but no one laid a hand on him, because his time had not yet come. Still, many in the crowd put their faith in him. They said, "When the Christ comes, will he do more miraculous signs than this man?"

The Pharisees heard the crowd whispering such things about him. Then the chief priests and the Pharisees sent temple guards to arrest him.

Jesus said, "I am with you for only a short time, and then I go to the one who sent me. You will look for me, but you will not find me; and where I am, you cannot come."

The Jews said to one another, "Where does this man intend to go that we cannot find him? Will he go where our people live scattered among the Greeks, and teach the Greeks? What did he mean when he said, 'You will look for me, but you will not find me,' and 'Where I am, you cannot come'?"

186

On the last and greatest day of the Feast, Jesus stood and said in a loud voice, "If anyone is thirsty, let him come to me and drink. Whoever believes in me, as[b] the Scripture has said, streams of living water will flow from within him." By this he meant the Spirit, whom those who believed in him were later to receive. Up to that time the Spirit had not been given, since Jesus had not yet been glorified.

On hearing his words, some of the people said, "Surely this man is the Prophet."

Others said, "He is the Christ."

Still others asked, "How can the Christ come from Galilee? Does not the Scripture say that the Christ will come from David's family[c] and from Bethlehem, the town where David lived?" Thus the people were divided because of Jesus. Some wanted to seize him, but no one laid a hand on him. JOHN 7:25-44

UNBELIEF OF THE JEWISH LEADERS

Finally the temple guards went back to the chief priests and Pharisees, who asked them, "Why didn't you bring him in?"

"No one ever spoke the way this man does," the guards declared.

"You mean he has deceived you also?" the Pharisees retorted. "Has any of the rulers or of the Pharisees believed in him? No! But this mob that knows nothing of the law—there is a curse on them."

Nicodemus, who had gone to Jesus earlier and who was one of their own number, asked, "Does our law condemn anyone without first hearing him to find out what he is doing?"

They replied, "Are you from Galilee, too? Look into it, and you will find that a prophet[d] does not come out of Galilee." JOHN 7:45-53

"He is the Christ."

FROM OSWALD CHAMBERS

    ❮ "I am the first and the last" (Rev. 1:11). Is Jesus Christ the first and the last of my personal creed, the first and last of all I look to and hope for? Frequently the discipline of discipleship has to be delayed until we learn that God's barriers are put there not by sovereign deity only; they are put there by a God whose will is absolutely holy and who has told us plainly, "Not that way." IWP 126

❧ Every Christian knows Jesus Christ as God, not as the equivalent of God; the call to proclaim Him to others means that I see Him and know Him as God. There is no God that is not Father, Son, and Holy Ghost—the Triune aspect of one God, from all eternity to all eternity. GW 30

❧ Jesus Christ claims that He can take a man or woman who is fouled in the springs of their nature by heredity and make them as pure as He is Himself. That is why He teaches what He does, and it is His standard we are to be judged by if we are His disciples. No wonder the disciples when they heard Jesus speak, said, "Who then can be saved?" The greatest philosophy ever produced does not come within a thousand leagues of the fathomless profundity of our Lord's statements, e.g., "Learn of Me; for I am meek and lowly in heart" (Matt. 11:29). HG 60

❧ The standard of Jesus Christ is that I may be perfect as my Father in heaven is perfect. Jesus Christ is not after making a fine character or a virtuous man; those are ingredients to another end: His end is that we may be children of our Father in heaven. PH 195

❧ Jesus Christ . . . can take you and me, and can fit us exactly to the expression of the divine life in us. It is not a question of putting the statements of our Lord in front of us and trying to live up to them, but of receiving His Spirit and finding that we can live up to them as He brings them to our remembrance and applies them to our circumstances. SSM 53

❧ Jesus Christ is the supreme sacrifice for the sin of the world; He is "the Lamb of God, which taketh away the sin of the world!" (John 1:29) How the death of Jesus looms all through the Bible! It is through His death that we are made partakers of His life and can have gifted to us a pure heart, which He says is the condition for seeing God. CHI 120

❧ Napoleon said of Jesus Christ that He had succeeded in making of every human soul an appendage of His own—why? Because He had the genius of holiness. There have been great military geniuses, intellectual giants, geniuses of statesmen, but these only exercise influence over a limited number of men; Jesus Christ exercises unlimited sway over all men because He is the altogether worthy One. CHI 119

❧ Jesus Christ proved Himself worthy, not only in the domain of God which we do not know, but in the domain of man which we do know. By means of His redemption Jesus Christ makes us the sons and daughters of God, and we have to "put on the new man" (Eph. 4:24) in accordance with the life of the Son of God formed in us, and as we do we become invincible—"more than conquerors through Him that loved us" (Rom. 8:37). SHL 69

❧ Jesus Christ is not only Savior; He is King, and He has the right to exact anything and everything from us at His own discretion. HGM 129

---

a. Some early manuscripts [of John 7:8] do not have *yet*
b. Or / *If anyone is thirsty, let him come to me.* / *And let him drink, who believes in me.* / *As*
c. Greek *seed*
d. Two early manuscripts [of John 7:52] *the Prophet*

189

45

THE COST OF FOLLOWING JESUS

s they were walking along the road, a teacher of the law came to Jesus and said, "Teacher, I will follow you wherever you go."

Jesus replied, "Foxes have holes and birds of the air have nests, but the Son of Man has no place to lay his head."

He said to another disciple, "Follow me."

But the man replied, "Lord, first let me go and bury my father."

But Jesus said to him, "Let the dead bury their own dead, but you go and proclaim the kingdom of God."

Still another said, "I will follow you, Lord; but first let me go back and say good-by to my family."

Jesus replied, "No one who puts his hand to the plow and looks back is fit for service in the kingdom of God." MATTHEW 8:19-22; LUKE 9:57-62

"No one who puts his hand to the plow and looks back is fit for service in the kingdom of God."

FROM OSWALD CHAMBERS

⌘ We are saved and sanctified not for service, but to be absolutely Jesus Christ's, the consuming passion of the life is for Him. DI 61

⌘ Jesus Christ counts as service not what we do for Him, but what we are to Him, and the inner secret of that is identity with Him in person. *"That I may know Him."* MFL 107

191

≈ With us, Christian service is something we do; with Jesus Christ it is not what we do for Him, but what we are to Him that He calls service. Our Lord always puts the matter of discipleship on the basis of devotion not to a belief or a creed, but to Himself. There is no argument about it, and no compulsion; simply—"If you would be My disciple, you must be devoted to Me." PH 144

≈ "Lord, I will follow Thee, but . . . " The wish ought to be followed by immediate obedience. I must take the wish and translate it into resolution and then into action. If I do not, the wish will translate itself into a corrupting instead of a redeeming power in my life. This principle holds good in the matter of emotions. A sentimentalist is one who delights to have high and devout emotions stirred while reading in an armchair or when in a prayer meeting, but he never translates his emotions into action. Consequently a sentimentalist is usually callous, self-centered and selfish, because the emotions he likes to have stirred do not cost him anything; and when he comes across the same things in the domain where things are real and not sentimental, the revenge comes along the line of selfishness and meanness, which is always the aftermath of an unfulfilled emotion. SH 31

≈ Beware of anything that competes with loyalty to Jesus Christ. The greatest competitor of devotion to Jesus is service for Him. It is easier to serve than to be drunk to the dregs. The one aim of the call of God is the satisfaction of God, not a call to do something for Him. We are not sent to battle for God, but to be used by God in His battlings. Are we being more devoted to service than to Jesus Christ? MUH 18

≈ The distinction between a saved soul and a disciple is fundamental. The stern conditions laid down by our Lord for discipleship are not the conditions of salvation; discipleship is a much closer and more conscious relationship. BSG 23

≈ The one mark of discipleship is the mastership of Jesus—His right to me from the crown of my head to the sole of my foot. DI 34

≈ A disciple is one who not only proclaims God's truth, but one who manifests that he is no longer his own; he has been "bought with a price." DI 35

❧ Jesus Christ always talked about discipleship with an "If." We are at perfect liberty to toss our spiritual head and say, "No, thank you, that is a bit too stern for me," and the Lord will never say a word, we can do exactly what we like. He will never plead, but the opportunity is there, "If . . . " IWP 61

❧ Discipleship must always be a personal matter; we can never become disciples in crowds, or even in twos. It is so easy to talk about what "we" mean to do—"we" are going to do marvelous things, and it ends in none of us doing anything. The great element of discipleship is the personal one. IWP 104

46

A WOMAN CAUGHT IN ADULTERY

But Jesus went to the Mount of Olives. At dawn he appeared again in the temple courts, where all the people gathered around him, and he sat down to teach them. The teachers of the law and the Pharisees brought in a woman caught in adultery. They made her stand before the group and said to Jesus, "Teacher, this woman was caught in the act of adultery. In the Law Moses commanded us to stone such women. Now what do you say?" They were using this question as a trap, in order to have a basis for accusing him.

But Jesus bent down and started to write on the ground with his finger. When they kept on questioning him, he straightened up and said to them, "If any one of you is without sin, let him be the first to throw a stone at her." Again he stooped down and wrote on the ground.

At this, those who heard began to go away one at a time, the older ones first, until only Jesus was left, with the woman still standing there. Jesus straightened up and asked her, "Woman, where are they? Has no one condemned you?"

"No one, sir," she said.

"Then neither do I condemn you," Jesus declared. "Go now and leave your life of sin." JOHN 8:1-11

"Neither do I condemn you ...
Go now and leave your life of sin."

FROM OSWALD CHAMBERS

❧ If the redemption cannot get hold of the worst and vilest, then

195

Jesus Christ is a fraud. But if [the Bible] means anything, it means that at the wall of the world stands God, and any man driven there by conviction of sin finds the arms of God outstretched to save him. God can forgive a man anything but despair that He can forgive him. HGM 65

❧ There is no obstacle—nothing in the past or the present or in his heredity—that can stand in a man's way if he will only make room for Jesus Christ. Once let him realize his need—"I can't be holy, I can't be pure in heart, I can't be the child of my Father in heaven and be kind to the unthankful and evil, I can't love my enemies"— Jesus Christ claims that He can do all that for him, but it depends on the man, i.e., upon how much he has come up against the things he cannot do for himself. HGM 109

❧ He has undertaken to take the vilest piece of stuff that humanity and the devil have put together, and to transform this into a son of God. If I receive forgiveness and continue to be bad, I prove that God is immoral in forgiving me, and make a travesty of redemption. SA 41

❧ The distinctive thing about Christianity is forgiveness, not sanctification or my holiness, but forgiveness—the greatest miracle God ever performs through the redemption. . . . By means of the redemption God undertakes to deal with a man's past, and He does it in two ways—first, He forgives it, and then He makes it a wonderful culture for the future. . . . Forgiveness means not merely that a man is saved from sin and made right for heaven—no man would accept forgiveness on such a level; forgiveness means that I am saved from sinning and put into the Redeemer to grow up into His image. HGM 105

❧ Forgiveness, which is so easy for us to accept, cost God the agony of Calvary. PH 184

❧ When Jesus Christ says, "Sin no more," He conveys the power that enables a man not to sin anymore, and that power comes by right of what He did on the cross. That is the unspeakable wonder of the forgiveness of God. PH 184

47

THE VALIDITY OF JESUS' TESTIMONY

hen Jesus spoke again to the people, he said, "I am the light of the world. Whoever follows me will never walk in darkness, but will have the light of life."

The Pharisees challenged him, "Here you are, appearing as your own witness; your testimony is not valid."

Jesus answered, "Even if I testify on my own behalf, my testimony is valid, for I know where I came from and where I am going. But you have no idea where I come from or where I am going. You judge by human standards; I pass judgment on no one. But if I do judge, my decisions are right, because I am not alone. I stand with the Father, who sent me. In your own Law it is written that the testimony of two men is valid. I am one who testifies for myself; my other witness is the Father, who sent me."

Then they asked him, "Where is your father?"

"You do not know me or my Father," Jesus replied. "If you knew me, you would know my Father also." He spoke these words while teaching in the temple area near the place where the offerings were put. Yet no one seized him, because his time had not yet come.

Once more Jesus said to them, "I am going away, and you will look for me, and you will die in your sin. Where I go, you cannot come."

This made the Jews ask, "Will he kill himself? Is that why he says, 'Where I go, you cannot come'?"

But he continued, "You are from below; I am from above. You are of this world; I am not of this world. I told you that you would die in your sins; if you do not believe that I am [the one I claim to be],[a] you will indeed die in your sins."

"Who are you?" they asked.

"Just what I have been claiming all along," Jesus replied. "I have much to say in judgment of you. But he who sent me is reliable, and what I have heard from him I tell the world."

They did not understand that he was telling them about his Father. So Jesus said, "When you have lifted up the Son of Man, then you will know who I am [the one I claim to be] and that I do nothing on my own but speak just what the Father has taught me. The one who sent me is with me; he has not left me alone, for I always do what pleases him." Even as he spoke, many put their faith in him. JOHN 8:12-30

"Whoever follows me will never walk in darkness,
but will have the light of life."

FROM OSWALD CHAMBERS

ᴥ To walk in the light means that everything that is of the darkness drives me closer into the center of the light. MUH 361

ᴥ If we have entered into the heavenly places in Christ Jesus, the light has shone, and, this is the marvelous thing, as we begin to do what we know the Lord would have us do, we find He does not enable *us* to do it, He simply puts through us all His power and the thing is done in His way. Thank God for everyone who has seen the light, who has understood how the Lord Jesus Christ clears away the darkness and brings the light by showing His own characteristics through us. OBH 40

ᴥ One step in the right direction in obedience to the light, and the manifestation of the Son of God in your mortal flesh is as certain as that God is on His throne. When once God's light has come to us through Jesus Christ, we must never hang back, but obey; and we shall not walk in darkness, but will have the light of life. OBH 43

ᴥ "I am come . . . to fulfill." An amazing word! Our shoes ought to be off our feet and every commonsense mood stripped from our minds when we hear Jesus Christ speak. In Him we deal with God as man, the God-Man, the representative of the whole human race in one Person. The men of His day traced their religious pedigree back to the constitution of God, and this young Nazarene Carpenter says, "I am the constitution of God"; consequently, to them He was a blasphemer. SSM 21

❧ Beware if in personal testimony you have to hark back and say— "Once, so many years ago, I was saved." If you are walking in the light, there is no harking back, the past is transfused into the present wonder of communion with God. If you get out of the light, you become a sentimental Christian and live on memories, your testimony has a hard, metallic note. Beware of trying to patch up a present refusal to walk in the light by recalling past experiences when you did walk in the light. Whenever the Spirit checks, call a halt and get the thing right, or you will go on grieving Him without knowing it. MUH 226

❧ If the Spirit of God detects anything in you that is wrong, He does not ask you to put it right; He asks you to accept the light, and He will put it right. A child of the light confesses instantly and stands bared before God; a child of the darkness says—"Oh, I can explain that away." When once the light breaks and the conviction of wrong comes, be a child of the light, and confess, and God will deal with what is wrong; if you vindicate yourself, you prove yourself to be a child of the darkness. MUH 83

❧ If you do not obey the light, it will turn into darkness. MUH 240

---

a. Or *I am he*

48

WHOSE CHILDREN?

T o the Jews who had believed him, Jesus said, "If you hold to my teaching, you are really my disciples. Then you will know the truth, and the truth will set you free."

They answered him, "We are Abraham's descendants[a] and have never been slaves of anyone. How can you say that we shall be set free?"

Jesus replied, "I tell you the truth, everyone who sins is a slave to sin. Now a slave has no permanent place in the family, but a son belongs to it forever. So if the Son sets you free, you will be free indeed. I know you are Abraham's descendants.[b] Yet you are ready to kill me, because you have no room for my word. I am telling you what I have seen in the Father's presence, and you do what you have heard from your father."

"Abraham is our father," they answered.

"If you were Abraham's children," said Jesus, "then you would[c] do the things Abraham did. As it is, you are determined to kill me, a man who has told you the truth that I heard from God. Abraham did not do such things. You are doing the things your own father does."

"We are not illegitimate children," they protested. "The only Father we have is God himself." JOHN 8:31-41

THE CHILDREN OF THE DEVIL

Jesus said to them, "If God were your Father, you would love me, for I came from God and now am here. I have not come on my own; but he sent me. Why is my language not clear to you? Because you are unable to hear what I say. You belong to your father, the devil, and you want to carry out your father's desire.

201

He was a murderer from the beginning, not holding to the truth, for there is no truth in him. When he lies, he speaks his native language, for he is a liar and the father of lies. Yet because I tell the truth, you do not believe me! Can any of you prove me guilty of sin? If I am telling the truth, why don't you believe me? He who belongs to God hears what God says. The reason you do not hear is that you do not belong to God." JOHN 8:42-47

"If you hold to my teaching, you are really my disciples.
Then you will know the truth, and the truth will set you free."

FROM OSWALD CHAMBERS

෨ No man begins his Christian life by believing a creed. The man with a dogmatic creed says, "You must believe this and that." Jesus says, "Do the will," i.e., "commit yourself to Me." Truth is not in a particular statement; Truth is a Person—"I am the Truth." It is a mistake to attempt to define what a man must believe before he can be a Christian; his beliefs are the effect of his being a Christian, not the cause of it. [When] you lose sight of the central, majestic figure of Jesus Christ you are swept off your feet by all kinds of doctrine, and when big things hit you find your religion does not stand you in good stead because your creed does not agree with the Truth. CHI 46

෨ There was in the disciples the "one fact more" which put them in one kingdom and Jesus Christ in another kingdom. Our Lord was never impatient. He simply planted seed thoughts in their minds and surrounded them with the atmosphere of His own life. He did not attempt to convince them, but left mistakes to correct themselves, because He knew that eventually the truth would bear fruit in their lives. How differently we would have acted! We get impatient and take men by the scruff of the neck and say: "You must believe this and that." You cannot make a man see moral truth by persuading his intellect. "When He, the Spirit of Truth, is come, He will guide you into all the truth" (John 16:13). IYA 106

෨ Jesus does not take men and say—"This is the truth and if you don't believe it you will be damned." He simply shows us the truth—"I am the Truth," and leaves us alone. We name His name,

202

but is He the Truth to us in our bodily life, in our commonsense life, in our intellectual and emotional life? It takes a long while for us to begin to see that Jesus Christ is the Truth. Truths exist that have no meaning for us until we get into the domain of their power. "Verily, verily, I say unto thee, Except a man be born anew, he cannot see the kingdom of God" (John 3:3). We want to get at truth by shortcuts; the wonder is our Lord's amazing patience. He never insists that we take His way; He simply says — "I am the Way." PH 102

✌ A man can never be the same again — I don't care who he is — after having heard Jesus Christ preached. He may say he pays no attention to it; he may appear to have forgotten all about it, but he is never quite the same, and at any moment truths may spring up into his consciousness that will destroy all his peace and happiness. RTR 77

✌ If you only take your own ideas, you will never know the truth. The whole truth is the only truth, and the whole truth is Jesus Christ — "I am the Truth." Any bit of truth is an error if taken alone. RTR 87

✌ In our Lord's day the habit was common, as it is today, of backing up ordinary assertions with an appeal to the name of God. Jesus checks that. He says never call on anything in the nature of God to attest what you say; speak simply and truly, realizing that truth in a man is the same as truth in God. To call God in as a witness to back up what you say is nearly always a sign that what you are saying is not true. Similarly if you can find reasons for the truth of what you say, it is proof that what you say is not strictly true; if it were, you would never have to find reasons to prove it. Jesus Christ puts in a truthfulness that never takes knowledge of itself. SSM 40

---

a. Greek *seed*
b. Or *presence. Therefore do what you have heard from the Father*
c. Some early manuscripts [of John 8:39] *"If you are Abraham's children," said Jesus, "then*

49

THE CLAIMS OF JESUS ABOUT HIMSELF

The Jews answered him, "Aren't we right in saying that you are a Samaritan and demon-possessed?"

"I am not possessed by a demon," said Jesus, "but I honor my Father and you dishonor me. I am not seeking glory for myself; but there is one who seeks it, and he is the judge. I tell you the truth, if anyone keeps my word, he will never see death."

At this the Jews exclaimed, "Now we know that you are demon-possessed! Abraham died and so did the prophets, yet you say that if anyone keeps your word, he will never taste death. Are you greater than our father Abraham? He died, and so did the prophets. Who do you think you are?"

Jesus replied, "If I glorify myself, my glory means nothing. My Father, whom you claim as your God, is the one who glorifies me. Though you do not know him, I know him. If I said I did not, I would be a liar like you, but I do know him and keep his word. Your father Abraham rejoiced at the thought of seeing my day; he saw it and was glad."

"You are not yet fifty years old," the Jews said to him, "and you have seen Abraham!"

"I tell you the truth," Jesus answered, "before Abraham was born, I am!" At this, they picked up stones to stone him, but Jesus hid himself, slipping away from the temple grounds. JOHN 8:48-59

"I tell you the truth,
if anyone keeps my word,
he will never see death."

205

FROM OSWALD CHAMBERS

❧ It is a marvelous thing to know that Jesus Christ is the Son of God, but a more marvelous thing to know that He is the Son of God in me. HGM 37

❧ God's thought expressed itself not only in the universe which He created, but in a Being called "the Word," whose name to us is "Jesus Christ." HGM 96

❧ "I am Alpha and Omega, the first and the last" (Rev. 1:11). Jesus Christ is the last word on God, on sin and death, on heaven and hell; the last word on every problem that human life has to face. IWP 125

❧ If we preach anything other than "Jesus Christ, and Him crucified," we make our doctrines God and ourselves the judge of others. Think of the times we have hindered the Spirit of God by trying to help others when only God could help them, because we have forgotten to discipline our own minds. It is the familiar truth that we have to be stern in proclaiming God's Word, let it come out in all its rugged bluntness, unwatered down and unrefined; but when we deal with others we have to remember that we are sinners saved by grace. The tendency today is to do exactly the opposite; we make all kinds of excuses for God's Word—"Oh, God does not expect us to be perfect," and when we deal with people personally we are amazingly hard.

All these things lead us back to Jesus Christ—He is the Truth; He is the Honorable One; He is the Just One; He is the Pure One; He is the altogether Lovely One; he is the only One of Good Report. No matter where we start from, we will always come back to Jesus Christ. MFL 81

❧ Jesus Christ is not a Being with two personalities; He is Son of God (the exact expression of Almighty God) and Son of Man (the presentation of God's normal man). As Son of God, He reveals what God is like; as Son of Man, He mirrors what the human race will be like on the basis of redemption—a perfect oneness between God and man. PR 13

206

❧ Jesus Christ stands as the type of man, and the only type of man, who can come near to God. PS 73

❧ "I am come . . . to fulfill" (Matt. 5:17). An amazing word! Our shoes ought to be off our feet and every commonsense mood stripped from our minds when we hear Jesus Christ speak. In Him we deal with God as man, the God-Man, the representative of the whole human race in one Person. The men of His day traced their religious pedigree back to the constitution of God, and this young Nazarene Carpenter says, "I am the constitution of God"; consequently to them He was a blasphemer. SSM 21

❧ At the beginning we were sure we knew all about Jesus Christ. It was a delight to sell all and to fling ourselves out in a hardihood of love, but now we are not quite so sure. Jesus is on in front and He looks strange: "Jesus went before them and they were amazed." MUH 75

❧ Jesus Christ is a source of deep offense to the educated mind of today that does not want Him in any other way than as a comrade. MUH 71

50

JESUS HEALS A MAN BORN BLIND

As he went along, he saw a man blind from birth. His disciples asked him, "Rabbi, who sinned, this man or his parents, that he was born blind?"

"Neither this man nor his parents sinned," said Jesus, "but this happened so that the work of God might be displayed in his life. As long as it is day, we must do the work of him who sent me. Night is coming, when no one can work. While I am in the world, I am the light of the world."

Having said this, he spit on the ground, made some mud with the saliva, and put it on the man's eyes. "Go," he told him, "wash in the Pool of Siloam" (this word means Sent). So the man went and washed, and came home seeing.

His neighbors and those who had formerly seen him begging asked, "Isn't this the same man who used to sit and beg?" Some claimed that he was.

Others said, "No, he only looks like him."

But he himself insisted, "I am the man."

"How then were your eyes opened?" they demanded.

He replied, "The man they call Jesus made some mud and put it on my eyes. He told me to go to Siloam and wash. So I went and washed, and then I could see."

"Where is this man?" they asked him.

"I don't know," he said. JOHN 9:1-12

THE PHARISEES INVESTIGATE THE HEALING

They brought to the Pharisees the man who had been blind. Now the day on which Jesus had made the mud and opened the man's eyes was a Sabbath. Therefore the Pharisees also asked him how he had received his sight. "He put mud on my eyes," the man replied, "and I washed, and now I see."

Some of the Pharisees said, "This man is not from God, for he does not keep the Sabbath."

But others asked, "How can a sinner do such miraculous signs?" So they were divided.

Finally they turned again to the blind man, "What have you to say about him? It was your eyes he opened."

The man replied, "He is a prophet."

The Jews still did not believe that he had been blind and had received his sight until they sent for the man's parents. "Is this your son?" they asked. "Is this the one you say was born blind? How is it that now he can see?"

"We know he is our son," the parents answered, "and we know he was born blind. But how he can see now, or who opened his eyes, we don't know. Ask him. He is of age; he will speak for himself." His parents said this because they were afraid of the Jews, for already the Jews had decided that anyone who acknowledged that Jesus was the Christ would be put out of the synagogue. That was why his parents said, "He is of age; ask him."

A second time they summoned the man who had been blind. "Give glory to God,[a]" they said. "We know this man is a sinner."

He replied, "Whether he is a sinner or not, I don't know. One thing I do know. I was blind but now I see!"

Then they asked him, "What did he do to you? How did he open your eyes?"

He answered, "I have told you already and you did not listen. Why do you want to hear it again? Do you want to become his disciples, too?"

Then they hurled insults at him and said, "You are this fellow's disciple! We are disciples of Moses! We know that God spoke to Moses, but as for this fellow, we don't even know where he comes from."

The man answered, "Now that is remarkable! You don't know where he comes from, yet he opened my eyes. We know that God does not listen to sinners. He listens to the godly man who does his will. Nobody has ever heard of opening the eyes of a man born blind. If this man were not from God, he could do nothing."

JOHN 9:13-34

SPIRITUAL BLINDNESS

Jesus heard that they had thrown him out, and when he found him, he said, "Do you believe in the Son of Man?"

"Who is he, sir?" the man asked. "Tell me so that I may believe in him."

Jesus said, "You have now seen him; in fact, he is the one speaking with you."

Then the man said, "Lord, I believe," and he worshiped him.

Jesus said, "For judgment I have come into this world, so that the blind will see and those who see will become blind."

Some Pharisees who were with him heard him say this and asked, "What? Are we blind too?"

Jesus said, "If you were blind, you would not be guilty of sin; but now that you claim you can see, your guilt remains." JOHN 9:35-41

"Jesus said, 'For judgment I have come into this world, so that the blind will see and those who see will become blind.' "

FROM OSWALD CHAMBERS

⮞ One of the first things Jesus Christ does is to open a man's eyes, and he sees things as they are. Until then he is not satisfied with the seeing of his eyes; he wants more, anything that is hidden he must drag to the light, and the wandering of desire is the burning waste of a man's life until he finds God. His heart lusts; his mind lusts, his eyes lust, everything in him lusts until he is related to God. It is the demand for an infinite satisfaction, and it ends in the perdition of a man's life. SHH 74

⮞ You must do what you see, or become blind in that particular. BE 58

⮞ Seeing is never believing: we interpret what we see in the light of what we believe. HGM 70

⮞ We *see* for the first time when we do not look. We see actual things, and we say that we see them, but we never really see them until we see God; when we see God, everything becomes different. It is not the external things that are different, but a different disposition

211

looks through the same eyes as the result of the internal surgery that has taken place. We see God, and then we see things actually as we never saw them before. NKW 54

❧ The great emancipation in the salvation of God is that it gives a man the sight of his eyes, and he sees for the first time the handiwork of God in a daisy. SHH 75

❧ We can enter into His kingdom whenever the time comes for us to see it. We cannot see a thing until we do see it, but we must not be blind and say we don't see it when we do; and if we are enthusiastic saints we must not be too much disturbed about the fellow who does not see. At any second he may turn the corner of an agony and say, "I thought those other fellows were mad, but now I am prepared to see as they do." SA 41

---

a. A solemn charge to tell the truth (see Joshua 7:19)

51

THE SHEPHERD AND HIS FLOCK

I tell you the truth, the man who does not enter the sheep pen by the gate, but climbs in by some other way, is a thief and a robber. The man who enters by the gate is the shepherd of his sheep. The watchman opens the gate for him, and the sheep listen to his voice. He calls his own sheep by name and leads them out. When he has brought out all his own, he goes on ahead of them, and his sheep follow him because they know his voice. But they will never follow a stranger; in fact, they will run away from him because they do not recognize a stranger's voice." Jesus used this figure of speech, but they did not understand what he was telling them.

Therefore Jesus said again, "I tell you the truth, I am the gate for the sheep. All who ever came before me were thieves and robbers, but the sheep did not listen to them. I am the gate; whoever enters through me will be saved.[a] He will come in and go out, and find pasture. The thief comes only to steal and kill and destroy; I have come that they may have life, and have it to the full.

"I am the good shepherd. The good shepherd lays down his life for the sheep. The hired hand is not the shepherd who owns the sheep. So when he sees the wolf coming, he abandons the sheep and runs away. Then the wolf attacks the flock and scatters it. The man runs away because he is a hired hand and cares nothing for the sheep.

"I am the good shepherd; I know my sheep and my sheep know me—just as the Father knows me and I know the Father—and I lay down my life for the sheep. I have other sheep that are not of this sheep pen. I must bring them also. They too will listen to my voice, and there shall be one flock and one shepherd. The reason my Father loves me is that I lay down my life—only to take it up again. No one takes it from me, but I lay it down of my own accord. I have authority to lay it down and authority to take it up again. This command I received from my Father."

At these words the Jews were again divided. Many of them said, "He is demon-possessed and raving mad. Why listen to him?"

But others said, "These are not the sayings of a man possessed by a demon. Can a demon open the eyes of the blind?" JOHN 10:1-21

"I am the good shepherd;
I know my sheep and my sheep know me . . .
and I lay down my life for the sheep."

FROM OSWALD CHAMBERS

ᵅ The sacrifice of Jesus is the essence of renunciation; it was "a sacrifice to God for a sweet smelling savor" (Eph. 5:2). The death of Jesus was not a satisfaction paid to the justice of God—a hideous statement which the Bible nowhere makes. The death of Jesus was an exact revelation of the justice of God. When we read of the sacrifice of Jesus Christ, it is the sacrifice of God also. "God was in Christ, reconciling the world unto Himself" (2 Cor. 5:19). BSG 78

ᵅ When we are identified with Jesus Christ, the Spirit of God would have us sacrifice ourselves for Him, point for point, as He did for His Father. We pray and wait, and need urging, and want the thrilling vision; but Jesus wants us to narrow and limit ourselves to one thing—clearly and intelligently knowing what we are doing; we deliberately lay down our lives for Him as He laid down His life for us in the purpose of God. GW 114

ᵅ Have we ever realized the glorious opportunity we have of laying down our lives for Jesus Christ? Jesus does not ask us to die for Him, but to lay down our lives for Him. Our Lord did not sacrifice Himself for death, He sacrificed His *life,* and God wants our life, not our death. "I beseech you," says Paul, "present your bodies a living sacrifice" (Rom. 12:1). OBH 59

214

❧ He [Jesus] deliberately laid down His life without any possibility of deliverance. There was no compulsion; it was a sacrifice made with a free mind, nor was there anything of the impulsive about it. He laid down His life with a clear knowledge of what He was doing. Jesus understood what was coming; it was not a foreboding, but a certainty; not a catastrophe which might happen, but an ordained certainty in the decrees of God, and He knew it. GW 113

❧ Jesus Christ laid down His holy life for His Father's purposes, then if we are God's children we have to lay down our lives for His sake — not for the sake of a truth, not for the sake of devotion to a doctrine, but for Jesus Christ's sake — the personal relationship all through. IWP 85

❧ Sacrifice in it essence is the exuberant passionate love-gift of the best I have to the one I love best. MFL 108

❧ The idea of sacrifice is giving back to God the best we have in order that He may make it His and ours forever. PR 102

---

a. Or *kept safe*

52

JESUS SENDS OUT THE SEVENTY-TWO

After this the Lord appointed seventy-two[a] others and sent them two by two ahead of him to every town and place where he was about to go. He told them, "The harvest is plentiful, but the workers are few. Ask the Lord of the harvest, therefore, to send out workers into his harvest field. Go! I am sending you out like lambs among wolves. Do not take a purse or bag or sandals; and do not greet anyone on the road.

"When you enter a house, first say, 'Peace to this house.' If a man of peace is there, your peace will rest on him; if not, it will return to you. Stay in that house, eating and drinking whatever they give you, for the worker deserves his wages. Do not move around from house to house.

"When you enter a town and are welcomed, eat what is set before you. Heal the sick who are there and tell them, 'The kingdom of God is near you.' But when you enter a town and are not welcomed, go into its streets and say, 'Even the dust of your town that sticks to our feet we wipe off against you. Yet be sure of this: The kingdom of God is near.' I tell you, it will be more bearable on that day for Sodom than for that town." Luke 10:1-12

WOE ON UNREPENTANT CITIES

Then Jesus began to denounce the cities in which most of his miracles had been performed, because they did not repent. "Woe to you, Korazin! Woe to you, Bethsaida! For if the miracles that were performed in you had been performed in Tyre and Sidon, they would have repented long ago, sitting in sackcloth and ashes. But I tell you, it will be more bearable for Tyre and Sidon on the day of judgment than for you. And you, Capernaum, will

217

you be lifted up to the skies? No, you will go down to the depths.[b] If the miracles that were performed in you had been performed in Sodom, it would have remained to this day. But I tell you that it will be more bearable for Sodom on the day of judgment than for you.

"He who listens to you listens to me; he who rejects you rejects me; but he who rejects me rejects him who sent me." MATTHEW 11:20-24; LUKE 10:13-16

THE SEVENTY-TWO RETURN

The seventy-two[c] returned with joy and said, "Lord, even the demons submit to us in your name."

He replied, "I saw Satan fall like lightning from heaven. I have given you authority to trample on snakes and scorpions and to overcome all the power of the enemy; nothing will harm you. However, do not rejoice that the spirits submit to you, but rejoice that your names are written in heaven."

At that time Jesus, full of joy through the Holy Spirit, said, "I praise you, Father, Lord of heaven and earth, because you have hidden these things from the wise and learned, and revealed them to little children. Yes, Father, for this was your good pleasure.

"All things have been committed to me by my Father. No one knows who the Son is except the Father, and no one knows who the Father is except the Son and those to whom the Son chooses to reveal him.

"Come to me, all you who are weary and burdened, and I will give you rest. Take my yoke upon you and learn from me, for I am gentle and humble in heart, and you will find rest for your souls. For my yoke is easy and my burden is light."

Then he turned to his disciples and said privately, "Blessed are the eyes that see what you see. For I tell you that many prophets and kings wanted to see what you see but did not see it, and to hear what you hear but did not hear it." MATTHEW 11:25-30; LUKE 10:17-24

"The harvest is plentiful, but the workers are few.
Ask the Lord . . . to send out workers into his harvest field."

218

From Oswald Chambers

❧ "As My Father hath sent Me, even so send I you" (John 20:21). A missionary is a saved and sanctified soul detached to Jesus. The one thing that must not be overlooked is the personal relationship to Jesus Christ and to His point of view; if that is overlooked, the needs are so great, the conditions so perplexing, that every power of mind and heart will fail and falter. SSY 73

❧ Concentrate on God; let Him engineer circumstances as He will, and wherever He places you He is binding up the brokenhearted through you, setting at liberty the captives through you, doing His mighty soul-saving work through you, as you keep rightly related to Him. Self-conscious service is killed, self-conscious devotion is gone, only one thing remains—"witnesses unto Me," Jesus Christ first, second, and third. MFL 108

❧ The Master Speaker, after conveying His life to us by means of His words, turns us loose into a tower of Babel and tells us to speak His messages there. The missionary is one whom Jesus Christ has taken aside from the multitude, and, having put His fingers into his ears and touched his tongue, has sent him straight forth from hearing his Master, with his own tongue loosened and his speech plain, to speak "all the words of this life." SSY 91

❧ The key to the missionary is the absolute sovereignty of the Lord Jesus Christ. We must get into real solitude with Him, feed our soul on His Word, and He will engineer our circumstances. "Consider the lilies . . . how they grow" (Matt. 6:28)—they live where they are put, and we have to live where God places us. It is not the going of the feet, but the going of the life in real vital relationship to Jesus Christ. SSY 140

❧ It is easy to forget that the first duty of the missionary is not to uplift the heathen, not to heal the sick, not to civilize savage races, because all that sounds so rational and so human, and it is easy to arouse interest in it and get funds for it. The primary duty of the missionary is to preach "repentance and remission of sins in His name" (Luke 24:47). The key to the missionary message, whether the missionary is a doctor, a teacher, an industrial worker, or a

219

nurse — the key is the remissionary purpose of our Lord Jesus Christ's death. SSY 142

---

a. Some manuscripts [of Luke 10:1] *seventy*
b. Greek *Hades* [and hereinafter]
c. Some manuscripts [of Luke 10:17] *seventy*

53

THE PARABLE OF THE GOOD SAMARITAN

n one occasion an expert in the law stood up to test Jesus. "Teacher," he asked, "what must I do to inherit eternal life?"

"What is written in the Law?" he replied. "How do you read it?"

He answered: " 'Love the Lord your God with all your heart and with all your soul and with all your strength and with all your mind'[a]; and, 'Love your neighbor as yourself.' "[b]

"You have answered correctly," Jesus replied. "Do this and you will live."

But he wanted to justify himself, so he asked Jesus, "And who is my neighbor?"

In reply Jesus said: "A man was going down from Jerusalem to Jericho, when he fell into the hands of robbers. They stripped him of his clothes, beat him and went away, leaving him half dead. A priest happened to be going down the same road, and when he saw the man, he passed by on the other side. So too, a Levite, when he came to the place and saw him, passed by on the other side. But a Samaritan, as he traveled, came where the man was; and when he saw him, he took pity on him. He went to him and bandaged his wounds, pouring on oil and wine. Then he put the man on his own donkey, took him to an inn and took care of him. The next day he took out two silver coins[c] and gave them to the innkeeper. 'Look after him,' he said, 'and when I return, I will reimburse you for any extra expense you may have.'

"Which of these three do you think was a neighbor to the man who fell into the hands of robbers?"

The expert in the law replied, "The one who had mercy on him." Jesus told him, "Go and do likewise." LUKE 10:25-37

*"Love the Lord your God with all your heart
and with all your soul and with all your strength
and with all your mind; and love your neighbor as yourself."*

FROM OSWALD CHAMBERS

- Jesus Christ teaches that if we have had a work of grace done in our hearts, we will show to our fellowmen the same love God has shown to us. BP 134

- When we are rightly related to Jesus Christ, human love is transfigured because the last aching abyss of the heart is satisfied; but if the relationship with God is cut off, our relationship to others is embittered. When once the relationship with God is right, the satisfaction of human love is marvelous. HGM 113

- Jesus Christ emancipates the personality; the individuality is transfigured in the mastership of God's purpose in Christ Jesus, and the transfiguring element is love; personal, passionate devotion to Himself, and to others. SA 102

- Love cannot be defined. Try to define your love for Jesus Christ, and you will find you cannot do it. SSY 158

- Love is the sovereign preference of my person for another person, and Jesus Christ demands that that other person be Himself. That does not mean we have no preference for anyone else, but that Jesus Christ has the sovereign preference; within that sovereign preference come all other loving preferences, down to flowers and animals. The Bible makes no distinction between divine love and human love; it speaks only of love. SSY 158

- The love of God is wrought in us by the Holy Ghost. He sheds abroad the love of God—the nature of God—in our hearts, and that love works efficaciously through us as we come in contact with others. The test of love for Jesus Christ is the practical one; all the rest is sentimental jargon. SSY 160

- When Jesus Christ said, "Thou shalt love the Lord thy God with all thy heart," He did not stop there. He went on to say "and with all thy soul, and with all thy *mind,* and with all thy strength." WG 96

222

a. Deuteronomy 6:5
b. Leviticus 19:18
c. Greek *two denarii*

54

JESUS' TEACHING ON PRAYER

ne day Jesus was praying in a certain place. When he finished, one of his disciples said to him, "Lord, teach us to pray, just as John taught his disciples."

He said to them, "When you pray, say:

" 'Father,[a]
hallowed be your name,
your kingdom come.[b]
Give us each day our daily bread.
Forgive us our sins,
for we also forgive everyone
who sins against us.[c]
And lead us not into temptation.' "[d]

Then he said to them, "Suppose one of you has a friend, and he goes to him at midnight and says, 'Friend, lend me three loaves of bread, because a friend of mine on a journey has come to me, and I have nothing to set before him.'

"Then the one inside answers, 'Don't bother me. The door is already locked, and my children are with me in bed. I can't get up and give you anything.' I tell you, though he will not get up and give him the bread because he is his friend, yet because of the man's boldness[e] he will get up and give him as much as he needs.

"So I say to you: Ask and it will be given to you; seek and you will find; knock and the door will be opened to you. For everyone who asks receives; he who seeks finds; and to him who knocks, the door will be opened.

"Which of you fathers, if your son asks for[f] a fish, will give him a snake instead? Or if he asks for an egg, will give him a scorpion? If you then, though you are evil, know how to give good gifts to your children, how much more will your Father in heaven give the Holy Spirit to those who ask him!" LUKE 11:1-13

"Everyone who asks receives; he who seeks finds;
and to him who knocks, the door will be opened."

FROM OSWALD CHAMBERS

✌ We have not the remotest conception of what is done by our prayers, nor have we the right to try to examine and understand it; all we know is that Jesus Christ laid all stress on prayer. "And greater works than these shall he do, because I go unto My Father. And whatsoever ye shall ask in My name, that will I do" (John 14:12-13). BP 159

✌ How much of our praying is from the empty spaces round our own hearts and how much from the basis of the redemption, so that we give no thought for ourselves or for others, but only for Jesus Christ? Inarticulate prayer, the impulsive prayer that looks so futile, is the great thing God heeds more than anything else because it is along the line of His program. HGM 80

✌ "Your Father knoweth what things ye have need of, before ye ask Him" (Matt. 6:8). Then why ask? Very evidently our ideas about prayer and Jesus Christ's are not the same. Prayer to Him is not a means of getting things from God, but in order that we may get to know God. IYA 10

✌ Jesus did not promise to be at every prayer meeting, but only at those "where two or three are gathered together in My name," meaning, in His nature (Matt. 18:20). Jesus Christ does not pay any attention to the gift of "religious gab," and His words "But when ye pray, use not vain repetitions, as the heathen do, for they think that they shall be heard for their much speaking" (Matt. 6:7), refer not to the mere repetition and form of the words, but to the fact that it is never our earnestness that brings us into touch with God, but our Lord Jesus Christ's vitalizing death. IYA 12

✌ There is a difference in the prayers of the Old and the New Testaments. . . . The Prophet Habakkuk bases his prayer on the character of God, and appeals to God's great mercies. In the New Testament, prayer is based on a relationship with God through Jesus Christ: "When ye pray, say, Our Father." There is another difference—the prayers in the Old Testament have to do with an earthly people in an earthly setting; the prayers in the New Testament have to do with a heavenly state of mind in a heavenly people while on this earth. . . . When through Jesus Christ we are rightly related to God, we learn to watch and wait, and wait wonderingly. "I wonder how God will answer this prayer." "I wonder how God will answer the prayer the Holy Spirit is praying in me." "I wonder what glory God will bring to Himself out of the strange perplexities I am in." "I wonder what new turn His providence will take in manifesting Himself in my ways." IYA 42

⁊ Prayer is an effort of will, and Jesus Christ instructs us by using the word *ask*. "Everyone that asketh receiveth." These words are an amazing revelation of the simplicity with which God would have us pray. The other domains of prayer, the intercession of the Holy Spirit and the intercession of Christ, are nothing to do with us; the effort of our will is to do with us. MFL 59

⁊ Prayer alters a man on the inside, alters his mind and his attitude to things. The point of praying is not that we get things from God, but that we learn by prayer to detect the difference between God's order and God's permissive will. God's order is—no pain, no sickness, no devil, no war, no sin; His permissive will is all these things including the "soup" we are in just now. What a man needs to do is to get hold of God's order in the kingdom on the inside, and then he will begin to see how to handle the riddle of the universe on the outside. SHH 19

---

a. Some manuscripts [of Luke 11:2] *Our Father in heaven*
b. Some manuscripts [of Luke 11:2] *come. May your will be done on earth as it is in heaven.*
c. Greek *everyone who is indebted to us*
d. Some manuscripts [of Luke 11:4] *temptation but deliver us from the evil one*
e. Or *persistence*
f. Some manuscripts [of Luke 11:11] *for bread, will give him a stone; or if he asks for*

55

SIX WOES

hen Jesus had finished speaking, a Pharisee invited him to eat with him; so he went in and reclined at the table. But the Pharisee, noticing that Jesus did not first wash before the meal, was surprised.

Then the Lord said to him, "Now then, you Pharisees clean the outside of the cup and dish, but inside you are full of greed and wickedness. You foolish people! Did not the one who made the outside make the inside also? But give what is inside [the dish][a] to the poor, and everything will be clean for you.

"Woe to you Pharisees, because you give God a tenth of your mint, rue and all other kinds of garden herbs, but you neglect justice and the love of God. You should have practiced the latter without leaving the former undone.

"Woe to you Pharisees, because you love the most important seats in the synagogues and greetings in the marketplaces.

"Woe to you, because you are like unmarked graves, which men walk over without knowing it."

One of the experts in the law answered him, "Teacher, when you say these things, you insult us also."

Jesus replied, "And you experts in the law, woe to you, because you load people down with burdens they can hardly carry, and you yourselves will not lift one finger to help them.

"Woe to you, because you build tombs for the prophets, and it was your forefathers who killed them. So you testify that you approve of what your forefathers did; they killed the prophets, and you build their tombs. Because of this, God in his wisdom said, 'I will send them prophets and apostles, some of whom they will kill and others they will persecute.' Therefore this generation will be held responsible for the blood of all the prophets that has been shed since the beginning of the world, from the blood of Abel to the blood of Zechariah, who was killed between the altar and the sanctuary. Yes, I tell you, this generation will be held responsible for it all.

"Woe to you experts in the law, because you have taken away the key to knowledge. You yourselves have not entered, and you have hindered those who were entering."

When Jesus left there, the Pharisees and the teachers of the law began to oppose him fiercely and to besiege him with questions, waiting to catch him in something he might say. LUKE 11:37-54

*"You . . . clean the outside of the cup and dish,
but inside you are full of greed and wickedness."*

FROM OSWALD CHAMBERS

❧ The moral law is not imperative, because it can be disobeyed and immediate destruction does not follow. And yet the moral law never alters, however much men disobey it; it can be violated, but it never alters. Remember, at the back of all human morality stands God. BE 7

❧ Jesus Christ did not come to pronounce judgment; He Himself is the judgment; whenever we come across Him we are judged instantly. . . . One of the most remarkable things about Jesus Christ is that although He was full of love and gentleness, yet in His presence everyone not only felt benefited, but ashamed. It is His presence that judges us; we long to meet Him, and yet we dread to. . . . It is not simply the things Jesus says to us directly, or what He does in the way of judgment particularly; it is Himself entirely, whenever He comes we are judged. HGM 42, 43

❧ Man has to fulfill God's law in his physical life, in his mental and moral life, in his social and spiritual life, and to offend in one point is to be guilty of all. BE 15

❧ We pronounce judgments, not by our character or our goodness, but by the intolerant ban of finality in our views, which awakens resentment and has none of the Spirit of Jesus in it. Jesus never judged like that. It was His presence, His inherent holiness that judged. Whenever we see Him we are judged instantly. HGM 46

❧ If you refrain from all sorts of bad things, that is no sign that you are regenerated, much less sanctified! Not one bit of it. Scores of people who have not a spark of salvation live a cleaner life than some folks who say they are Christians. Entire sanctification is not mere outward cleanness or moral living. That is your definition, not God's. But spirituality is based on the most intense morality. Christianity is not the annulling of the Ten Commandments; to the contrary, it is a transfiguration of the will, which allows Jesus Christ to be manifested in every fiber of your being. DDL 21

---

a. Or *what you have*

56

WARNINGS AND ENCOURAGEMENTS

Meanwhile, when a crowd of many thousands had gathered, so that they were trampling on one another, Jesus began to speak first to his disciples, saying: "Be on your guard against the yeast of the Pharisees, which is hypocrisy. There is nothing concealed that will not be disclosed, or hidden that will not be made known. What you have said in the dark will be heard in the daylight, and what you have whispered in the ear in the inner rooms will be proclaimed from the roofs.

"I tell you, my friends, do not be afraid of those who kill the body and after that can do no more. But I will show you whom you should fear: Fear him who, after the killing of the body, has power to throw you into hell. Yes, I tell you, fear him. Are not five sparrows sold for two pennies?[a] Yet not one of them is forgotten by God. Indeed, the very hairs of your head are all numbered. Don't be afraid; you are worth more than many sparrows.

"I tell you, whoever acknowledges me before men, the Son of Man will also acknowledge him before the angels of God. But he who disowns me before men will be disowned before the angels of God. And everyone who speaks a word against the Son of Man will be forgiven, but anyone who blasphemes against the Holy Spirit will not be forgiven.

"When you are brought before synagogues, rulers and authorities, do not worry about how you will defend yourselves or what you will say, for the Holy Spirit will teach you at that time what you should say." LUKE 12:1-12

"Whoever acknowledges me before men,
the Son of Man will also acknowledge."

From Oswald Chambers

❧ It is easy to be priggish and profess, but it takes the indwelling of the Holy Spirit to so identify us with Jesus Christ that when we are put in a corner we confess Him, not denounce others. "No, I cannot take part in what you are doing because it would imperil my relationship to Jesus Christ." We are afraid of being "speckled birds" in the company we belong to. Jesus says, "Don't be ashamed to confess Me." HGM 30

❧ A man may betray Jesus Christ by speaking too many words, and he may betray Him through keeping his mouth shut. The revelation that perceives is that which recklessly states what it believes. When you stand up before your fellowmen and confess something about Jesus Christ, you feel you have no one to support you in the matter, but as you testify you begin to find the reality of your spiritual possessions, and there rushes into you the realization of a totally new life. PH 211

❧ The disadvantage of a saint in the present order of things is that his confession of Jesus Christ is not to be in secret, but glaringly public. It would doubtless be to our advantage from the standpoint of self-realization to keep quiet, and nowadays the tendency to say — "Be a Christian, live a holy life, but don't talk about it" — is growing stronger. Our Lord uses in illustration the most conspicuous things known to men, viz., salt, light, and a city set on a hill, and He says — "Be like that in your home, in your business, in your church; be conspicuously a Christian for ridicule or respect according to the mood of the people you are with." SSM 18

❧ There is no allowance whatever in the New Testament for the man who says he is saved by grace but who does not produce the graceful goods. Jesus Christ by His redemption can make our actual life in keeping with our religious profession. SSM 90

---

a. Greek *two assaria*

57

THE PARABLE OF THE RICH FOOL

S omeone in the crowd said to him, "Teacher, tell my brother to divide the inheritance with me."

Jesus replied, "Man, who appointed me a judge or an arbiter between you?" Then he said to them, "Watch out! Be on your guard against all kinds of greed; a man's life does not consist in the abundance of his possessions."

And he told them this parable: "The ground of a certain rich man produced a good crop. He thought to himself, 'What shall I do? I have no place to store my crops.'

"Then he said, 'This is what I'll do. I will tear down my barns and build bigger ones, and there I will store all my grain and my goods. And I'll say to myself, "You have plenty of good things laid up for many years. Take life easy; eat, drink and be merry." '

"But God said to him, 'You fool! This very night your life will be demanded from you. Then who will get what you have prepared for yourself?'

"This is how it will be with anyone who stores up things for himself but is not rich toward God." LUKE 12:13-21

"A man's life does not consist
in the abundance of his possessions."

FROM OSWALD CHAMBERS

> Professional Christianity is a religion of possessions that are devoted to God; the religion of Jesus Christ is a religion of personal relationship to God, and has nothing whatever to do with possessions. AUG 24

ɹ When Jesus Christ talked about discipleship, He indicated that a disciple must be detached from property and possessions, for if a man's life is in what he possesses, when disaster comes to his possessions, his life goes too. BFB 11

ɹ When Jesus Christ came He possessed nothing; the only symbol for our Lord is the symbol of poverty and this is true of the saint — "having nothing, and yet possessing all things" (2 Cor. 6:10). Every possession produces an appetite that clings. NKW 33

ɹ In civilized life it is the building up of possessions that is the snare — This is *my* house, *my* land; these are *my* books, and *my* things — imagine when they are touched! I am consumed with distress. Over and over again Jesus Christ drives this point home — Remember, don't have your heart in your possessions, let them come and go. SHH 63

ɹ "Seek ye first the kingdom of God, and His righteousness; and all these things shall be added unto you" (Matt. 6:33). "Seek ye first the kingdom of God" — "But suppose I do, what about this thing and that? Who is going to look after me? I would like to obey God, but don't ask me to take a step in the dark." We enthrone commonsense as Almighty God and treat Jesus Christ as a spiritual appendage to it. SSM 73

ɹ Am I prepared to strip myself of what I possess in property, in virtues, in the estimation of others — to count all things to be loss in order to win Christ? I can be so rich in poverty, so rich in the consciousness that I am nobody, that I shall never be a disciple; and I can be so rich in the consciousness that I am somebody that I shall never be a disciple. Am I willing to be destitute even of the sense that I am destitute? It is not a question of giving up outside things, but of making myself destitute to myself, reducing myself to a mere consciousness and giving that to Jesus Christ. I must reduce myself until I am a mere conscious man, fundamentally renounce possessions of all kinds — not to save my soul; only one thing saves a man's soul, absolute reliance on the Lord Jesus — and then give yourself to Jesus. SSY 59

58

DO NOT WORRY

T hen Jesus said to his disciples: "Therefore I tell you, do not worry about your life, what you will eat; or about your body, what you will wear. Life is more than food, and the body more than clothes. Consider the ravens: They do not sow or reap, they have no storeroom or barn; yet God feeds them. And how much more valuable you are than birds! Who of you by worrying can add a single hour to his life?[a] Since you cannot do this very little thing, why do you worry about the rest?

"Consider how the lilies grow. They do not labor or spin. Yet I tell you, not even Solomon in all his splendor was dressed like one of these. If that is how God clothes the grass of the field, which is here today, and tomorrow is thrown into the fire, how much more will he clothe you, O you of little faith! And do not set your heart on what you will eat or drink; do not worry about it. For the pagan world runs after all such things, and your Father knows that you need them. But seek his kingdom, and these things will be given to you as well.

"Do not be afraid, little flock, for your Father has been pleased to give you the kingdom. Sell your possessions and give to the poor. Provide purses for yourselves that will not wear out, a treasure in heaven that will not be exhausted, where no thief comes near and no moth destroys. For where your treasure is, there your heart will be also." LUKE 12:22-34

"I tell you, do not worry about your life,
what you will eat;
or about your body, what you will wear."

FROM OSWALD CHAMBERS

🙠 Once [we] become worried . . . the choking of the grace of God begins. If we have really had wrought into our hearts and heads the amazing revelation which Jesus Christ gives that God is love and that we can never remember anything He will forget, then worry is impossible. . . . Notice how frequently Jesus Christ warns against worry. The "cares of this world" will produce worry, and the "lusts of other things" entering in will choke the word God has put in.
BP 143

🙠 Jesus would never allow His disciples to be in a panic. The one great crime on the part of a disciple, according to Jesus Christ, is worry. Whenever we begin to calculate without God we commit sin.
CD, VOL. 1 110

🙠 Suppose that God is the God we know Him to be when we are nearest to Him; what an impertinence worry is! Think of the unspeakable marvel of the remaining hours of this day, and think how easily we can shut God right out of His universe by the logic of our own heads, by a trick of our nerves, by remembering the way we have limited Him in the past—banish Him right out, and let the old drudging, carking care come in, until we are a disgrace to the name of Jesus. But once let the attitude be a continual "going out" in dependence on God, and the life will have an ineffable charm, which is a satisfaction to Jesus Christ.

We have to learn how to "go out" of everything, out of convictions, out of creeds, out of experiences, out of everything, until so far as our faith is concerned, there is nothing between us and God.
LG 150

---

a. Or *single cubit to his height*

59

JESUS TEACHES WATCHFULNESS

Be dressed ready for service and keep your lamps burning, like men waiting for their master to return from a wedding banquet, so that when he comes and knocks they can immediately open the door for him. It will be good for those servants whose master finds them watching when he comes. I tell you the truth, he will dress himself to serve, will have them recline at the table and will come and wait on them. It will be good for those servants whose master finds them ready, even if he comes in the second or third watch of the night. But understand this: If the owner of the house had known at what hour the thief was coming, he would not have let his house be broken into. You also must be ready, because the Son of Man will come at an hour when you do not expect him."

Peter asked, "Lord, are you telling this parable to us, or to everyone?"

The Lord answered, "Who then is the faithful and wise manager, whom the master puts in charge of his servants to give them their food allowance at the proper time? It will be good for that servant whom the master finds doing so when he returns. I tell you the truth, he will put him in charge of all his possessions. But suppose the servant says to himself, 'My master is taking a long time in coming,' and he then begins to beat the menservants and maidservants and to eat and drink and get drunk. The master of that servant will come on a day when he does not expect him and at an hour he is not aware of. He will cut him to pieces and assign him a place with the unbelievers.

"That servant who knows his master's will and does not get ready or does not do what his master wants will be beaten with many blows. But the one who does not know and does things deserving punishment will be beaten with few blows. From everyone who has been given much, much will be demanded; and from the one who has been entrusted with much, much more will be asked." LUKE 12:35-48

> *"Everyone who has been given much,*
> *much will be demanded."*

___

FROM OSWALD CHAMBERS

> Remember you are accountable to no one but God; keep yourself for His service along the line of His providential leading for you, not on the line of your temperament. AUG 25

> Beware of the tendency of trying to do what God alone can do, and of blaming God for not doing what we alone can do. BP 119

> With us, Christian service is something we do; with Jesus Christ it is not what we do *for* Him, but what we *are to* Him that He calls service. Our Lord always puts the matter of discipleship on the basis of devotion not to a belief or a creed, but to Himself. There is no argument about it, and no compulsion, simply — "If you would be My disciple, you must be devoted to Me." PH 144

> Looking for opportunities to serve God is an impertinence; every time and all the time is our opportunity of serving God. RTR 52

> The idea is not that we do work for God, but that we are so loyal to Him that He can do His work through us — "I reckon on you for extreme service, with no complaining on your part and no explanation on Mine." God wants to use us as He used His own Son. RTR 92

> "To serve the living God." This means a life laid down for Jesus, a life of narrowed interests, a life that deliberately allows itself to be swamped by a crowd of paltry things. It is not fanaticism; it is the steadfast, flintlike attitude of heart and mind and body for one purpose — spoiled for everything saving as we can be used to win souls for Jesus. PS 22

> My contact with the nature of God has made me realize what I can do for God. Service is the outcome of what is fitted to my nature;

God's call is fitted to His nature, and I never hear His call until I have received His nature. When I have received His nature, then His nature and mine work together; the Son of God reveals Himself in me, and I, the natural man, serve the Son of God in ordinary ways, out of sheer downright devotion to Him. SSY 12

❧ Be ready for the sudden surprise visits of our Lord, and remember there is no such things as prominent service and obscure service; it is all the same with God, and God knows better than ourselves what we are ready to do. SSY 39

❧ God grant that His choice may fall on everyone of us, and that we may learn with patience and discipline how He is going to teach us to be patient, to be powerful, and to be passionate in His service! Never losing heart, never being discouraged, never being excited over a big catch. Many a worker has rendered himself useless to God by his undue hilarity over a big revival for God. "Notwithstanding, in this rejoice not, that the spirits are subject unto you," said Jesus, "but rather rejoice, because your names are written in heaven" (Luke 10:20). WG 85

60

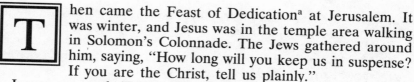

THE UNBELIEF OF THE JEWS

T hen came the Feast of Dedication[a] at Jerusalem. It was winter, and Jesus was in the temple area walking in Solomon's Colonnade. The Jews gathered around him, saying, "How long will you keep us in suspense? If you are the Christ, tell us plainly."

Jesus answered, "I did tell you, but you do not believe. The miracles I do in my Father's name speak for me, but you do not believe because you are not my sheep. My sheep listen to my voice; I know them, and they follow me. I give them eternal life, and they shall never perish; no one can snatch them out of my hand. My Father, who has given them to me, is greater than all[b]; no one can snatch them out of my Father's hand. I and the Father are one."

Again the Jews picked up stones to stone him, but Jesus said to them, "I have shown you many great miracles from the Father. For which of these do you stone me?"

"We are not stoning you for any of these," replied the Jews, "but for blasphemy, because you, a mere man, claim to be God."

Jesus answered them, "Is it not written in your Law, 'I have said you are gods'[c]? If he called them 'gods,' to whom the word of God came—and the Scripture cannot be broken—what about the one whom the Father set apart as his very own and sent into the world? Why then do you accuse me of blasphemy because I said, 'I am God's Son'? Do not believe me unless I do what my Father does. But if I do it, even though you do not believe me, believe the miracles, that you may know and understand that the Father is in me, and I in the Father." Again they tried to seize him, but he escaped their grasp.

Then Jesus went back across the Jordan to the place where John had been baptizing in the early days. Here he stayed and

many people came to him. They said, "Though John never performed a miraculous sign, all that John said about this man was
true." And in that place many believed in Jesus. JOHN 10:22-42

"My sheep listen to my voice;
I know them, and they follow me."

FROM OSWALD CHAMBERS

- I will always hear what I listen for, and the ruling disposition of the
soul determines what I listen for, just as the ruling disposition
either keeps the eyes from beholding vanity or makes them behold
nothing else. When Jesus Christ alters our disposition, He gives us
the power to hear as He hears. BP 74

- "He that hath ear to hear, let him hear." Before we can hear
certain things, we must be trained. Our disposition determines what
we listen for; and when Jesus alters the disposition, He gives us the
power to hear as He hears. OBH 54

- When we *hear* a thing is not necessarily when it is spoken, but when
we are in a state to listen to it and to understand. Our Lord's
statements seem to be so simple and gentle, and they slip unob-
served into the subconscious mind. Then something happens in our
circumstances, and up comes one of these words into our consciousness and we *hear* it for the first time, and it makes us reel
with amazement. SSY 60

- We show how little we love God by preferring to listen to His
servants only. We like to listen to personal testimonies, but we do
not desire that God Himself should speak to us. Why are we so
terrified lest God should speak to us? Because we know that if God
does speak, either the thing must be done or we must tell God we
will not obey Him. If it is only the servant's voice we hear, we feel it
is not imperative, we can say, "Well, that is simply your own idea,
though I don't deny it is probably God's truth."
    Am I putting God in the humiliating position of having treated
me as a child of His while all the time I have been ignoring Him?
When I do hear Him, the humiliation I have put on Him comes
back on me—"Lord, why was I so dull and so obstinate?" This is
always the result when once we do hear God. The real delight of

hearing Him is tempered with shame in having been so long in hearing Him. MUH 48

---

a. That is, Hanukkah
b. Many early manuscripts [of John 10:29] *What my Father has given me is greater than all*
c. Psalm 82:6

61

THE NARROW DOOR

T hen Jesus went through the towns and villages, teaching as he made his way to Jerusalem. Someone asked him, "Lord, are only a few people going to be saved?"

He said to them, "Make every effort to enter through the narrow door, because many, I tell you, will try to enter and will not be able to. Once the owner of the house gets up and closes the door, you will stand outside knocking and pleading, 'Sir, open the door for us.'

"But he will answer, 'I don't know you or where you come from.'

"Then you will say, 'We ate and drank with you, and you taught in our streets.'

"But he will reply, 'I don't know you or where you come from. Away from me, all you evildoers!'

"There will be weeping there, and gnashing of teeth, when you see Abraham, Isaac and Jacob and all the prophets in the kingdom of God, but you yourselves thrown out. People will come from east and west and north and south, and will take their places at the feast in the kingdom of God. Indeed there are those who are last who will be first, and first who will be last." LUKE 13:22-30

"Make every effort
to enter through the narrow door."

FROM OSWALD CHAMBERS

ᴥ Are you experiencing daily salvation, or are you shut out from Jesus Christ just now in your bodily life, in your mind, in your circumstances? Is there any fog, any darkness, any weariness, any trouble? Every day there are things that seem to shut the way up, but you can always enter in by the door and experience salvation. In the East it is the body of the shepherd himself that is the door of the fold. GW 110

❧ The Gospel gives access into privileges which no man can reach by any other way than the way Jesus Christ has appointed. Unsaved human nature resents this and tries to make out that Jesus Christ will bow in submissive weakness to the way it wants to go. The preaching of the Gospel awakens an intense craving and an equally intense resentment. The door is opened wide by a God of holiness and love, and any and every man can enter in through that door, if he will. "I am the way." Jesus Christ is the exclusive Way to the Father. IWP 127

❧ "Behold, *I* stand at the door and knock" (Rev. 3:20). If it is true that no man can open the doors Jesus Christ has closed, it is also true that He never opens the door for His own incoming into the heart and life of a church or an individual. "If any man . . . open the door, I will come in to him." The experience into which Jesus Christ by His sovereignty can bring us is at-one-ment with God, a full-orbed, unworrying oneness with God. IWP 128

❧ Redemption means that Jesus Christ can give us His own disposition, and all the standards He gives are based on that disposition — i.e., His teaching is for the life He puts in us. We enter into the life of Jesus by means of His death, that is our only door of entrance. We may try [to] batter through some other way if we choose — through Bethlehem, through the teachings of Jesus, but we cannot get in. Those ways in would produce frauds and humbugs. PR 25

62

JESUS AT A PHARISEE'S HOUSE

One Sabbath, when Jesus went to eat in the house of a prominent Pharisee, he was being carefully watched. There in front of him was a man suffering from dropsy. Jesus asked the Pharisees and experts in the law, "Is it lawful to heal on the Sabbath or not?" But they remained silent. So taking hold of the man, he healed him and sent him away.

Then he asked them, "If one of you has a son[a] or an ox that falls into a well on the Sabbath day, will you not immediately pull him out?" And they had nothing to say.

When he noticed how the guests picked the places of honor at the table, he told them this parable: "When someone invites you to a wedding feast, do not take the place of honor, for a person more distinguished than you may have been invited. If so, the host who invited both of you will come and say to you, 'Give this man your seat.' Then, humiliated, you will have to take the least important place. But when you are invited, take the lowest place, so that when your host comes, he will say to you, 'Friend, move up to a better place.' Then you will be honored in the presence of all your fellow guests. For everyone who exalts himself will be humbled, and he who humbles himself will be exalted."

Then Jesus said to his host, "When you give a luncheon or dinner, do not invite your friends, your brothers or relatives, or your rich neighbors; if you do, they may invite you back and so you will be repaid. But when you give a banquet, invite the poor, the crippled, the lame, the blind, and you will be blessed. Although they cannot repay you, you will be repaid at the resurrection of the righteous." LUKE 14:1-14

The Parable of the Great Banquet

When one of those at the table with him heard this, he said to Jesus, "Blessed is the man who will eat at the feast in the kingdom of God."

Jesus replied: "A certain man was preparing a great banquet and invited many guests. At the time of the banquet he sent his servant to tell those who had been invited, 'Come, for everything is now ready.'

"But they all alike began to make excuses. The first said, 'I have just bought a field, and I must go and see it. Please excuse me.'

"Another said, 'I have just bought five yoke of oxen, and I'm on my way to try them out. Please excuse me.'

"Still another said, 'I just got married, so I can't come.'

"The servant came back and reported this to his master. Then the owner of the house became angry and ordered his servant, 'Go out quickly into the streets and alleys of the town and bring in the poor, the crippled, the blind and the lame.'

" 'Sir,' the servant said, 'what you ordered has been done, but there is still room.'

"Then the master told his servant, 'Go out to the roads and country lanes and make them come in, so that my house will be full. I tell you, not one of those men who were invited will get a taste of my banquet.' " LUKE 14:15-24

"Everyone who exalts himself will be humbled
and he who humbles himself will be exalted."

From Oswald Chambers

- There is nothing more awful than conscious humility; it is the most satanic type of pride. BP 187

- Jesus Christ presented humility as a description of what we shall be unconsciously when we have become rightly related to God and are rightly centered in Jesus Christ. BP 187

- Humility is the exhibition of the Spirit of Jesus Christ, and is the touchstone of saintliness. MFL 102

   It is easier to be a fanatic than a faithful soul, because there is something amazingly humbling, particularly to our religious conceit, in being loyal to God. NKW 144

   Humility is the one stamp of a saint. Beware of the complacency of superiority when God's grace has done anything for you. RTR 9

   Humility is not an ideal; it is the unconscious result of the life being rightly related to God. RTR 21

   The great characteristic of the saint is humility. SSM 80

   We have the idea that we are meant to work for God along the heroic line; we are meant to do un-heroic work for God in the martyr spirit. The sphere of humiliation is always the place of more satisfaction to Jesus Christ, and it is in our power to refuse to be humiliated, to say, " 'No, thank you,' I much prefer to be on the mountaintop with God." LG 58

   The way we continually talk about our own inability is an insult to the Creator. The deploring of our own incompetence is a slander against God for having overlooked us. Get into the habit of examining in the sight of God the things that sound humble before men, and you will be amazed at how staggeringly impertinent they are. MUH 335

---

a. Some manuscripts [of Luke 14:5] *donkey*

63

THE COST OF DISCIPLESHIP

arge crowds were traveling with Jesus, and turning to them he said: "If anyone comes to me and does not hate his father and mother, his wife and children, his brothers and sisters—yes, even his own life—he cannot be my disciple. And anyone who does not carry his cross and follow me cannot be my disciple.

"Suppose one of you wants to build a tower. Will he not first sit down and estimate the cost to see if he has enough money to complete it? For if he lays the foundation and is not able to finish it, everyone who sees it will ridicule him, saying, 'This fellow began to build and was not able to finish.'

"Or suppose a king is about to go to war against another king. Will he not first sit down and consider whether he is able with ten thousand men to oppose the one coming against him with twenty thousand? If he is not able, he will send a delegation while the other is still a long way off and will ask for terms of peace. In the same way, any of you who does not give up everything he has cannot be my disciple.

"Salt is good, but if it loses its saltiness, how can it be made salty again? It is fit neither for the soil nor for the manure pile; it is thrown out.

"He who has ears to hear, let him hear." LUKE 14:25-35

"If anyone comes to me
and does not hate his father and mother . . .
even his own life. . . .
And anyone who does not carry his cross
and follow me cannot be my disciple."

FROM OSWALD CHAMBERS

❧ Our Lord places our love for Him way beyond our love for father and mother; in fact, He uses a tremendous word. He says, "Unless you hate your father and mother, you cannot be My disciple." The word *hate* appears to have been a stumbling block to a great number of people. It is quite conceivable that many persons may have such a slight regard for their fathers and mothers that it is nothing to separate from them; but the word *hate* shows what love we ought to have for our parents, an intense love; yet your love for [Him], says Jesus, is to be so intense that any other relationship is "hatred" in comparison when in conflict with [His] claims. GR 6-8-1911

❧ Most of us are smugly satisfied with praising Jesus Christ without ever having realized what the Cross means. We say, "O Lord, I want to be sanctified," and at any moment in answer to that prayer the Holy Ghost may rip and tear your conscience and stagger you dumb by conviction of sin, and the question is, will you accept God's verdict on sin on the cross of Christ, or will you whine and compromise? The only test of spirituality is holiness, practical, living holiness, and that holiness is impossible unless the Holy Ghost has brought you to your "last day," and you can look back and say—"That was the day when I died right out to my right to myself, crucified with Christ." HG 109

❧ There is a difference between devotion to principles and devotion to a person. Hundreds of people today are devoting themselves to phases of truth, to causes. Jesus Christ never asks us to devote ourselves to a cause or a creed; He asks us to devote ourselves to Him, to sign away the right to ourselves and yield to Him absolutely, and take up that cross daily. AUG 97

❧ It is one thing to recognize what God is doing with us, but another thing to deliberately accept it as His appointment. We can never accept the appointment of Jesus Christ and bear away the sin of the world; that was His work; but He does ask us to accept our cross. What is my cross? The manifestation of the fact that I have given up my right to myself to Him forever: self-interest, self-sympathy, self-pity—anything and everything that does not arise from a determination to accept my life entirely from Him will lead to a dissipation of my life. PR 57

꙳ Never mistake the wonderful visions God gives you for reality, but watch, for after the vision you will be brought straight down into the valley. We are not made for the mountains; we are made for the valley. Thank God for the mountains, for the glorious spiritual realization of who Jesus Christ is. But can we face things as they actually are in the light of the reality of Jesus Christ? Or do things as they are efface altogether our faith in Him and drive us into a panic? When Jesus said, "I go to prepare a place for you" (John 14:2), it was to the cross He went. Through His cross He prepared a place for us to "sit with Him in the heavenly places in Christ Jesus" (Eph. 2:6) *now* — not by and by. When we get to the cross we do not go through and out the other side; we abide in the life to which the cross is the gateway; and the characteristic of the life is deep and profound sacrifice to God. We know who our Lord is by the power of His Spirit; we are strongly confident in Him, and the reality of our relationship to Him works out all the time in the actualities of our ordinary life. PR 82

꙳ The Cross is the point where God and sinful man merge with a crash, and the way to life is opened, but the crash is on the heart of God. God is always the sufferer. PR 107

꙳ Our cross is the steady exhibition of the fact that we are not our own but Christ's, and we know it, and are determined to be unenticed from living a life of dedication to Him. This is the beginning of the emergence of the real life of faith. PS 38

꙳ The cross is the deliberate recognition of what my personal life is for, viz., to be given to Jesus Christ; I have to take up that cross daily and prove that I am no longer my own. Individual independence has gone, and all that is left is personal passionate devotion to Jesus Christ through identification with His Cross. SHL 79

64

THE PARABLE OF THE LOST SON

Jesus continued: "There was a man who had two sons. The younger one said to his father, 'Father, give me my share of the estate.' So he divided his property between them.

"Not long after that, the younger son got together all he had, set off for a distant country and there squandered his wealth in wild living. After he had spent everything, there was a severe famine in that whole country, and he began to be in need. So he went and hired himself out to a citizen of that country, who sent him to his fields to feed pigs. He longed to fill his stomach with the pods that the pigs were eating, but no one gave him anything.

"When he came to his senses, he said, 'How many of my father's hired men have food to spare, and here I am starving to death! I will set out and go back to my father and say to him: Father, I have sinned against heaven and against you. I am no longer worthy to be called your son; make me like one of your hired men.' So he got up and went to his father.

"But while he was still a long way off, his father saw him and was filled with compassion for him; he ran to his son, threw his arms around him and kissed him.

"The son said to him, 'Father, I have sinned against heaven and against you. I am no longer worthy to be called your son.'[a]

"But the father said to his servants, 'Quick! Bring the best robe and put it on him. Put a ring on his finger and sandals on his feet. Bring the fattened calf and kill it. Let's have a feast and celebrate. For this son of mine was dead and is alive again; he was lost and is found.' So they began to celebrate.

"Meanwhile, the older son was in the field. When he came near the house, he heard music and dancing. So he called one of the servants and asked him what was going on. 'Your brother has come,' he replied, 'and your father has killed the fattened calf because he has him back safe and sound.'

"The older brother became angry and refused to go in. So his father went out and pleaded with him. But he answered his father, 'Look! All these years I've been slaving for you and never disobeyed your orders. Yet you never gave me even a young goat so I could celebrate with my friends. But when this son of yours who has squandered your property with prostitutes comes home, you kill the fattened calf for him!'

" 'My son,' the father said, 'you are always with me, and everything I have is yours. But we had to celebrate and be glad, because this brother of yours was dead and is alive again; he was lost and is found.' " LUKE 15:11-32

"When he came to his senses, he said . . .
'I will set out and go back to my father.' "

FROM OSWALD CHAMBERS

❧ *Repentance* does not simply mean sorrow for sin. No! The prodigal son had remorse and sorrow while he fed pigs. In despair, he said, "How many hired servants of my father's have bread enough and to spare, and I perish with hunger!" (Luke 15:17) But was that repentance? Obviously not. The prodigal left the pigs and husks, and *went back* to his father. He said, "I will say unto him, Father, I have sinned against heaven, and before thee, and am no more worthy to be called thy son; make me as one of thy hired servants" (Luke 15:18-19). Almost before he realized it, two strong arms of love embraced him, and the father clasped him to his bosom. That is repentance! The New Testament meaning of repentance is "going back." DDL 9

❧ Jesus Christ came to do what no man can do for himself, viz., alter his disposition. "How can a man be born when he is old?" By receiving the gift of the Holy Spirit, and allowing Him to do *in* him what Jesus did *for* him. The mighty sovereign power of God can remake a man from within and readjust him to God. The Holy Spirit is God Himself working to make the Redemption efficacious in human lives. No wonder men leap for joy when they get saved in the New Testament way! HGM 13

✌ Modern ethical teaching bases everything on the power of the will, but we need to recognize also the perils of the will. The man who has achieved a moral victory by the sheer force of his will is less likely to want to become a Christian than the man who has come to the moral frontier of his own need. It is the obstinate man who makes vows, and by the very fulfillment of his vow he may increase his inability to see things from Jesus Christ's standpoint. GW 132

✌ The knowledge of our own poverty brings us to the moral frontier where Jesus Christ works. LG 111

---

a. Some early manuscripts [of Luke 15:21] *son. Make me like one of your hired men.*

65

THE DEATH AND RESURRECTION OF LAZARUS

ow a man named Lazarus was sick. He was from Bethany, the village of Mary and her sister Martha. This Mary, whose brother Lazarus now lay sick, was the same one who poured perfume on the Lord and wiped his feet with her hair. So the sisters sent word to Jesus, "Lord, the one you love is sick."

When he heard this, Jesus said, "This sickness will not end in death. No, it is for God's glory so that God's Son may be glorified through it." Jesus loved Martha and her sister and Lazarus. Yet when he heard that Lazarus was sick, he stayed where he was two more days.

Then he said to his disciples, "Let us go back to Judea."

"But, Rabbi," they said, "a short while ago the Jews tried to stone you, and yet you are going back there?"

Jesus answered, "Are there not twelve hours of daylight? A man who walks by day will not stumble, for he sees by this world's light. It is when he walks by night that he stumbles, for he has no light."

After he had said this, he went on to tell them, "Our friend Lazarus has fallen asleep; but I am going there to wake him up."

His disciples replied, "Lord, if he sleeps, he will get better." Jesus had been speaking of his death, but his disciples thought he meant natural sleep.

So then he told them plainly, "Lazarus is dead, and for your sake I am glad I was not there, so that you may believe. But let us go to him."

Then Thomas (called Didymus) said to the rest of the disciples, "Let us also go, that we may die with him." JOHN 11:1-16

Jesus Comforts the Sisters

On his arrival, Jesus found that Lazarus had already been in the tomb for four days. Bethany was less than two miles[a] from Jerusalem, and many Jews had come to Martha and Mary to comfort them in the loss of their brother. When Martha heard that Jesus was coming, she went out to meet him, but Mary stayed at home.

"Lord," Martha said to Jesus, "if you had been here, my brother would not have died. But I know that even now God will give you whatever you ask."

Jesus said to her, "Your brother will rise again."

Martha answered, "I know he will rise again in the resurrection at the last day."

Jesus said to her, "I am the resurrection and the life. He who believes in me will live, even though he dies; and whoever lives and believes in me will never die. Do you believe this?"

"Yes, Lord," she told him, "I believe that you are the Christ, the Son of God, who was to come into the world."

And after she had said this, she went back and called her sister Mary aside. "The Teacher is here," she said, "and is asking for you." When Mary heard this, she got up quickly and went to him. Now Jesus had not yet entered the village, but was still at the place where Martha had met him. When the Jews who had been with Mary in the house, comforting her, noticed how quickly she got up and went out, they followed her, supposing she was going to the tomb to mourn there.

When Mary reached the place where Jesus was and saw him, she fell at his feet and said, "Lord, if you had been here, my brother would not have died."

When Jesus saw her weeping, and the Jews who had come along with her also weeping, he was deeply moved in spirit and troubled. "Where have you laid him?" he asked.

"Come and see, Lord," they replied.

Jesus wept.

Then the Jews said, "See how he loved him!"

But some of them said, "Could not he who opened the eyes of the blind man have kept this man from dying?" JOHN 11:17-37

JESUS RAISES LAZARUS FROM THE DEAD

Jesus, once more deeply moved, came to the tomb. It was a cave with a stone laid across the entrance. "Take away the stone," he said.

"But, Lord," said Martha, the sister of the dead man, "by this time there is a bad odor, for he has been there four days."

Then Jesus said, "Did I not tell you that if you believed, you would see the glory of God?"

So they took away the stone. Then Jesus looked up and said, "Father, I thank you that you have heard me. I knew that you always hear me, but I said this for the benefit of the people standing here, that they may believe that you sent me."

When he had said this, Jesus called in a loud voice, "Lazarus, come out!" The dead man came out, his hands and feet wrapped with strips of linen, and a cloth around his face.

Jesus said to them, "Take off the grave clothes and let him go." JOHN 11:38-44

THE PLOT TO KILL JESUS

Therefore many of the Jews who had come to visit Mary, and had seen what Jesus did, put their faith in him. But some of them went to the Pharisees and told them what Jesus had done. Then the chief priests and the Pharisees called a meeting of the Sanhedrin.

"What are we accomplishing?" they asked. "Here is this man performing many miraculous signs. If we let him go on like this, everyone will believe in him, and then the Romans will come and take away both our place[b] and our nation."

Then one of them, named Caiaphas, who was high priest that year, spoke up, "You know nothing at all! You do not realize that it is better for you that one man die for the people than that the whole nation perish."

He did not say this on his own, but as high priest that year prophesied that Jesus would die for the Jewish nation, and not only for that nation but also for the scattered children of God, to bring them together to make them one. So from that day on they plotted to take his life.

Therefore Jesus no longer moved about publicly among the Jews. Instead He withdrew to a region near the desert, to a village called Ephraim, where he stayed with his disciples. JOHN 11:45-54

"I am the resurrection and the life."

From Oswald Chambers

❧ We know nothing about the mystery of death apart from what Jesus Christ tells us; but blessed be the name of God, what He tells us makes us more than conquerors, so that we can shout the victory through the darkest valley of the shadow that ever a human being can go through. SHL 24

❧ Death has no terror for the man who is rightly related to God through Jesus Christ. SHL 26

❧ Our Lord makes little of physical death, but He makes much of moral and spiritual death. SSY 97

❧ Every time you venture out in the life of faith, you will find something in your commonsense circumstances that flatly contradicts your faith. Common sense is not faith, and faith is not common sense; they stand in the relation of the natural and the spiritual. Can you trust Jesus Christ where your common sense cannot trust Him? . . . Faith must be tested, because it can be turned into a personal possession only through conflict. What is your faith up against just now? The test will either prove your faith is right, or it will kill it. "Blessed is he whosoever shall not be offended in Me" (Matt. 11:6). The final thing is confidence in Jesus. Believe steadfastly on Him and all you come up against will develop your faith. There is continual testing in the life of faith, and the last great test is death. May God keep us in fighting trim! Faith is unutterable trust in God, trust which never dreams that He will not stand by us. MUH 242

❧ Picture Martha and Mary waiting day after day for Jesus to come, yet not till Lazarus' body had been in the grave four days does Jesus Christ appear on the scene. Days of absolute silence, of awful repose on the part of God! Is there anything analogous to it in your life? Can God trust you like that, or are you still wanting a visible answer? "Everyone that asketh receiveth" (Matt. 7:8). IYA 50

❧ Could the answer that Jesus Christ gave ever have entered into the heart of Martha and Mary—a raised brother, the manifestation of the glory of God, and the understanding of Jesus Christ in a way that has blessed the church for twenty centuries! IYA 51

❧ Some prayers are followed by silence because they are wrong, others because they are bigger than we can understand. Jesus stayed where He was—a positive staying, because He loved Martha and Mary. Did they get Lazarus back? They got infinitely more; they got to know the greatest truth mortal beings ever knew—that Jesus Christ is the Resurrection and the Life. It will be a wonderful moment for some of us when we stand before God and find that the prayers we clamored for in early days and imagined were never answered, have been answered in the most amazing way, and that God's silence has been the sign of the answer. IYA 49

---

a. Greek *fifteen stadia* (about 3 kilometers)
b. Or *temple*

66

TEN HEALED OF LEPROSY

 ow on his way to Jerusalem, Jesus traveled along the border between Samaria and Galilee. As he was going into a village, ten men who had leprosy met him. They stood at a distance and called out in a loud voice, "Jesus, Master, have pity on us!"

When he saw them, he said, "Go, show yourselves to the priests." And as they went, they were cleansed.

One of them, when he saw he was healed, came back, praising God in a loud voice. He threw himself at Jesus' feet and thanked him—and he was a Samaritan.

Jesus asked, "Were not all ten cleansed? Where are the other nine? Was no one found to return and give praise to God except this foreigner?" Then he said to him, "Rise and go; your faith has made you well." LUKE 17:11-19

"One of them . . . came back,
praising God in a loud voice."

FROM OSWALD CHAMBERS

ً Praising God is the ultimate end and aim of all we go through. "Whoso offereth praise glorifieth Me" (Ps. 50:23). AUG 10

ً If we only praise when we feel like praising, it is simply an undisciplined expression; but if we deliberately go over the neck of our disinclination and offer the sacrifice of praise, we are emancipated by our very statements. PH 208

ً Are you thankful to God for your salvation and sanctification, thankful He has purged your conscience from dead works? Then go a step further; let Jesus Christ take you straight through into identification with His death until there is nothing left but the light at the foot of the cross, and the whole sphere of the life is hid with Christ in God. PS 23

   Discipleship and salvation are two different things: a disciple is one who, realizing the meaning of the Atonement, deliberately gives himself up to Jesus Christ in unspeakable gratitude. SSY 34

   God's grace does not turn out milksops, but men and women with a strong family likeness to Jesus Christ. Thank God He does give us difficult things to do! A man's heart would burst if there were no way to show his gratitude. "I beseech you therefore, brethren," says Paul, "by the mercies of God, that ye present your bodies *a living sacrifice*" (Rom. 12:1). SSM 97

67

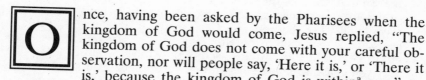

THE COMING OF THE KINGDOM OF GOD

Once, having been asked by the Pharisees when the kingdom of God would come, Jesus replied, "The kingdom of God does not come with your careful observation, nor will people say, 'Here it is,' or 'There it is,' because the kingdom of God is within[a] you."

Then he said to his disciples, "The time is coming when you will long to see one of the days of the Son of Man, but you will not see it. Men will tell you, 'There he is!' or 'Here he is!' Do not go running off after them. For the Son of Man in his day[b] will be like the lightning, which flashes and lights up the sky from one end to the other. But first he must suffer many things and be rejected by this generation.

"Just as it was in the days of Noah, so also will it be in the days of the Son of Man. People were eating, drinking, marrying and being given in marriage up to the day Noah entered the ark. Then the flood came and destroyed them all.

"It was the same in the days of Lot. People were eating and drinking, buying and selling, planting and building. But the day Lot left Sodom, fire and sulfur rained down from heaven and destroyed them all.

"It will be just like this on the day the Son of Man is revealed. On that day no one who is on the roof of his house, with his goods inside, should go down to get them. Likewise, no one in the field should go back for anything. Remember Lot's wife! Whoever tries to keep his life will lose it, and whoever loses his life will preserve it. I tell you, on that night two people will be in one bed; one will be taken and the other left. Two women will be grinding grain together; one will be taken and the other left.[c]"

"Where, Lord?" they asked.

He replied, "Where there is a dead body, there the vultures will gather." LUKE 17:20-37

"The kingdom of God
is within you."

FROM OSWALD CHAMBERS

❧ The entrance into the kingdom is through the panging pains of repentance crashing into a man's respectable goodness; then the Holy Ghost, who produces these agonies, begins the formation of the Son of God in the life. The new life will manifest itself in conscious repentance and unconscious holiness, never the other way about. The bedrock of Christianity is repentance. Strictly speaking, a man cannot repent when he chooses; repentance is a gift of God. The old Puritans used to pray for "the gift of tears." If ever you cease to know the virtue of repentance, you are in darkness. Examine yourself and see if you have forgotten how to be sorry. MUH 342

❧ It may be hard for a rich man to enter into the kingdom of heaven, but it is just as hard for a poor man to seek first the kingdom of God. HG 23

❧ We must realize the frontiers of death, that there is no more chance of our entering the life of God than a mineral has of entering into the vegetable kingdom; we can only enter into the kingdom of God if God will stoop down and lift us up. That is exactly what Jesus Christ promises to do. RTR 33

❧ In this dispensation the emphasis is on the kingdom within, but in another dispensation there is to be an external manifestation of the kingdom. To say that the kingdom is going to be brought in by the earth being swept clean through wars and cataclysms is not true; you cannot introduce the kingdom in that way; it is impossible. Nothing can bring in the kingdom saving the redemption, which works in personal lives through the cross and in no other way. GW 54

---

a. Or *among*
b. Some manuscripts [of Luke 17:24] do not have *in his day*
c. Some manuscripts [of Luke 17:35] *left. Two men will be in the field; one will be taken and the other left*

68

THE PARABLE OF THE PHARISEE AND THE TAX COLLECTOR

To some who were confident of their own righteousness and looked down on everybody else, Jesus told this parable: "Two men went up to the temple to pray, one a Pharisee and the other a tax collector. The Pharisee stood up and prayed about[a] himself: 'God, I thank you that I am not like other men — robbers, evildoers, adulterers — or even like this tax collector. I fast twice a week and give a tenth of all I get.'

"But the tax collector stood at a distance. He would not even look up to heaven, but beat his breast and said, 'God, have mercy on me, a sinner.'

"I tell you that this man, rather than the other, went home justified before God. For everyone who exalts himself will be humbled, and he who humbles himself will be exalted." LUKE 18:9-14

> *"He . . . beat his breast and said,*
> *'God have mercy on me, a sinner.' "*

FROM OSWALD CHAMBERS

- "I am not come to call the righteous, but sinners to repentance" (Matt. 9:13). Remember, that kind of statement hits the Pharisees to the very core of their being. HG 79

- Jesus Christ takes the man who has been broken on the wheel by conviction of sin and rendered plastic by the Holy Spirit, and re-molds him and makes him a vessel for God's glory. BP 183

❧ What our Lord Jesus Christ wants us to present to Him is not our goodness, or our honesty, or our endeavor, but our real solid sin, that is all He can take. "For He hath made Him to be sin for us, who knew no sin." And what does He give in exchange for our solid sin? Great solid righteousness — "that we might be made the righteousness of God in Him" (2 Cor. 5:21); but we must relinquish all pretense of being anything; we must relinquish in every way all claim to being worthy of God's consideration. That is the meaning of conviction of sin. CD, VOL. 1 129

❧ When conviction of sin by the Holy Spirit comes, it gives us an understanding of the deeps of our personality we are otherwise not conscious of. DI 64

❧ The first thing the Holy Spirit does when He comes in is to convict, not to comfort, because He has to let us know what we are like in God's sight; and then He brings the revelation that God will fill us with His own nature if we will let Him. OBH 58

❧ It is of the mercy of God that no man is convicted of *sin* before he is born again; we are convicted of *sins* in order to be born again, then the indwelling Holy Spirit convicts us of sin. If God gave us conviction of sin apart from a knowledge of His redemption, we would be driven insane. When conviction of what sin is in the sight of God comes home to me, language cannot support the strain of the verbal expression of its enormity; the only word that expresses it is "Calvary." If I see sin apart from the cross, suicide seems the only fool's way out. GW 84

---

a. Or *to*

69

A Rich Young Ruler

A s Jesus started on his way, a certain ruler ran up to him and fell on his knees before him. "Good teacher," he asked, "what good thing must I do to inherit eternal life?"

"Why do you call me good?" Jesus answered. "There is only One who is good—God alone. Why do you ask me about what is good? If you want to enter life, obey the commandments."

"Which ones?" the man inquired.

Jesus replied, "You know the commandments: 'Do not murder, do not commit adultery, do not steal, do not give false testimony, do not defraud, honor your father and mother,'[a] and 'love your neighbor as yourself.'[b] "

"Teacher," the young man declared, "all these I have kept since I was a boy. What do I still lack?"

When Jesus heard this, he looked at him and loved him. "You still lack one thing," he said. "If you want to be perfect, go, sell your possessions, everything you have, and give to the poor, and you will have treasure in heaven. Then come, follow me."

When he heard this, the young man's face fell. He went away very sad, because he was a man of great wealth.

Jesus looked at him, looked around and said to his disciples, "I tell you the truth, how hard it is for the rich to enter the kingdom of heaven!"

The disciples were amazed at his words. But Jesus said again, "Children, how hard it is[c] to enter the kingdom of God! Indeed, it is easier for a camel to go through the eye of a needle than for a rich man to enter the kingdom of God."

When the disciples heard this, they were greatly astonished and asked each other, "Who then can be saved?"

Jesus looked at them and replied, "With man this is impossible, but not with God; all things are possible with God."

Peter answered him, "We have left everything we had to follow you! What then will there be for us?"

"I tell you the truth," Jesus replied to them, "at the renewal of all things, when the Son of Man sits on his glorious throne, you who have followed me will also sit on twelve thrones, judging the twelve tribes of Israel. And everyone who has left home or wife or brothers or sisters or father or mother or children or fields for me and the gospel, for the sake of the kingdom of God, will receive a hundred times as much in this present age (homes, brothers, sisters, mothers, children and fields — and with them, persecutions) and in the age to come, eternal life. But many who are first will be last, and many who are last will be first." MATTHEW 19:16-30; MARK 10:17-31; LUKE 18:18-30

"Then come, follow me."

FROM OSWALD CHAMBERS

 ~ "Sell all that thou hast and distribute unto the poor." There is a general principle here and a particular reference. We are always in danger of taking the particular reference for the general principle and evading the general principle. The particular reference here is to selling material goods. The rich young ruler had deliberately to be destitute, deliberately to distribute, deliberately to discern where his treasure was, and to devote himself to Jesus Christ. The principle underlying it is that I must detach myself from everything I possess. SH 57

 ~ "Go, sell that thou hast, and give to the poor . . . and come, follow Me." These words mean a voluntary abandoning of riches and a deliberate, devoted attachment to Jesus Christ. We are so desperately wise in our own conceit that we continually make out that Jesus did not mean what He said, and we spiritualize His meaning into thin air. Jesus saw that this man depended on his riches. If He came to you or to me, He might not say that, but He would say something that dealt with whatever He saw we were depending on. "Sell that thou hast" — strip yourself of every possession, disengage yourself from all things until you are a naked soul; be a man merely and then give your manhood to God. Reduce yourself until nothing remains but your consciousness of yourself, and then cast that consciousness at the feet of Jesus Christ. SSY 58

❧ The rich young ruler had the master passion to be perfect. When he saw Jesus Christ, he wanted to be like Him. Our Lord never puts personal holiness to the fore when He calls a disciple; He puts absolute annihilation of my right to myself and identification with Himself—a relationship with Himself in which there is no other relationship. Luke 14:26 ["If any man come to Me, and hate not his father, and mother . . . and his own life also, he cannot be my disciple."] has nothing to do with salvation or sanctification, but with unconditional identification with Jesus Christ. Very few of us know the absolute "go" of abandonment to Jesus. MUH 272

a. Exodus 20:12-16; Deuteronomy 5:16-20
b. Leviticus 19:18
c. Some manuscripts [of Mark 10:24] *is for those who trust in riches*

70

THE REQUEST OF JAMES, JOHN, AND THEIR MOTHER

hen James and John, the sons of Zebedee, came to Jesus *with their mother.* "Teacher," they said, "we want you to do for us whatever we ask."

"What is it you want me to do for you?" he asked.

Then the mother, kneeling down, asked a favor of him.

She said, "Grant that one of these two sons of mine may sit at your right and the other at your left in your kingdom glory." They replied *similarly.*

"You don't know what you are asking," Jesus said to them. "Can you drink the cup I am going to drink or be baptized with the baptism I am baptized with?"

"We can," they answered.

Jesus said to them, "You will indeed drink the cup I drink and be baptized with the baptism I am baptized with, but to sit at my right or left is not for me to grant. These places belong to those for whom they have been prepared by my Father."

When the ten heard about this, they became indignant with James and John. Jesus called them together and said, "You know that those who are regarded as rulers of the Gentiles lord it over them, but their high officials exercise authority over them. Not so with you. Instead, whoever wants to become great among you must be your servant, and whoever wants to be first must be slave of all. For even the Son of Man did not come to be served, but to serve, and to give his life as a ransom for many." MATTHEW 20:20-28; MARK 10:35-45

"Whoever wants to become great among you must be your servant."

277

From Oswald Chambers

❧ Paul's idea of service is the same as our Lord's: "I am among you as He that serveth"; "ourselves your servants for Jesus' sake" (2 Cor. 4:5). . . . The mainspring of Paul's service is not love for men, but love for Jesus Christ. If we are devoted to the cause of humanity, we shall soon be crushed and brokenhearted, for we shall often meet with more ingratitude from men than we would from a dog; but if our motive is love to God, no ingratitude can hinder us from serving our fellowmen.

Paul's realization of how Jesus Christ had dealt with him is the secret of his determination to serve others. . . . When we realize that Jesus Christ has served us to the end of our meanness, our selfishness, and sin, nothing that we meet with from others can exhaust our determination to serve men for His sake. MUH 54

❧ We have a way of saying "What a wonderful power that man or woman would be in God's service." Reasoning on man's broken virtues makes us fix on the wrong thing. The only way any man or woman can ever be of service to God is when he or she is willing to renounce all natural excellencies and determine to be weak in Him — "I am here for one thing only — for Jesus Christ to manifest Himself in me." That is to be the steadfast habit of a Christian's life. MFL 106

❧ Beware of anything that competes with loyalty to Jesus Christ. The greatest competitor of devotion to Jesus is service for Him. It is easier to serve than to be drunk to the dregs. The one aim of the call of God is the satisfaction of God — not a call to do something for Him. We are not sent to battle for God, but to be used by God in His battlings. MUH 18

❧ The tendency today is to put the emphasis on service. Beware of the people who make usefulness their ground of appeal. If you make usefulness the test, then Jesus Christ was the greatest failure that ever lived. The lodestar of the saint is God Himself — not estimated usefulness. It is the work that God does through us that counts, not what we do for Him. MUH 243

❧ The stars do their work without fuss; God does His work without fuss, and saints do their work without fuss. PH 41

❧ God does not expect us to work *for* Him, but to work *with* Him. IYA 56

71

ZACCHAEUS THE TAX COLLECTOR

J esus entered Jericho and was passing through. A man was there by the name of Zacchaeus; he was a chief tax collector and was wealthy. He wanted to see who Jesus was, but being a short man he could not, because of the crowd. So he ran ahead and climbed a sycamore-fig tree to see him, since Jesus was coming that way.

When Jesus reached the spot, he looked up and said to him, "Zacchaeus, come down immediately. I must stay at your house today." So he came down at once and welcomed him gladly.

All the people saw this and began to mutter, "He has gone to be the guest of a 'sinner.' "

But Zacchaeus stood up and said to the Lord, "Look, Lord! Here and now I give half of my possessions to the poor, and if I have cheated anybody out of anything, I will pay back four times the amount."

Jesus said to him, "Today salvation has come to this house, because this man, too, is a son of Abraham. For the Son of Man came to seek and to save what was lost." LUKE 19:1-10

*"The Son of Man came to seek
and to save what was lost."*

FROM OSWALD CHAMBERS

⁊ Jesus Christ's thought about man is that he is lost, and that He is the only One who can find him. "For the Son of Man came to seek and to save that which was lost." CHI 97

⁊ From Jesus Christ's point of view all men are lost, but we have so narrowed and so specialized the term *lost* that we have missed its evangelical meaning; we have made it mean that only the people who are down and out in sin are lost. WG 30

    No man can be saved by praying, by believing, by obeying, or by consecration; salvation is a free gift of God's almighty grace. We have the sneaking idea that we earn things and get into God's favor by what we do—by our praying, by our repentance: the only way we get into God's favor is by the sheer gift of His grace. GW 11

    There is a difference between the way we try to appreciate the things of God and the way in which the Spirit of God teaches. We begin by trying to get fundamental conceptions of the creation and the world; why the devil is allowed; why sin exists. When the Spirit of God comes in, He does not begin by expounding any of these subjects. He begins by giving us a dose of the plague of our own heart; He begins where our vital interests lie—in the salvation of our souls. MFL 98

    If you have been making a great profession in your religious life but begin to find that the Holy Spirit is scrutinizing you, let His searchlight go straight down, and He will not only search you, He will put everything right that is wrong; He will make the past as though it had never been; He will "restore the years the cankerworm hath eaten" (see Joel 2:25); He will "blot out the handwriting of ordinances that is against you" (see Col. 2:14); He will put His Spirit within you and cause you to walk in His ways; He will make you pure in the deepest recesses of your personality. Thank God, Jesus Christ's salvation is a flesh-and-blood reality! SHL 51

    Salvation is not merely deliverance from sin, nor the experience of personal holiness; the salvation of God is deliverance out of self entirely into union with Himself. My experiential knowledge of salvation will be along the line of deliverance from sin and of personal holiness; but salvation means that the Spirit of God has brought me into touch with God's personality, and I am thrilled with something infinitely greater than myself; I am caught up into the abandonment of God. MUH 73

72

THE TRIUMPHAL ENTRY

T he next day, as they approached Jerusalem and came to Bethphage and Bethany at the hill called the Mount of Olives, Jesus sent two of his disciples, saying to them, "Go to the village ahead of you, and just as you enter it, you will find a donkey tied there, with her colt by her, which no one has ever ridden. Untie them and bring them here to me. If anyone asks you, 'Why are you doing this?' tell him, 'The Lord needs them, and he will send them back here right away.' "

The disciples went and did as Jesus had instructed them. They found a colt just as he had told them, outside in the street, tied at a doorway. As they were untying the colt, its owners asked them, "What are you doing? Why are you untying that colt?"

They answered as Jesus had told them, "The Lord needs it," and the people let them go. They brought the donkey and the colt to Jesus, threw their cloaks on the colt and put Jesus on it.

This took place to fulfill what was spoken through the prophet:

"Say to the Daughter of Zion,
'Do not be afraid.
See, your king comes to you,
gentle and riding on a donkey,
on a colt, the foal of a donkey.' "[a]

At first his disciples did not understand all this. Only after Jesus was glorified did they realize that these things had been written about him and that they had done these things to him.

The great crowd that had come for the Feast heard that Jesus was on his way to Jerusalem. Now the crowd that was with him when he called Lazarus from the tomb and raised him from the dead continued to spread the word. Many people, because they had heard that he had given this miraculous sign, went out to meet him.

As he went along, people spread their cloaks on the road, while others cut palm branches from the trees in the fields and spread them on the road.

When he came near the place where the road goes down the Mount of Olives, the whole crowd of disciples that went ahead of him, and those that followed, began joyfully to praise God in loud voices for all the miracles they had seen, shouting:

"Hosanna!"
"Hosanna to the Son of David!"
"Blessed is he who comes
in the name of the Lord!b"
"Blessed is the King of Israel!"
"Blessed is the coming kingdom
of our father David!"
"Peace in heaven and glory in the highest!"
"Hosanna in the highest!"

Some of the Pharisees in the crowd said to Jesus, "Teacher, rebuke your disciples!"

"I tell you," he replied, "if they keep quiet, the stones will cry out."

So the Pharisees said to one another, "See, this is getting us nowhere. Look how the whole world has gone after him!"

As he approached Jerusalem and saw the city, he wept over it and said, "If you, even you, had only known on this day what would bring you peace—but now it is hidden from your eyes. The days will come upon you when your enemies will build an embankment against you and encircle you and hem you in on every side. They will dash you to the ground, you and the children within your walls. They will not leave one stone on another, because you did not recognize the time of God's coming to you."

When Jesus entered Jerusalem, the whole city was stirred and asked, "Who is this?"

The crowds answered, "This is Jesus, the prophet from Nazareth in Galilee."

Jesus went to the temple. He looked around at everything, but

since it was already late, he went out to Bethany with the Twelve.
MATTHEW 21:1-11; MARK 11:1-11; LUKE 19:29-44; JOHN 12:12-19

*"The whole city was stirred
and asked, 'Who is this?' "*

FROM OSWALD CHAMBERS

- In presenting Jesus Christ never present Him as a miraculous Being who came down from heaven and worked miracles and who was not related to life as we are; that is not the Gospel Christ. The Gospel Christ is the Being who came down to earth and lived our life and was possessed of a frame like ours. He became Man in order to show the relationship man was to hold to God, and by His death and resurrection He can put any man into that relationship. Jesus Christ is the last word in human nature. AUG 44

- Jesus Christ was not a being who became Divine; He was the God-head incarnated; He emptied Himself of His glory in becoming incarnate. Never separate the Incarnation from the Atonement. The Incarnation was not meant to enable God to realize Himself, but that man might realize God and gain readjustment to Him. Jesus Christ became Man for one purpose, that He might put away sin and bring the whole human race back into the oneness of identification. AUG 70

- Jesus Christ is a Fact; He is the most honorable and the holiest Man, and two things necessarily follow—first, He is the least likely to be deceived about Himself; second, He is least likely to deceive anyone else. AUG 82

- Jesus Christ had a twofold personality: He was Son of God revealing what God is like, and Son of Man revealing what man is to be like. BSG 77

- What weakness! Our Lord lived thirty years in Nazareth with His brethren who did not believe on Him; He lived three years of popularity, scandal, and hatred; fascinated a dozen illiterate men who at the end of three years all forsook Him and fled; and finally He was taken by the powers that be and crucified outside the city wall. Judged from every standpoint save the standpoint of the Spirit

283

of God, His life was a most manifest expression of weakness, and the idea would be strong to those in the pagan world who thought anything about Him that surely now He and His crazy tale were stamped out. CD, VOL. 2 144

    There is an amazing sanity in Jesus Christ that shakes the foundations of death and hell, no panic, absolute dominant mastery over everything—such a stupendous mastery that He let men take His strength from Him: "He was crucified through weakness" (2 Cor. 13:4); that was the acme of Godlike strength. IWP 98

    Jesus Christ is the last word on God, on sin and death, on heaven and hell; the last word on every problem that human life has to face. IWP 125

    Jesus Christ is the love of God incarnated. LG 68

---

a. Zechariah 9:9
b. Psalm 118:25-26

73

THE PARABLE OF THE TWO SONS

e then began to speak to them in parables. "What do you think? There was a man who had two sons. He went to the first and said, 'Son, go and work today in the vineyard.'

" 'I will not,' he answered, but later he changed his mind and went.

"Then the father went to the other son and said the same thing. He answered, 'I will, sir,' but he did not go.

"Which of the two did what his father wanted?"

"The first," they answered.

Jesus said to them, "I tell you the truth, the tax collectors and the prostitutes are entering the kingdom of God ahead of you. For John came to you to show you the way of righteousness, and you did not believe him, but the tax collectors and the prostitutes did. And even after you saw this, you did not repent and believe him." MATTHEW 21:28-32; MARK 12:1a

"You did not believe him."

FROM OSWALD CHAMBERS

> ❧ The reason people disbelieve God is not because they do not understand with their heads—we understand very few things with our heads, but because they have turned their hearts in another direction. BP 144

> ❧ If we would only get into the way of bringing our limitations before God . . . we should begin to see the awful wickedness of unbelief, and why our Lord was so vigorous against it, and why the Apostle

285

John places fearfulness and unbelief at the head of all the most awful sins. BP 222

≈ Unbelief is the most active thing on earth; it is a fretful, worrying, questioning, annoying, self-centered spirit. To believe is to stop all this and let God work. RTR 44

≈ Belief is a wholesale committal. It means making things inevitable, cutting off every possible retreat. Belief is as irrevocable as bereavement. DI 1

≈ Belief is the abandonment of all claim to merit. That is why it is so difficult to believe. DI 1

≈ According to the New Testament, belief arises from intellectual conviction and goes through moral self-surrender to identification with the Lord Jesus Christ. AUG 110

≈ To believe is literally to commit. Belief is a moral act, and Jesus makes an enormous demand of a man when He asks him to believe in Him. PH 222

≈ It is a great thing to be a believer, but easy to misunderstand what the New Testament means by it. It is not that we believe Jesus Christ can *do* things, or that we believe in a plan of salvation; it is that we believe *Him;* whatever happens we will hang [on] to the fact that He is true. If we say, "I am going to believe He will put things right," we shall lose our confidence when we see things go wrong. AUG 114

≈ Our Lord's word *believe* does not refer to an intellectual act, but to a moral act; with our Lord to believe means to commit. "Commit yourself to Me," and it takes a man all he is worth to believe in Jesus Christ. AUG 114

74

THE GREATEST COMMANDMENT

O ne of the teachers of the law came and heard them debating. *He noticed* that Jesus had given them a good answer. Hearing that Jesus had silenced the Sadducees, the Pharisees got together. One of them, *the* expert in the law, tested him with this question: "Teacher, of all the commandments, which is the most important?"

"The most important one," answered Jesus, "is this: 'Hear, O Israel, the Lord our God, the Lord is one.[a] Love the Lord your God with all your heart and with all your soul and with all your mind and with all your strength.'[b] This is the first and greatest commandment. And the second is like it: 'Love your neighbor as yourself.'[c] There is no commandment greater than these. All the Law and the Prophets hang on these two commandments."

"Well said, teacher," the man replied. "You are right in saying that God is one and there is no other but him. To love him with all your heart, with all your understanding and with all your strength, and to love your neighbor as yourself is more important than all burnt offerings and sacrifices."

When Jesus saw that he had answered wisely, he said to him, "You are not far from the kingdom of God." MATTHEW 22:34-40; MARK 12:28-34a

"Love the Lord your God with all your heart
and with all your soul and with all your mind
and with all your strength."

From Oswald Chambers

❧ If my love is first of all God, I shall take no account of the base ingratitude of others, because the mainspring of my service to my fellowmen is love to God. BP 181

❧ Man was created to be the friend and lover of God and for no other end, and until he realizes this he will go through turmoil and upset. Human nature must rise to its own Source, the bosom of God, and Jesus Christ by His redemption brings it back there. God is the only One who has the right to myself; and when I love Him with all my heart and soul and mind and strength, self in its essence is realized. All the teaching of Jesus is woven around self; I have a moral self-love to preserve for God. Not, "Oh, I'm of no account," "[I'm] a worm" (see Acts 20:24); that would spell selflessness. "I hold not my life of any account, as dear unto myself," says Paul, "so that I may accomplish my course, and the ministry which I received from the Lord Jesus to testify the Gospel of the grace of God." That is, he refused to use himself for any other interest but God's, and for that which glorified God. SH 105

❧ Love in the Bible is ONE; it is unique, and the human element is but one aspect of it. It is a love so mighty, so absorbing, so intense that all the mind is emancipated and entranced by God; all the heart is transfigured by the same devotion; all the soul in its living, working, waking, sleeping moments is indwelt and surrounded and enwheeled in the rest of this love. CD, VOL. 2 154

❧ You don't love a person with your heart and leave the rest of your nature out; you love with your whole being, from the crown of the head to the sole of the foot. GW 9

❧ It is the most ordinary business to fall in love; it is the most extraordinary business to abide there. The same thing with regard to the love of our Lord. The Holy Ghost gives us the great power to love Jesus Christ. That is not a rare experience at all; the rare experience is to get into the conception of loving Him in such a way that the whole heart and mind and soul are taken up with Him. PH 109

a. Or *the Lord our God is one Lord*
b. Deuteronomy 6:4-5
c. Leviticus 19:18

75

WARNING ABOUT TEACHERS OF THE LAW

While all the people were listening, Jesus said to the crowds and to his disciples, "The teachers of the law and the Pharisees sit in Moses' seat. So you must obey them and do everything they tell you. But do not do what they do, for they do not practice what they preach. They tie up heavy loads and put them on men's shoulders, but they themselves are not willing to lift a finger to move them.

"Beware of the teachers of the law. Everything they do is done for men to see: They make their phylacteries[a] wide and the tassels on their garments long. They like to walk around in flowing robes and love to be greeted in the marketplaces and to have men call them 'Rabbi.' They love the place of honor at banquets and the most important seats in the synagogues. They devour widows' houses and for a show make lengthy prayers. Such men will be punished most severely.

"But you are not to be called 'Rabbi,' for you have only one Master and you are all brothers. And do not call anyone on earth 'father,' for you have one Father, and he is in heaven. Nor are you to be called 'teacher,' for you have one Teacher, the Christ. The greatest among you will be your servant. For whoever exalts himself will be humbled, and whoever humbles himself will be exalted." MATTHEW 23:1-12; MARK 12:38-40; LUKE 20:45-47

> *"Beware of the teachers of the law.*
> *Everything they do is done for men to see."*

FROM OSWALD CHAMBERS

❧ The test of any teaching is its estimate of Jesus Christ. The teaching may sound wonderful and beautiful, but watch lest it have at its center the dethroning of Jesus Christ. PR 76

❧ The Nature of Pharisaism is that it must stand on tiptoe and be superior. The man who does not want to face the foundation of things becomes tremendously stern and keen on principles and on moral reforms. BFB 72

❧ A Pharisee shuts you up, not by loud shouting, but by the unanswerable logic he presents; he is bound to principles, not to a relationship. BFB 72

❧ "I am not come to call the righteous, but sinners to repentance" (Matt. 9:13). Remember, that kind of statement hits the Pharisees to the very core of their being. HG 79

❧ It was the ruthless way [Jesus] went straight to the very root of Pharisaism that enraged them until they became the devil incarnate and crucified the Son of God. HG 79

❧ This is always the dodge of a Pharisee, whether he is a demagogue or a religious man, he must make a moral issue somewhere. If he can rouse up a passion for a neglected principle, it is exactly what he wants, but there is not reality in it. BFB 73

❧ The one test of a teacher sent from God is that those who listen see and know Jesus Christ better than ever they did. IWP 111

❧ If you are a teacher sent from God, your worth in God's sight is estimated by the way you enable people to see Jesus. IWP 112

❧ If a teacher fascinates with his doctrine, his teaching never came from God. The teacher sent from God is the one who clears the way to Jesus and keeps it clear; souls forget altogether about him because the vision of Jesus is the only abiding result. When people are attracted to Jesus Christ through you, see always that you stay on God all the time, and their hearts and affections will never stop at you. IWP 112

---

a. That is, boxes containing Scripture verses, worn on forehead and arm

76

A WIDOW'S OFFERING

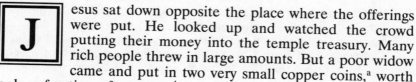esus sat down opposite the place where the offerings were put. He looked up and watched the crowd putting their money into the temple treasury. Many rich people threw in large amounts. But a poor widow came and put in two very small copper coins,[a] worth only a fraction of a penny.[b]

Calling his disciples to him, Jesus said, "I tell you the truth, this poor widow has put more into the treasury than all the others. All these people gave their gifts out of their wealth; but she out of her poverty put in everything—all she had to live on."
MARK 12:41-44; LUKE 21:1-4

"This poor widow ... put in everything—
all she had to live on."

FROM OSWALD CHAMBERS

❧ As Christians our giving is to be proportionate to all we have received of the infinite giving of God. "Freely ye have received, freely give" (Matt. 10:8). Not how much we give, but what we do not give, is the test of our Christianity. When we speak of giving, we nearly always think only of money. Money is the lifeblood of most of us. We have a remarkable trick—when we give money we don't give sympathy; and when we give sympathy we don't give money. CHI 77

❧ Much of our modern philanthropy is based on the motive of giving to the poor man because he deserves it, or because we are distressed at seeing him poor. Jesus never taught charity from those motives: He said, "Give to him that asketh thee, not because he deserves it, but because I tell you to." The great motive in all giving is Jesus Christ's command. SSM 46

 ❧ We never get credit spiritually for impulsive giving. If suddenly we feel we should give a shilling to a poor man, we get no credit from God for giving it; there is no virtue in it whatever. As a rule, that sort of giving is a relief to our feelings; it is not an indication of a generous character, but rather an indication of a lack of generosity. God never estimates what we give from impulse. We are given credit for what we determine in our hearts to give; for the giving that is governed by a fixed determination. The Spirit of God revolutionizes our philanthropic instincts. Much of our philanthropy is simply the impulse to save ourselves an uncomfortable feeling. The Spirit of God alters all that. As saints our attitude toward giving is that we give for Jesus Christ's sake, and from no other motive. God holds us responsible for the way we use this power of voluntary choice. BP 108

---

a. Greek *two lepta*
b. Greek *kodrantes*

77

SOME GREEKS SEEK JESUS

ow there were some Greeks among those who went up to worship at the Feast. They came to Philip, who was from Bethsaida in Galilee, with a request. "Sir," they said, "we would like to see Jesus." Philip went to tell Andrew; Andrew and Philip in turn told Jesus.

Jesus replied, "The hour has come for the Son of Man to be glorified. I tell you the truth, unless a kernel of wheat falls to the ground and dies, it remains only a single seed. But if it dies, it produces many seeds. The man who loves his life will lose it, while the man who hates his life in this world will keep it for eternal life. Whoever serves me must follow me; and where I am, my servant also will be. My Father will honor the one who serves me.

"Now my heart is troubled, and what shall I say? 'Father, save me from this hour'? No, it was for this very reason I came to this hour. Father, glorify your name!"

Then a voice came from heaven, "I have glorified it, and will glorify it again." The crowd that was there and heard it said it had thundered; others said an angel had spoken to him.

Jesus said, "This voice was for your benefit, not mine. Now is the time for judgment on this world; now the prince of this world will be driven out. But I, when I am lifted up from the earth, will draw all men to myself." He said this to show the kind of death he was going to die.

The crowd spoke up, "We have heard from the Law that the Christ will remain forever, so how can you say, 'The Son of Man must be lifted up'? Who is this 'Son of Man'?"

Then Jesus told them, "You are going to have the light just a little while longer. Walk while you have the light, before darkness overtakes you. The man who walks in the dark does not know where he is going. Put your trust in the light while you have it, so that you may become sons of light." When he had finished speaking, Jesus left and hid himself from them. JOHN 12:20-36

"Put your trust in the light . . .
so that you may become sons of light."

FROM OSWALD CHAMBERS

🙿 The condemnation is not that a man is born with a heredity of sin; a man begins to get the seal of condemnation when he sees the light and prefers the darkness (John 3:19). BE 62

🙿 "If therefore the light that is in thee be darkness, how great is that darkness!" (Matt. 6:23) Darkness is my own point of view; when once I allow the prejudice of my head to shut down the witness of my heart, I make my heart dark. BP 138

🙿 "If we walk in the light, as He is in the light" (1 John 1:7). Walking in the light means walking according to His standard, which is now ours. RTR 36

🙿 How often God's Book refers to God as light, to Jesus Christ as light, to the Spirit of God as light, and to the saints as light. By sanctification God places us in the light that He is in, the light in which our Lord Jesus lived His life. "And the life was the light of men" (John 1:4). OBH 39

🙿 Beware of not acting upon what you see in your moments on the mount with God. If you do not obey the light, it will turn into darkness. "If therefore the light that is in thee be darkness, how great is that darkness!" (Matt. 6:23) The second you waive the question of sanctification or any other thing upon which God gave you light, you begin to get dry rot in your spiritual life. Continually bring the truth out into actuality; work it out in every domain, or the very light you have will prove a curse. MUH 240

78

SIGNS OF THE END OF THE AGE

Jesus was leaving the temple and walking away when his disciples came up to him to call his attention to its buildings. Some of his disciples were remarking about how the temple was adorned with beautiful stones and with gifts dedicated to God. One of his disciples said to him, "Look, Teacher! What massive stones! What magnificent buildings!"

"Do you see all these great buildings?" replied Jesus. "I tell you the truth, as for what you see here, the time will come when not one stone here will be left on another; every one of them will be thrown down."

As Jesus was sitting on the Mount of Olives opposite the temple, Peter, James, John and Andrew asked him privately, "Teacher, tell us, when will these things happen? And what will be the sign that they are all about to take place, and what will be the sign of your coming and of the end of the age?"

Jesus answered: "Watch out that no one deceives you. For many will come in my name, claiming, 'I am he, I am the Christ. The time is near,' and will deceive many. Do not follow them. You will hear of wars and revolutions and rumors of wars, but see to it that you are not alarmed. Do not be frightened. These things must happen first, but the end will not come right away. The end is still to come." For more details, read MATTHEW 24:1-51; MARK 13:1-37; LUKE 21:5-36

"Many will come . . . claiming,
'I am he, I am the Christ.' . . .
Do not follow them. You will hear of wars. . . .
Do not be frightened."

FROM OSWALD CHAMBERS

❧ The Jesus who saves our souls and identifies us with Himself is "this same Jesus" who went to sleep as a Babe on His mother's bosom; and it is "this same Jesus," the almighty, powerful Christ, with all power in heaven and on earth, who is at work in the world today by His Spirit. BSG 72

❧ War is a conflict of wills, either in individuals or in nations, and just now there is a terrific conflict of wills in nations. If I cannot make my will by diplomacy bear on other people, then the last resort is war, and always will be until Jesus Christ brings in His kingdom. CD, VOL. 1 107

❧ Today we have all kinds of christs in our midst, the christ of labor and of socialism; the mind-cure Christ and the Christ of Christian Science and of Theosophy; but they are all abstract christs. The one great sign of Christ is not with them—there are no marks of the Atonement about these christs. Jesus Christ is the only One with the marks of Atonement on Him, the wounded hands and feet, a symbol of the Redeemer who is to come again. There will be signs and wonders wrought by these other christs, and great problems may be solved, but the heartbreaking agony and long-suffering patience that they might be reconciled to His way of salvation. GW 73

❧ "Is war of the devil or of God?" It is of neither. It is of man, though both God and the devil are behind it. SA 55

❧ To call war either diabolical or divine is nonsense; war is human. War is a conflict of wills, not something that can be solved by law or philosophy. If you take what I want, you may talk till all's blue; either I will hit you or you'll hit me. It is no use to arbitrate when you get below into the elemental. In the time between birth and death, this conflict of wills will go on until men by their relationship to God receive the disposition of the Son of God, which is holiness. SHH 28

79

THE PARABLE OF THE TEN VIRGINS

At that time the kingdom of heaven will be like ten virgins who took their lamps and went out to meet the bridegroom. Five of them were foolish and five were wise. The foolish ones took their lamps but did not take any oil with them. The wise, however, took oil in jars along with their lamps. The bridegroom was a long time in coming, and they all became drowsy and fell asleep.

"At midnight the cry rang out: 'Here's the bridegroom! Come out to meet him!'

"Then all the virgins woke up and trimmed their lamps. The foolish ones said to the wise, 'Give us some of your oil; our lamps are going out.'

" 'No,' they replied, 'there may not be enough for both us and you. Instead, go to those who sell oil and buy some for yourselves.'

"But while they were on their way to buy the oil, the bridegroom arrived. The virgins who were ready went in with him to the wedding banquet. And the door was shut.

"Later the others also came. 'Sir! Sir!' they said. 'Open the door for us!'

"But he replied, 'I tell you the truth, I don't know you.'

"Therefore keep watch, because you do not know the day or the hour." MATTHEW 25:1-13

"And the door was shut. . . .
'I don't know you.' "

FROM OSWALD CHAMBERS

❧ The Parable of the Ten Virgins reveals that it is fatal from our

Lord's standpoint to live this life without preparation for the life to come. That is not the exegesis; it is the obvious underlying principle.

The Parable of the Talents is our Lord's statement with regard to the danger of leaving undone the work of a lifetime.

And the description of the last judgment is the picture of genuine astonishment on the part of both the losers and the gainers of what they had never once thought about. SH 88

❧ What idea have you of the salvation of your soul? The experience of salvation means that in your actual life things are really altered; you no longer look at things as you used to; your desires are new; old things have lost their power. One of the touchstones of experience is—Has God altered the thing that matters? If you still hanker after the old things, it is absurd to talk about being born from above; you are juggling with yourself. If you are born again, the Spirit of God makes the alteration manifest in your actual life and reasoning, and when the crisis comes you are the most amazed person on earth at the wonderful difference there is in you. MUH 317

❧ Nowhere does the Bible say that God holds man responsible for having the disposition of sin; but what God does hold man responsible for is refusing to let Him deliver him from that heredity the moment he sees and understands that that is what Jesus Christ came to do. BP 228

❧ Salvation means that if a man will turn—and every man has the power to turn, if it is only a look toward the cross, he has the power for that—if a man will but turn, he will find that Jesus is able to deliver him not only from the snare of the wrong disposition within him, but from the power of evil and wrong outside him. CHI 97

❧ The last possible reach of faith is the cry of a sinner who begins to realize that God can save him. Immediately he cries out to God he will find the marvel of Jesus Christ's salvation wrought out in his personal experience. BSG 50

80

THE PARABLE OF THE TALENTS

A gain, it will be like a man going on a journey, who called his servants and entrusted his property to them. To one he gave five talents[a] of money, to another two talents, and to another one talent, each according to his ability. Then he went on his journey. The man who had received the five talents went at once and put his money to work and gained five more. So also, the one with the two talents gained two more. But the man who had received the one talent went off, dug a hole in the ground and hid his master's money.

"After a long time the master of those servants returned and settled accounts with them. The man who had received the five talents brought the other five. 'Master,' he said, 'you entrusted me with five talents. See, I have gained five more.'

"His master replied, 'Well done, good and faithful servant! You have been faithful with a few things; I will put you in charge of many things. Come and share your master's happiness!'

"The man with the two talents also came. 'Master,' he said, 'you entrusted me with two talents; see, I have gained two more.'

"His master replied, 'Well done, good and faithful servant! You have been faithful with a few things; I will put you in charge of many things. Come and share your master's happiness!'

"Then the man who had received the one talent came. 'Master,' he said, 'I knew that you are a hard man, harvesting where you have not sown and gathering where you have not scattered seed. So I was afraid and went out and hid your talent in the ground. See, here is what belongs to you.'

"His master replied, 'You wicked, lazy servant! So you knew that I harvest where I have not sown and gather where I have not scattered seed? Well then, you should have put my money on deposit with the bankers, so that when I returned I would have received it back with interest.

" 'Take the talent from him and give it to the one who has the ten talents. For everyone who has will be given more, and he will have an abundance. Whoever does not have, even what he has will be taken from him. And throw that worthless servant outside, into the darkness, where there will be weeping and gnashing of teeth.' " MATTHEW 25:14-30

"Well done, good and faithful servant."

FROM OSWALD CHAMBERS

⮚ This slothful servant, who gave such a verdict about his Lord, is recognizable among men today; we have to realize that our capacity in spiritual things must be measured by God's promise, and our accountability to God by exactly the same dimensions. Jesus Christ demands that we shall allow the indwelling Holy Ghost to enable us to come up to the last limit of obedience. Unregenerated human nature can never attain the full obedience to the commands of Jesus Christ, yet He demands us to come up to His standard; and it is only by this reception of the Holy Spirit that we learn to do it. . . .

Christianity is supernatural from beginning to end; when a man knows that the Lord Jesus Christ can enable him to fulfill to the hilt every one of His commands, by the indwelling Holy Spirit, he knows that there is not an aching abyss in His nature that Christ cannot satisfy, and not one supernatural command that He cannot reach, if he relies on the gifts that Christ has given him. God grant that we learn this marvelous secret. Only be strong and have good courage. Can earth, or hell or heaven, time or eternity, stand against the man or woman presenced with mighty divinity through the marvelous Atonement of Christ? Nay, we are made conquering and to conquer until at last we hear from His lips: *"Well done, good and faithful servant. . . . enter thou into the joy of thy Lord."* GR 2-24-1910

⮚ A servant is one who, recognizing God's *sovereign will,* leaps to do that will of his own *free choice.* CD, VOL. 1 30

---

a. A talent was worth more than a thousand dollars

81

THE SHEEP AND THE GOATS

When the Son of Man comes in his glory, and all the angels with him, he will sit on his throne in heavenly glory. All the nations will be gathered before him, and he will separate the people one from another as a shepherd separates the sheep from the goats. He will put the sheep on his right and the goats on his left.

"Then the King will say to those on his right, 'Come, you who are blessed by my Father; take your inheritance, the kingdom prepared for you since the creation of the world. For I was hungry and you gave me something to eat, I was thirsty and you gave me something to drink, I was a stranger and you invited me in, I needed clothes and you clothed me, I was sick and you looked after me, I was in prison and you came to visit me.'

"Then the righteous will answer him, 'Lord, when did we see you hungry and feed you, or thirsty and give you something to drink? When did we see you a stranger and invite you in, or needing clothes and clothe you? When did we see you sick or in prison and go to visit you?'

"The King will reply, 'I tell you the truth, whatever you did for one of the least of these brothers of mine, you did for me.'

"Then he will say to those on his left, 'Depart from me, you who are cursed, into the eternal fire prepared for the devil and his angels. For I was hungry and you gave me nothing to eat, I was thirsty and you gave me nothing to drink, I was a stranger and you did not invite me in, I needed clothes and you did not clothe me, I was sick and in prison and you did not look after me.'

"They also will answer, 'Lord, when did we see you hungry or thirsty or a stranger or needing clothes or sick or in prison, and did not help you?'

301

"He will reply, 'I tell you the truth, whatever you did not do for one of the least of these, you did not do for me.'

"Then they will go away to eternal punishment, but the righteous to eternal life."

Each day Jesus was teaching at the temple, and each evening he went out to spend the night on the hill called the Mount of Olives, and all the people came early in the morning to hear him at the temple. MATTHEW 25:31-46; LUKE 21:37-38

"I tell you the truth, whatever you did for one
of the least of these brothers of mine, you did for me."

FROM OSWALD CHAMBERS

❧ God does not transform a man's life by magic, but through the surrender of the man to Himself. The thirteenth chapter of 1 Corinthians is the description of the way love works out in actual life. To most of us love is a curiously useless word. The love Paul refers to is the sovereign preference of my person for another person, and that other Person Jesus Christ. That sovereign preference works out in the deliberate identification of myself with God's interests in other people, and God is interested in some strange people; He is interested in the man whom I am inclined to despise. PH 133

❧ The best way to know whether I am recognizing myself in the fullness of sanctity is to watch how I behave toward the mean folks who come around. If I am learning to behave to them as God behaved to me in Jesus Christ, then I am all right; but if I have no time for them, it means that I am growing meaner and more selfish. Our Father is kind to the unthankful, to the mean. Now, He says, you be the same. The idea of sanctity is that we must be perfect in these relationships in life. PH 195

❧ Jesus Christ came down to a most miserably insignificant people in order to redeem them. When He has lifted us into relationship with Himself, He expects us to identify ourselves with His interests in others. PR 107

❧ Watch the humor of our Heavenly Father. It is seen in the way He

302

brings across our path the type of person who exhibits to us what we have been like to Him. "Now," He says, "show that one the same love that I have shown you." If Jesus Christ has lifted us in love and grace, we must show that love to someone else. SSY 84

When the Spirit of God has shed abroad the love of God in our hearts, we begin deliberately to identify ourselves with Jesus Christ's interests in other people, and Jesus Christ is interested in every kind of man there is. MUH 55

82

MARY ANOINTS JESUS AT BETHANY

While he was in Bethany in the home of a man known as Simon the Leper, a dinner was given in Jesus' honor. Martha served, while Lazarus was among those reclining at the table with him. Then Mary took an alabaster jar of very expensive perfume, about a pint[a] of pure nard. She broke the jar and poured the perfume on *Jesus'* head as he was reclining at the table. She poured it on Jesus' feet and wiped his feet with her hair. And the house was filled with the fragrance of the perfume.

When some of those disciples present saw this, they were indignant. "Why this waste?" they asked one another. And they rebuked her harshly. One of his disciples, Judas Iscariot, who was later to betray him, objected, "Why wasn't this perfume sold and the money given to the poor? It could have been sold for more than a year's wages."[b] He did not say this because he cared about the poor but because he was a thief; as keeper of the money bag, he used to help himself to what was put into it.

Aware of this, Jesus said to them, "Why are you bothering this woman? Leave her alone. She has done a beautiful thing to me. It was intended that she should save this perfume for the day of my burial. You will always have the poor among you, and you can help them any time you want. But you will not always have me. She did what she could. When she poured this perfume on my body, she did it to prepare me for burial. I tell you the truth, wherever this gospel is preached throughout the world, what she has done will also be told, in memory of her." MATTHEW 26:6-13; MARK 14:3-9; JOHN 12:2-8

"She has done a beautiful thing to me."

From Oswald Chambers

⮞ If human love does not carry a man beyond himself, it is not love. If love is always discreet, always wise, always sensible, and calculating, never carried beyond itself, it is not love at all. It may be affection, it may be warmth of feeling, but it has not the true nature of love in it.

Have I ever been carried away to do something for God not because it was my duty, nor because it was useful, nor because there was anything in it at all beyond the fact that I love Him? Have I ever realized that I can bring to God things which are of value to Him, or am I mooning round the magnitude of His redemption while there are any number of things I might be doing? Not divine, colossal things which could be recorded as marvelous, but ordinary, simple human things which will give evidence to God that I am abandoned to Him? Have I ever produced in the heart of the Lord Jesus what Mary of Bethany produced?

There are times when it seems as if God watches to see if we will give Him the abandoned tokens of how genuinely we do love Him. Abandon to God is of more value than personal holiness. Personal holiness focuses the eye on our own whiteness; we are greatly concerned about the way we walk and talk and look, fearful lest we offend Him. Perfect love casts out all that when once we are abandoned to God. We have to get rid of this notion—"Am I of any use?" and make up our minds that we are not, and we may be near the truth. It is never a question of being of use, but of being of value to God Himself. When we are abandoned to God, He works through us all the time. MUH 52

⮞ The reason some of us are such poor specimens of Christianity is because we have no Almighty Christ. We have Christian attributes and experiences, but there is no abandonment to Jesus Christ. MUH 58

⮞ What is needed in spiritual matters is reckless abandonment to the Lord Jesus Christ, reckless and uncalculating abandonment, with no reserve anywhere about it. PS 23

---

a. Greek *a litra* (probably about 0.5 liter)
b. Greek *three hundred denarii*

83

THE PASSOVER MEAL IS PREPARED

 Then came the first day of the Feast of Unleavened Bread, when it was customary to sacrifice the Passover Lamb. Jesus' disciples came to him and asked, "Where do you want us to go and make preparations for you to eat the Passover?"

Jesus sent Peter and John, telling them, "Go into the city, and a man carrying a jar of water will meet you. Follow him to the house that he enters, and say to the owner of the house, 'The Teacher says: My appointed time is near. I am going to celebrate the Passover with my disciples at your house. Where is my guest room, where I may eat the Passover with my disciples?' He will show you a large upper room, all furnished and ready. Make preparations for us there."

So the disciples did as Jesus had directed them. They left, went into the city and found things just as Jesus had told them. So they prepared the Passover. MATTHEW 26:17-19; MARK 14:12-16; LUKE 22:7-13

JESUS WASHES HIS DISCIPLES' FEET

When evening came, Jesus arrived with the Twelve. It was just before the Passover Feast. Jesus knew that the time had come for him to leave this world and go to the Father. Having loved his own who were in the world, he now showed them the full extent of his love.[a]

The evening meal was being served, and the devil had already prompted Judas Iscariot, son of Simon, to betray Jesus. Jesus knew that the Father had put all things under his power, and that he had come from God and was returning to God; so he got up from the meal, took off his outer clothing, and wrapped a towel around his waist. After that, he poured water into a basin and began to wash his disciples' feet, drying them with the towel that was wrapped around him.

He came to Simon Peter, who said to him, "Lord, are you going to wash my feet?"

Jesus replied, "You do not realize now what I am doing, but later you will understand."

"No," said Peter, "you shall never wash my feet."

Jesus answered, "Unless I wash you, you have no part with me."

"Then, Lord," Simon Peter replied, "not just my feet but my hands and my head as well!"

Jesus answered, "A person who has had a bath needs only to wash his feet; his whole body is clean. And you are clean, though not every one of you." For he knew who was going to betray him, and that was why he said not every one was clean.

When he had finished washing their feet, he put on his clothes and returned to his place. "Do you understand what I have done for you?" he asked them. "You call me 'Teacher' and 'Lord,' and rightly so, for that is what I am. Now that I, your Lord and Teacher, have washed your feet, you also should wash one another's feet. I have set you an example that you should do as I have done for you. I tell you the truth, no servant is greater than his master, nor is a messenger greater than the one who sent him. Now that you know these things, you will be blessed if you do them.

"I am not referring to all of you; I know those I have chosen. But this is to fulfill the scripture: 'He who shares my bread has lifted up his heel against me.'[b]

"I am telling you now before it happens, so that when it does happen you will believe that I am He. I tell you the truth, whoever accepts anyone I send accepts me; and whoever accepts me accepts the one who sent me." MARK 14:17; JOHN 13:1-20

"No servant is greater than his master."

FROM OSWALD CHAMBERS

❧ Whenever we go into work for God from any standpoint saving that of the dominance of God, we begin to patronize at once; unless we go as the bondservants of Jesus Christ we have no business to go at all. Jesus Christ became the towel-girt Servant of His own disciples. GW 74

❧ We are here with no right to ourselves, for no spiritual blessing for ourselves; we are here for one purpose only—to be made servants of God as Jesus was. PS 17

❧ My contact with the nature of God has made me realize what I can do for God. Service is the outcome of what is fitted to my nature; God's call is fitted to His nature, and I never hear His call until I have received His nature. When I have received His nature, then His nature and mine work together; the Son of God reveals Himself in me, and I, the natural man, serve the Son of God in ordinary ways, out of sheer downright devotion to Him. SSY 12

❧ The things that Jesus did were of the most menial and common-place order, and this is an indication that it takes all God's power in me to do the most commonplace things in His way. Can I use a towel as He did? Towels and dishes and sandals—all the ordinary sordid things of our lives—reveal more quickly than anything what we are made of. It takes God Almighty incarnate in us to do the meanest duty as it ought to be done.

"I have given you an example, that ye should do as I have done to you" (John 13:15). Watch the kind of people God brings around you, and you will be humiliated to find that this is His way of revealing to you the kind of person you have been to Him. Now, He says, exhibit to that one exactly what I have shown to you. MUH 255

---

a. Or *he loved them to the last*
b. Psalm 41:9

84

THE LAST SUPPER

After taking the cup, he gave thanks and said, "Take this and divide it among you. For I tell you I will not drink again of the fruit of the vine until the kingdom of God comes."

While they were eating, Jesus took bread, gave thanks and broke it, and gave it to his disciples, saying, "Take and eat; this is my body, which is given for you; do this in remembrance of me."

In the same way, after the supper he took the cup, gave thanks and offered it to them, saying, "Drink from it, all of you. This cup is the new covenant in my blood, which is poured out for you, *and* for many, for the forgiveness of sins. Do this, whenever you drink it, in remembrance of me." And they all drank from it. "I tell you the truth, I will not drink again of the fruit of the vine from now on until that day when I drink it anew with you in my Father's kingdom." MATTHEW 26:26-29; MARK 14:22-25; LUKE 22:17-20; 1 CORINTHIANS 11:24-25

"This cup is the new covenant in my blood . . .
poured out for you."

FROM OSWALD CHAMBERS

❧ The only explanation of the forgiveness of God and of the unfathomable depth of His forgetting is the death of Jesus Christ. Our repentance is merely the outcome of our personal realization of the Atonement which He has worked out for us. "Christ Jesus . . . is made unto us wisdom, and righteousness, and sanctification and redemption" (1 Cor. 1:30). When we realize that Christ is made all this to us, the boundless joy of God begins; wherever the joy of God is not present, the death sentence is at work.

It does not matter who or what we are; there is absolute reinstatement into God by the death of Jesus Christ and by no other way, not because Jesus Christ pleads, but because He died. It is not earned, but accepted. All the pleading which deliberately refuses to recognize the Cross is of no avail; it is battering at another door than the one which Jesus has opened. I don't want to come that way, it is too humiliating to be received as a sinner. "There is none other name" (Acts 4:12). The apparent heartlessness of God is the expression of His real heart, there is boundless entrance in His way. "We have forgiveness through His blood" (see Eph. 1:7). Identification with the death of Jesus Christ means identification with Him to the death of everything that never was in Him. MUH 343

❧ When God forgives a man He gives him the heredity of His own Son, and there is no man on earth but can be presented "perfect in Christ Jesus." Then on the ground of the redemption, it is up to me to live as a son of God. HGM 102

❧ When Jesus Christ shed His blood on the cross, it was not the blood of a martyr, or the blood of one man for another; it was the life of God poured out to redeem the world. BE 60

❧ God redeemed the world by shedding His blood, by putting the whole passion of the Godhead into it. He did not become interested and put one arm in to help the human race up; He went into the redemption absolutely; there was nothing of Himself left out. BE 63

❧ "The Cross" and "the blood of Jesus" are indeed names for profound mysteries, but when a soul shattered by the crushing sense of his guilt believes that through the blood of Jesus there is forgiveness for sins, he receives a new life-energy; he is purged from his old sins, and with the Spirit of Jesus in him, he begins to work out his own salvation. Then begins the true evolution of a man's soul. GW 117

❧ When the blood is spilled, the soul is gone; when the breath is taken, the soul is gone. The whole life of a man consists physically in his breath and in his blood. The soul in working itself into the blood never fails to impart to it the peculiar character of its own life. This psychologically is brought out very clearly by our Lord's statement, "Except ye eat the flesh of the Son of Man, and drink His blood, ye have no life in you" (John 6:53). BP 69

෨ It was not the blood of a martyr, not the blood of goats and calves, that was shed, but "the blood of Christ." The very life of God was shed for the world — "the church of God which He purchased with His own blood." . . . All the perfections of the essential nature of God were in that blood; all the holiest attainments of man were in that blood. PS 18

85

JESUS PREDICTS PETER'S DENIAL

When *Judas* was gone, Jesus said, "Now is the Son of Man glorified and God is glorified in him. If God is glorified in him,[a] God will glorify the Son in himself, and will glorify him at once.

"My children, I will be with you only a little longer. You will look for me, and just as I told the Jews, so I tell you now: Where I am going, you cannot come.

"A new command I give you: Love one another. As I have loved you, so you must love one another. By this all men will know that you are my disciples, if you love one another."

Simon Peter asked him, "Lord, where are you going?"

Jesus replied, "Where I am going, you cannot follow now, but you will follow later."

Peter asked, "Lord, why can't I follow you now? I will lay down my life for you."

Then Jesus told them, "This very night you will all fall away on account of me, for it is written:

" 'I will strike the shepherd,
and the sheep of the flock will be scattered.'[b]

But after I have risen, I will go ahead of you into Galilee."

Peter declared, "Even if all fall away on account of you, I never will."

"Simon, Simon, Satan has asked to sift you[c] as wheat. But I have prayed for you, Simon, that your faith may not fail. And when you have turned back, strengthen your brothers."

But he replied, "Lord, I am ready to go with you to prison and to death."

Then Jesus answered, "Will you really lay down your life for

me? I tell you the truth, Peter, today—yes, this very night—
before the rooster crows twice[d] you yourself will disown me three
times."

But Peter insisted emphatically, "Even if I have to die with
you, I will never disown you." And all the other disciples said the
same.

Then Jesus asked them, "When I sent you without purse, bag
or sandals, did you lack anything?"

"Nothing," they answered.

He said to them, "But now if you have a purse, take it, and
also a bag; and if you don't have a sword, sell your cloak and buy
one. It is written: 'And he was numbered with the transgressors'[e];
and I tell you that this must be fulfilled in me. Yes, what is
written about me is reaching its fulfillment."

The disciples said, "See, Lord, here are two swords."

"That is enough," he replied. MATTHEW 26:31-35; MARK 14:27-31;
LUKE 22:31-38; JOHN 13:31-38

JESUS COMFORTS HIS DISCIPLES

"Do not let your hearts be troubled. Trust in God[f]; trust also in
me. In my Father's house are many rooms; if it were not so, I
would have told you. I am going there to prepare a place for you.
And if I go and prepare a place for you, I will come back and
take you to be with me that you also may be where I am. You
know the way to the place where I am going."

Thomas said to him, "Lord, we don't know where you are
going, so how can we know the way?"

Jesus answered, "I am the way and the truth and the life. No
one comes to the Father except through me. If you really knew
me, you would know[g] my Father as well. From now on, you do
know him and have seen him."

Philip said, "Lord, show us the Father and that will be enough
for us."

Jesus answered: "Don't you know me, Philip, even after I have
been among you such a long time? Anyone who has seen me has
seen the Father. How can you say, 'Show us the Father'? Don't
you believe that I am in the Father, and that the Father is in me?
The words I say to you are not just my own. Rather, it is the
Father, living in me, who is doing his work. Believe me when I

316

say that I am in the Father and the Father is in me; or at least believe on the evidence of the miracles themselves. I tell you the truth, anyone who has faith in me will do what I have been doing. He will do even greater things than these, because I am going to the Father. And I will do whatever you ask in my name, so that the Son may bring glory to the Father. You may ask me for anything in my name, and I will do it." JOHN 14:1-14

"I am the way and the truth and the life."

FROM OSWALD CHAMBERS

    However far we may drift, we must always come back to these words of our Lord: "I am the way"—not a road that we leave behind us, but the way itself. Jesus Christ is the way *of God,* not a way that leads to God; that is why He says "Come unto Me"; "abide in Me"; "I am the truth," not the truth about God, not a set of principles, but the truth itself. Jesus Christ is the truth *of God.* "No man cometh unto the Father, but by Me." We can get to God as Creator in other ways, but no man can come to God as Father in any other way than by Jesus Christ. "I am the life." Jesus Christ is the life *of God* as He is the way and the truth of God. Eternal life is not a gift *from* God; it is the gift of *God Himself.* The life imparted to me by Jesus is the life of God. "He that hath the Son hath the life" (1 John 5:12); "I am come that they might have life" (John 10:10); "And this is life eternal, that they should know thee the only true God" (John 17:3). We have to abide in the *way;* to be incorporated into the *truth;* to be infused by the *life.* SSY 92

    The Master says He is the way; then abide in Him. He says He is the truth; then believe in Him. He says He is the life; then live on Him. SSY 131

    "I am the way, the truth, and the life"—the way in the waylessness of this wild universe; the truth amidst all the contending confusions of man's thought and existence; the life amidst all the living deaths that sap men's characters and their relationships and connections with the highest. BE 112

    Our Lord said, *"I am the way,"* not the way to anyone or anything. He is not a road we leave behind us; He is the way to the Father in

317

which we abide. He *is* the way, not He was the way, and there is not any way of living in the Fatherhood of God except by living in Christ. . . . The way to the Father is not by the law, nor by obedience, or creed, but Jesus Christ Himself. He is the way of the Father whereby any and every soul may be in peace, in joy, and in divine courage. CD, VOL. 1 137

> "I am the way." If a man will resign himself in implicit trust to the Lord Jesus, he will find that He leads the wayfaring soul into the green pastures and beside the still waters, so that even when he goes through the dark valley of the shadow of some staggering episode, he will fear no evil. Nothing in life or death, time or eternity, can stagger that soul from the certainty of the way for one moment. PH 8

---

a. Many early manuscripts [of John 13:32] do not have *If God is glorified in him*
b. Zechariah 13:7
c. The Greek is plural
d. Some early manuscripts [of Mark 14:30] do not have *twice*
e. Isaiah 53:12
f. Or *You trust in God*
g. Some early manuscripts [of John 14:7] *If you really have known me, you will know*

86

JESUS PROMISES THE HOLY SPIRIT

I f you love me, you will obey what I command. And I will ask the Father, and he will give you another Counselor to be with you forever — the Spirit of truth. The world cannot accept him, because it neither sees him nor knows him. But you know him, for he lives with you and will be[a] in you. I will not leave you as orphans; I will come to you. Before long, the world will not see me anymore, but you will see me. Because I live, you also will live. On that day you will realize that I am in my Father, and you are in me, and I am in you. Whoever has my commands and obeys them, he is the one who loves me. He who loves me will be loved by my Father, and I too will love him and show myself to him."

Then Judas (not Judas Iscariot) said, "But, Lord, why do you intend to show yourself to us and not to the world?"

Jesus replied, "If anyone loves me, he will obey my teaching. My Father will love him, and we will come to him and make our home with him. He who does not love me will not obey my teaching. These words you hear are not my own; they belong to the Father who sent me.

"All this I have spoken while still with you. But the Counselor, the Holy Spirit, whom the Father will send in my name, will teach you all things and will remind you of everything I have said to you. Peace I leave with you; my peace I give you. I do not give to you as the world gives. Do not let your hearts be troubled and do not be afraid.

"You heard me say, 'I am going away and I am coming back to you.' If you loved me, you would be glad that I am going to the Father, for the Father is greater than I. I have told you now before it happens, so that when it does happen you will believe. I will not speak with you much longer, for the prince of this world

319

is coming. He has no hold on me, but the world must learn that I love the Father and that I do exactly what my Father has commanded me.

"Come now; let us leave."

When they had sung a hymn, they went out to the Mount of Olives. MATTHEW 26:30; MARK 14:26; JOHN 14:15-31

"The Counselor, the Holy Spirit ... will teach you
all things and will remind you of everything
I have said to you."

FROM OSWALD CHAMBERS

❧ The Holy Spirit is not a substitute for Jesus; the Holy Spirit is all that Jesus was, and all that Jesus did, made real in personal experience now. BE 99

❧ Mind the Holy Spirit, mind His light, mind His convictions, mind His guidance, and slowly and surely the sensual personality will be turned into a spiritual personality. BP 50

❧ The thought is unspeakably full of glory, that God the Holy Ghost can come into my heart and fill it so full that the life of God will manifest itself all through this body which used to manifest exactly the opposite. If I am willing and determined to keep in the light and obey the Spirit, then the characteristics of the indwelling Christ will manifest themselves. BP 146

❧ The great thing that the Holy Spirit reveals is that the supernatural power of God is ours through Jesus Christ, and if we will receive the Holy Spirit He will teach us how to think as well as how to live. BE 97

❧ The Holy Spirit enables us to fulfill all the commands of God, and we are without excuse for not fulfilling them. Absolute almighty ability is packed into our spirit, and to say "can't," if we have received the Holy Spirit, is unconscious blasphemy. MFL 44

❧ Just as the disposition of sin entered into the human race by one man, so the Holy Spirit entered the race by another Man, and redemption means that I can be delivered from the heredity of sin, and through Jesus Christ can receive an unsullied heredity, viz., the Holy Spirit. RTR 34

⊱ As soon as Jesus Christ was glorified, the personal Holy Spirit descended, and in the decrees of God the fullness of time was reached when the Son of Man, on whom the Holy Spirit had descended as a dove, ascended to the right hand of the Father and sent forth the mighty Holy Spirit. HGM 10

---

a. Some early manuscripts [of John 14:17] *and is*

87

THE VINE AND THE BRANCHES

I am the true vine, and my Father is the gardener. He cuts off every branch in me that bears no fruit, while every branch that does bear fruit he prunes[a] so that it will be even more fruitful. You are already clean because of the word I have spoken to you. Remain in me, and I will remain in you. No branch can bear fruit by itself; it must remain in the vine. Neither can you bear fruit unless you remain in me.

"I am the vine; you are the branches. If a man remains in me and I in him, he will bear much fruit; apart from me you can do nothing. If anyone does not remain in me, he is like a branch that is thrown away and withers; such branches are picked up, thrown into the fire and burned. If you remain in me and my words remain in you, ask whatever you wish, and it will be given you. This is to my Father's glory, that you bear much fruit, showing yourselves to be my disciples.

"As the Father has loved me, so have I loved you. Now remain in my love. If you obey my commands, you will remain in my love, just as I have obeyed my Father's commands and remain in his love. I have told you this so that my joy may be in you and that your joy may be complete. My command is this: Love each other as I have loved you. Greater love has no one than this, that he lay down his life for his friends. You are my friends if you do what I command. I no longer call you servants, because a servant does not know his master's business. Instead, I have called you friends, for everything that I learned from my Father I have made known to you. You did not choose me, but I chose you and appointed you to go and bear fruit—fruit that will last. Then the Father will give you whatever you ask in my name. This is my command: Love each other." JOHN 15:1-17

"If a man remains in me and I in him,
he will bear much fruit;
apart from me you can do nothing."

From Oswald Chambers

❧ Think of the things that take you out of abiding in Christ — "Yes, Lord, just a minute, I have got this to do"; Yes, I will abide when once this is finished; when this week is over, it will be all right; I will abide then. *Get a move on;* begin to abide *now.* In the initial stages it is a continual effort until it becomes so much the law of life that you abide in Him unconsciously. Determine to abide in Jesus wherever you are placed. MUH 166

❧ "Severed from Me you can do nothing," i.e., "You will not bear My fruit; you will bear something that did not come from Me at all"; but — "Abide in Me," and you will bring forth fruit that testifies to the nature of the vine, fruit whereby the Father is glorified. "The effectual fervent prayer of a righteous man," one who is abiding, "availeth much" (James 5:16). OBH 123

❧ The secret of bringing forth fruit is to abide in Jesus. "Abide in Me," says Jesus, in spiritual matters, in intellectual matters, in money matters, in every one of the matters that make human life what it is. OBH 107

❧ Our Lord did not say, "Ask God that you may abide in Me"; He said "Abide in Me"; it is something we have to do. Abiding in Jesus embraces physical, mental, and moral phases as well as spiritual. MFL 38

❧ We have to form the habit of abiding until we come into the relationship with God where we rely upon Him almost unconsciously in every particular. MFL 39

❧ The disciple who is in the condition of abiding in Jesus *is* the will of God, and his apparent free choices are God's foreordained decrees. Mysterious? Logically absurd? But a glorious truth to a saint. OBH 122

---

a. The Greek for *prunes* also means *cleans*

324

88

THE WORK OF THE HOLY SPIRIT

Now I am going to him who sent me, yet none of you asks me, 'Where are you going?' Because I have said these things, you are filled with grief. But I tell you the truth: It is for your good that I am going away. Unless I go away, the Counselor will not come to you; but if I go, I will send him to you. When he comes, he will convict the world of guilt[a] in regard to sin and righteousness and judgment: in regard to sin, because men do not believe in me; in regard to righteousness, because I am going to the Father, where you can see me no longer; and in regard to judgment, because the prince of this world now stands condemned.

"I have much more to say to you, more than you can now bear. But when he, the Spirit of truth, comes, he will guide you into all truth. He will not speak on his own; he will speak only what he hears, and he will tell you what is yet to come. He will bring glory to me by taking from what is mine and making it known to you. All that belongs to the Father is mine. That is why I said the Spirit will take from what is mine and make it known to you."
JOHN 16:5-15

"When he, the Spirit of truth, comes,
he will guide you into all truth."

FROM OSWALD CHAMBERS

❧ We can only discern the spiritual world by the Spirit of God, not by our own spirit; and if we have not received the Spirit of God, we shall never discern spiritual things or understand them. We shall move continually in a dark world, and come slowly to the conclusion that the New Testament language is very exaggerated. But when we have received the Spirit of God, we begin to "know the things that are freely given to us of God," and to compare "spiritual things with spiritual," "not in the words which man's wisdom teaches, but which the Holy Ghost teaches" (1 Cor. 2:13). BP 210

❧ Our great need is to ask for and receive the Holy Ghost in simple faith in the marvelous atonement of Jesus Christ, and He will turn us into passionate lovers of the Lord. It is this passion for Christ worked out in us that makes us witnesses to Jesus wherever we are, men and women in whom He delights, upon whom He can look down with approval; men and women whom He can put in the shadow or the sun; men and women whom He can put upon their beds or on their feet; men and women whom He can send anywhere He chooses. PH 33

❧ It is extraordinary how things fall off from a man like autumn leaves once he comes to the place where there is no rule but that of the personal domination of the Holy Spirit. DI 20

❧ The Holy Spirit is honest, and we know intuitively whether we have or have not been identified with the death of Jesus, whether we have or have not given over our self-will to the holy will of God. PH 160

❧ Very few of us know anything about conviction of sin. We know the experience of being disturbed because of having done wrong things, but conviction of sin by the Holy Ghost blots out every relationship on earth and leaves one relationship only—"Against Thee, Thee only, have I sinned!" (Ps. 51:4) MUH 324

---

a. Or *will expose the guilt of the world*

89

JESUS PRAYS FOR HIMSELF AND ALL BELIEVERS

J esus looked toward heaven and prayed:
"Father, the time has come. Glorify your Son, that your Son may glorify you. For you granted him authority over all people that he might give eternal life to all those you have given him. Now this is eternal life: that they may know you, the only true God, and Jesus Christ, whom you have sent. I have brought you glory on earth by completing the work you gave me to do. And now, Father, glorify me in your presence with the glory I had with you before the world began.

"I have revealed you[a] to those whom you gave me out of the world. They were yours; you gave them to me and they have obeyed your word. Now they know that everything you have given me comes from you. For I gave them the words you gave me and they accepted them. They knew with certainty that I came from you, and they believed that you sent me. I pray for them. I am not praying for the world, but for those you have given me, for they are yours. All I have is yours, and all you have is mine. And glory has come to me through them. I will remain in the world no longer, but they are still in the world, and I am coming to you. Holy Father, protect them by the power of your name—the name you gave me—so that they may be one as we are one. While I was with them, I protected them and kept them safe by that name you gave me. None has been lost except the one doomed to destruction so that Scripture would be fulfilled.

"I am coming to you now, but I say these things while I am still in the world, so that they may have the full measure of my joy within them. I have given them your word and the world has hated them, for they are not of the world any more than I am of the world. My prayer is not that you take them out of the world

327

but that you protect them from the evil one. They are not of the world, even as I am not of it. Sanctify[b] them by the truth; your word is truth. As you sent me into the world, I have sent them into the world. For them I sanctify[b] myself, that they too may be truly sanctified.

"My prayer is not for them alone. I pray also for those who will believe in me through their message, that all of them may be one, Father, just as you are in me and I am in you. May they also be in us so that the world may believe that you have sent me. I have given them the glory that you gave me, that they may be one as we are one: I in them and you in me. May they be brought to complete unity to let the world know that you sent me and have loved them even as you have loved me.

"Father, I want those you have given me to be with me where I am, and to see my glory, the glory you have given me because you loved me before the creation of the world.

"Righteous Father, though the world does not know you, I know you, and they know that you have sent me. I have made you[c] known to them, and will continue to make you known in order that the love you have for me may be in them and that I myself may be in them." JOHN 17:1-26

> *"They are not of the world, even as I am not of it.*
> *Sanctify them by the truth; your word is truth."*

FROM OSWALD CHAMBERS

> ☙ Sanctification is the impartation to us of the holy qualities of Jesus Christ. It is His patience, His love, His holiness, His faith, His purity, His godliness that are manifested in and through every sanctified soul. The presentation [is an error] that God by sanctification plants within us His Spirit, and then setting Jesus Christ before us says, "There is your Example; follow Him and I will help you, but you must do your best to follow Him and do what He did." . . . It is not true to experience, and thank God, it is not true to the wonderful Gospel of the grace of God. The mystery of sanctification is *"Christ in you, the hope of glory"* (Col. 1:27). OBH 31

> ☙ Sanctification means not only that we are delivered from sin, but

that we start on a life of stern discipline. It is not a question of praying but of performing, of deliberately disciplining ourselves. BE 48

❧ Consider the last verse in John 17, *"That the love wherewith Thou hast loved Me may be in them, and I in them."* Ask God to answer *Jesus Christ's prayer* [for you]. There is no excuse for any person not having the problem answered in their own lives. My natural heart is not the lover of God; the Holy Ghost is the lover of God, [when] He comes in He will turn my heart into a loving center for God — personal, passionate, overwhelming devotion to Jesus Christ. (God and Jesus Christ are synonymous terms in our practical experience.) When the Holy Spirit comes in, and sin and self-interest are in the road, He will instantly discern them to us, and we will have to give our consent that He clears them out, and He will. He will clear the whole lot out as soon as we give our consent, until the body is incandescent with this love to God. Jude says, *"Keep yourselves in the love of God"* (v. 21). That does not mean, keep on loving God; it is infinitely profounder than that. It means, "Keep your soul open to the fact that God loves you," and His love will be continually flowing through you to others. GR 7-6-1911

❧ The test of sanctification is not our talk about holiness and singing pious hymns; but, what are we like where no one sees us? with those who know us best? DI 60

❧ When we are sanctified we do not get into something like a landslide of holiness from heaven; we are introduced into a relationship of oneness with God, and as our Lord met antagonistic forces and overcame them, so must we. The life Jesus lived is the type of our life after sanctification. We are apt to make sanctification the end; it is only the beginning. Our holiness as saints consists in the exclusive dedication to God of all our powers. BSG 37

---

a. Greek *your name*
b. Greek *hagiazo (set apart for sacred use* or *make holy)*
c. Greek *your name*

90

GETHSEMANE

hen he had finished praying, Jesus went out as usual to the Mount of Olives, and his disciples followed him. They crossed the Kidron Valley. On the other side there was an olive grove called Gethsemane, and he and his disciples went into it.

On reaching the place, he said to his disciples, "Sit here while I go over there and pray. Pray that you will not fall into temptation." He took Peter, James and John along with him, and he began to be deeply distressed and troubled. Then he said to them, "My soul is overwhelmed with sorrow to the point of death. Stay here and keep watch with me."

Going a little farther, he withdrew about a stone's throw beyond them, knelt down, fell with his face to the ground and prayed that if possible the hour might pass from him. "Abba[a], My Father," he said, "everything is possible for you. If you are willing, take this cup from me. Yet not what I will, but what you will."

Then he returned to his disciples and found them sleeping. "Simon," he said to Peter, "are you asleep? Could you men not keep watch with me for one hour? Watch and pray so that you will not fall into temptation. The spirit is willing, but the body is weak."

He went away a second time and prayed, "My Father, if it is not possible for this cup to be taken away unless I drink it, may your will be done." An angel from heaven appeared to him and strengthened him. And being in anguish, he prayed more earnestly, and his sweat was like drops of blood falling to the ground.[b]

When he rose from prayer and went back to the disciples, he again found them sleeping. Exhausted from sorrow, their eyes

331

were heavy. "Why are you sleeping?" he asked them. They did not know what to say to him. "Get up and pray so that you will not fall into temptation." So he left them and went away once more and prayed the third time, saying the same thing.

Returning the third time, he said to them, "Are you still sleeping and resting? Enough! The hour has come. Look, the Son of Man is betrayed into the hands of sinners. Rise! Let us go! Here comes my betrayer!" MATTHEW 26:36-46; MARK 14:32-42; LUKE 22:39-46; JOHN 18:1

"My Father, if it is not possible for this cup
to be taken away unless I drink it,
may your will be done."

FROM OSWALD CHAMBERS

    In the temptation of our Lord, Satan's first attack was in the physical domain. In Gethsemane his onslaught is against our Lord as Son of Man, not against Him as Son of God. Satan could not touch Him as Son of God; he could only touch Him as Son of Man, and this is his final onslaught on the Son of God as Son of Man. "You will get through as Son of God; I cannot touch You there, but You will never get one member of the human race through with You. Look at Your disciples; they are asleep [and] they cannot even watch with You. When You come to the cross, Your body will be so tortured and fatigued, so paralyzed with pain, and Your soul will be so darkened and confused, that You will not be able to retain a clear understanding of what You are doing. Your whole personality will be so clouded and crushed by the weight of sin that You will never get through as Man."

If Satan had been right, all that would have happened on the cross would have been the death of a martyr only; the way into life for us would never have been opened. But if Jesus Christ does get through as Son of Man, it means that the way is open for everyone who has been born or ever will be born to get back to God. Satan's challenge to our Lord was that he would not be able to do it; He would only get through as Son of God, because Satan could not touch Him there. The fear that came upon the Lord was that He might die before He reached the cross. He feared that as Son of Man He might die before He had opened the gate for us to get

332

through, and He "was heard in that He feared" (Heb. 5:7), and was delivered from death in Gethsemane. PR 87

❧ Our Lord's object in becoming Deity incarnate was to redeem mankind, and Satan's final onslaught in the Garden of Gethsemane was against our Lord *as Son of Man,* viz., that the purpose of His incarnation would fail. The profundity of His agony has to do with the fulfilling of His destiny. MFL 106

❧ The agony of our Lord in Gethsemane is not typical of what we go through, any more than His cross is typical of our cross. We know nothing about Gethsemane in personal experience. Gethsemane and Calvary stand for something unique; they are the gateway into life for us. PR 84

---

a. Aramaic for *Father*
b. Some early manuscripts do not have [the previous two sentences in Luke 22:43-44]

91

JESUS ARRESTED

hile *Jesus* was still speaking, a crowd came up. The man who was called Judas, one of the Twelve, was leading them. Now Judas, who betrayed him, knew the place, because Jesus had often met there with his disciples. So Judas came to the grove, guiding a detachment of soldiers, and some officials, sent from the chief priests, Pharisees, teachers of the law, and elders of the people. Carrying torches and lanterns, a large crowd armed with swords and clubs was with him.

Jesus, knowing all that was going to happen to him, went out and asked them, "Who is it you want?"

"Jesus of Nazareth," they replied.

"I am he," Jesus said. (And Judas the traitor was standing there with them.) When Jesus said, "I am he," they drew back and fell to the ground.

Again he asked them, "Who is it you want?"

And they said, "Jesus of Nazareth."

"I told you that I am he," Jesus answered. "If you are looking for me, then let these men go." This happened so that the words he had spoken would be fulfilled: "I have not lost one of those you gave me."[a]

Now the betrayer had arranged a signal with them: "The one I kiss is the man; arrest him and lead him away under guard." He approached Jesus at once to kiss him, but Jesus asked him, "Judas, are you betraying the Son of Man with a kiss?" Judas said, "Greetings, Rabbi!" and kissed him.

Jesus replied, "Friend, do what you came for."[b]

Then the men stepped forward, seized Jesus and arrested him. When Jesus' followers saw what was going to happen, they said, "Lord, should we strike with our swords?" Then Simon Peter, standing near, reached for his sword, drew it out and struck the servant of the high priest, cutting off his right ear. (The servant's name was Malchus.)

But Jesus commanded Peter, "No more of this! Put your sword back in its place, for all who draw the sword will die by the sword. Do you think I cannot call on my Father, and he will at once put at my disposal more than twelve legions of angels? But how then would the Scriptures be fulfilled that say it must happen in this way? Shall I not drink the cup the Father has given me?" And he touched the man's ear and healed him.

At that time Jesus said to the chief priests, the officers of the temple guard, and the elders, who had come for him, "Am I leading a rebellion, that you have come out with swords and clubs to capture me? Every day I was with you; I sat in the temple courts teaching, and you did not lay a hand on me *to* arrest me. But this has all taken place that the writings of the prophets might be fulfilled. This is your hour—when darkness reigns." Then all the disciples deserted him and fled. MATTHEW 26:47-56; MARK 14:43-52; LUKE 22:47-54a; JOHN 18:2-11

"And he touched the man's ear
and healed him."

FROM OSWALD CHAMBERS

❧ If you get off on the line of personal holiness or divine healing or the second coming of our Lord, and make any of these your end, you are disloyal to Jesus Christ. Supposing the Lord has healed your body and you make divine healing your end, the dead set of your life is no longer for God but for what you are pleased to call the manifestation of God in your life. Bother your life! "It can never be God's will that I should be sick." If it was God's will to bruise His own Son, why should it not be His will to bruise you! The thing that tells is not relevant consistency to an idea of what a saint's life is, but abandonment abjectly to Jesus Christ whether you are well or ill. NKW 148

❧ When people come to the Atonement and say, "Now I have deliverance in the Atonement, therefore I have no business to be sick," they make a fundamental confusion, because there is no case of healing in the Bible that did not come from a direct intervention of the sovereign touch of God. IYA 85

❧ The attitude to sickness in the Bible is totally different from the attitude of people who believe in faith-healing. The Bible attitude is not that God sends sickness or that sickness is of the devil, but that sickness is a fact usable by both God and the devil. Never base a principle on your own experience. My personal experience is this: I have never once in my life been sick without being to blame for it. As soon as I turned my mind to asking why the sickness was allowed, I learned a lesson that I have never forgotten, viz., that my physical health depends absolutely on my relationship to God. PS 77

❧ The Master Physician—when He touches, there is no convalescence. SSY 88

---

a. John 6:39
b. Or "Friend, why have you come?"

92

PETER'S THREE DENIALS

S imon Peter and another disciple were following Jesus at a distance, right up to the courtyard of the high priest. Because this disciple was known to the high priest, he went with Jesus into the high priest's courtyard, but Peter had to wait outside at the door. The other disciple, who was known to the high priest, came back, spoke to the girl on duty there and brought Peter into the courtyard.

It was cold, and the servants and officials stood around a fire they had kindled in the middle of the courtyard to keep warm. Peter entered and was standing with them, warming himself. When they sat down together, Peter sat down with the guards to see the outcome.

While Peter was sitting out in the courtyard, one of the servant girls of the high priest, the girl at the door, came by. When she saw Peter seated there in the firelight warming himself, she asked, "You are not one of this man's disciples, are you?"

He replied, "I am not."

She looked closely at him and said, "This man was with him. You also were with that Nazarene, Jesus of Galilee."

But he denied it before them all. "Woman, I don't know him. I don't know or understand what you are talking about," he said, and went out into the entryway.[a]

A little later, Simon Peter stood warming himself. When the servant girl saw him, she said again to those people standing around, "This fellow is one of them."

Another servant girl saw him and said to the people there, "This fellow was with Jesus of Nazareth."

Someone else said, "You also are one of them."

He was asked, "You are not one of his disciples, are you?"

Peter denied it again, with an oath: "Man, I am not! I don't know the man!"

About an hour later, another asserted, "Certainly this fellow was with him, for he is a Galilean." Those standing there went up to Peter and said, "Surely you are one of them, for your accent gives you away." One of the high priest's servants, a relative of the man whose ear Peter had cut off, challenged him, "Didn't I see you with him in the olive grove?"

Again Peter denied it. He began to call down curses on himself, and he swore to them, "Man, I don't know what you're talking about! I don't know this man!"

At that moment, just as he was speaking, the rooster began to crow the second time.[b] The Lord turned and looked straight at Peter. Then Peter remembered the word the Lord Jesus had spoken to him: "Before the rooster crows twice[c] today, you will disown me three times." And he went outside, broke down and wept bitterly. MATTHEW 26:58, 69-75; MARK 14:54, 66-72; LUKE 22:54c-62; JOHN 18:15-18, 25-27

"He went outside, broke down,
and wept bitterly."

FROM OSWALD CHAMBERS

❧ Repentance is the experimental side of redemption and is altogether different from remorse or reformation. Repentance is a New Testament word and cannot be applied outside the New Testament. We all experience remorse, disgust with ourselves over the wrong we have done when we are found out by it, but the rarest miracle of God's grace is the sorrow that puts an end forever to the thing for which I am sorry. Repentance involves the receiving of a totally new disposition so that I never do the wrong thing again. CHI 26

❧ Strictly speaking, repentance is a gift of God. No man can repent when he chooses. A man can be remorseful when he chooses, but remorse is a lesser thing than repentance. Repentance means that I show my sorrow for the wrong thing by becoming the opposite. BFB 108

340

❧ Repentance does not bring a sense of sin, but a sense of unutterable unworthiness. MUH 235

❧ Repentance means that I estimate exactly what I am in God's sight, and I am sorry for it, and on the basis of redemption I become the opposite. SA 121

---

a. Some early manuscripts [of Mark 14:68] *entryway and the rooster crowed*
b. Some early manuscripts [of Mark 14:72] do not have *the second time*
c. Some early manuscripts [of Mark 14:72] do not have *twice*

93

JESUS SENTENCED TO BE CRUCIFIED

Wanting to satisfy the crowd, Pilate released Barabbas to them. Then Pilate took Jesus and had him flogged. The soldiers led Jesus away into the palace (that is, the Praetorium) and called together the whole company of soldiers around him. They stripped him and put a purple robe on him, and then twisted together a crown of thorns and set it on his head. They put a staff in his right hand. "Hail, O king of the Jews!" they began to call out to him. Falling on their knees in front of him, they worshiped him and mocked him. They spit on him, and took the staff and struck him on the head *and* face again and again.

Once more Pilate came out and said to the Jews, "Look, I am bringing him out to you to let you know that I find no basis for a charge against him." When Jesus came out wearing the crown of thorns and the purple robe, Pilate said to them, "Here is the man!"

As soon as the chief priests and their officials saw him, they shouted, "Crucify! Crucify!"

But Pilate answered, "You take him and crucify him. As for me, I find no basis for a charge against him."

The Jews insisted, "We have a law, and according to that law he must die, because he claimed to be the Son of God."

When Pilate heard this, he was even more afraid, and he went back inside the palace. "Where do you come from?" he asked Jesus, but Jesus gave him no answer. "Do you refuse to speak to me?" Pilate said. "Don't you realize I have power either to free you or to crucify you?"

Jesus answered, "You would have no power over me if it were not given to you from above. Therefore the one who handed me over to you is guilty of a greater sin."

343

From then on, Pilate tried to set Jesus free, but the Jews kept shouting, "If you let this man go, you are no friend of Caesar. Anyone who claims to be a king opposes Caesar."

When Pilate heard this, he brought Jesus out and sat down on the judge's seat at a place known as the Stone Pavement (which in Aramaic is Gabbatha). It was the day of Preparation of Passover Week, about the sixth hour.

"Here is your king," Pilate said to the Jews.

But they shouted, "Take him away! Take him away! Crucify him!"

"Shall I crucify your king?" Pilate asked.

"We have no king but Caesar," the chief priests answered.

With loud shouts they insistently demanded that he be crucified, and their shouts prevailed. When Pilate saw that he was getting nowhere, but that instead an uproar was starting, *he* decided to grant their demand. He took water and washed his hands in front of the crowd. "I am innocent of this man's blood," he said. "It is your responsibility!"

All the people answered, "Let his blood be on us and on our children!"

Finally Pilate surrendered Jesus to their will and handed him over to them to be crucified.

So the soldiers took charge of Jesus. They took off the purple robe and put his own clothes on him. Then they led him away to crucify him. MATTHEW 27:24-31; MARK 15:15-20; LUKE 23:23-25; JOHN 19:1-16

THE CRUCIFIXION

They led him away, carrying his own cross. As they were going out, they met a man from Cyrene, named Simon, the father of Alexander and Rufus. *He* was passing by on his way in from the country. They seized Simon, put the cross on him and forced him to carry it behind Jesus. A large number of people followed him, including women who mourned and wailed for him. Jesus turned and said to them, "Daughters of Jerusalem, do not weep for me; weep for yourselves and for your children. For the time will come when you will say, 'Blessed are the barren women, the wombs that never bore and the breasts that never nursed!' Then

" 'they will say to the mountains, "Fall on us!"
and to the hills, "Cover us!" '[a]

For if men do these things when the tree is green, what will happen when it is dry?"

Two other men, both robbers, were also led out with him to be executed.

They came to a place called Golgotha in Aramaic (which means The Place of the Skull). Then they offered Jesus wine to drink, mixed with gall (myrrh); but after tasting it, he refused to drink it. There they crucified him, along with the criminals—one on his right, the other on his left[b] and Jesus in the middle. It was the third hour when they crucified him.

Jesus said, "Father, forgive them, for they do not know what they are doing."[c]

When the soldiers had crucified Jesus, they took his clothes, dividing them into four shares, one for each of them, with the undergarment remaining. This garment was seamless, woven in one piece from top to bottom.

"Let's not tear it," they said to one another. "Let's decide by lot who will get it." They cast lots.

This happened that the scripture might be fulfilled which said,

"They divided my garments among them and cast lots for my clothing."[d]

So this is what the soldiers did. And sitting down, they kept watch over him there.

Pilate had a written notice of the charge against him prepared and fastened to the cross above his head. Many of the Jews read this sign, for the place where Jesus was crucified was near the city, and the sign was written in Aramaic, Latin and Greek. It read:

JESUS OF NAZARETH, THE KING OF THE JEWS
THIS IS JESUS, THE KING OF THE JEWS
THIS IS THE KING OF THE JEWS

The chief priests of the Jews protested to Pilate, "Do not write 'The King of the Jews,' but that this man claimed to be king of the Jews."

Pilate answered, "What I have written, I have written."

Those who passed by hurled insults at him, shaking their heads

345

and saying, "So! You who are going to destroy the temple and build it in three days, come down from the cross and save yourself, if you are the Son of God!"

The people stood watching, and the rulers even sneered at him. In the same way the chief priests, the teachers of the law and the elders mocked him among themselves. "He saved others," they said, "but he can't save himself!" "Let him save himself if he is the Christ of God, the Chosen One." "He's the King of Israel! Let this Christ, this King of Israel, come down now from the cross, that we may see and believe in him." "He trusts in God. Let God rescue him now if he wants him, for he said, 'I am the Son of God.' "

The soldiers also came up and mocked him. They offered him wine vinegar and said, "If you are the king of the Jews, save yourself."

In the same way the robbers who were crucified with him also heaped insults on him. One of the criminals who hung there hurled insults at him: "Aren't you the Christ? Save yourself and us!"

But the other criminal rebuked him. "Don't you fear God," he said, "since you are under the same sentence? We are punished justly, for we are getting what our deeds deserve. But this man has done nothing wrong."

Then he said, "Jesus, remember me when you come into your kingdom."e

Jesus answered him, "I tell you the truth, today you will be with me in paradise."

Near the cross of Jesus stood his mother, his mother's sister, Mary the wife of Cleopas, and Mary Magdalene. When Jesus saw his mother there, and the disciple whom he loved standing nearby, he said to his mother, "Dear woman, here is your son," and to the disciple, "Here is your mother." From that time on, this disciple took her into his home. MATTHEW 27:32-44; MARK 15:21-32; LUKE 23:26-43; JOHN 19:17-27

"There they crucified him,
along with the criminals."

From Oswald Chambers

❧ In the cross we may see the dimensions of divine love. The cross is not the cross of a man, but the exhibition of the heart of God. At the back of the wall of the world stands God with His arms outstretched, and every man driven there is driven into the arms of God. The cross of Jesus is the supreme evidence of the love of God. PH 65

❧ The great marvel of Jesus was that He was voluntarily weak. "He was crucified through weakness," and, says Paul, "we also are weak in Him" (2 Cor. 13:4). Any coward among us can hit back when hit, but it takes an exceedingly strong nature not to hit back. Jesus Christ never did. "Who, when He was reviled, reviled not again; when He suffered, He threatened not" (1 Peter 2:23); and if we are going to follow His example we shall find that all his teaching leads along that line. IWP 110

❧ There is nothing more certain in time or eternity than what Jesus Christ did on the cross: He switched the whole human race back into right relationship to God and made the basis of human life redemptive; consequently any member of the human race can get into touch with God *now*. BE 61

❧ The cross of Jesus Christ is the point where God and sinful man merge with a crash, and the way to life is opened; but the crash is on the heart of God. The cross is the presentation of God having done His "bit," that which man could never do. SA 38

❧ We have so hallowed the cross by twenty centuries of emotion and sentiment that it sounds a very beautiful and pathetic thing to talk about carrying our cross. But a wooden cross with iron nails in it is a clumsy thing to carry. The real cross was like that, and do we imagine that the external cross was more ugly than our actual one? Or that the thing that tore our Lord's hands and feet was not really so terrible as our imagination of it? PR 100

❧ If once a man has heard the appeal of Jesus from the cross, he begins to find there is something there that answers the cry of the whole world. What we have to do as God's servants is to lift up Christ crucified. IWP 61

347

a. Hosea 10:8
b. Some manuscripts [of Mark 15:28] *left, and the scripture was fulfilled which says, "He was counted with the lawless ones"* (Isaiah 53:12)
c. Some early manuscripts [of Luke 23:34] do not have this sentence
d. Psalm 22:18
e. Some manuscripts [of Luke 23:42] *come with your kingly power*

94

THE DEATH OF JESUS

rom the sixth hour until the ninth hour darkness came over all the land, for the sun stopped shining. And at the ninth hour Jesus cried out in a loud voice, "Eloi, Eloi,[a] lama sabach-thani?" — which means, "My God, my God, why have you forsaken me?"[b]

When some of those standing there heard this, they said, "Listen, he's calling Elijah."

Later, knowing that all was now completed, and so that the Scripture would be fulfilled, Jesus said, "I am thirsty." A jar of wine vinegar was there. Immediately one man ran and got a sponge. He soaked it with wine vinegar, put the sponge on a stalk of the hyssop plant, and lifted it to Jesus' lips. The rest said, "Leave him alone now. Let's see if Elijah comes to save him, to take him down." When he had received the drink, Jesus said, "It is finished."

Jesus cried out again with a loud voice, "Father, into your hands I commit my spirit." When he had said this, he breathed his last; he bowed his head and gave up his spirit.

At that moment the curtain of the temple was torn in two from top to bottom. The earth shook and the rocks split. The tombs broke open and the bodies of many holy people who had died were raised to life. They came out of the tombs, and after Jesus' resurrection they went into the holy city and appeared to many people.

When the centurion and those with him who were guarding Jesus saw the earthquake and all that had happened, they were terrified. The centurion stood there in front of Jesus, heard his cry and[c] saw how he died. He praised God and exclaimed, "Surely this was a righteous man. Surely he was the Son[d] of God!"

When all the people who had gathered to witness this sight

349

saw what took place, they beat their breasts and went away. But all those who knew him, including many women, stood at a distance, watching these things. Among them were Mary Magdalene, Mary the mother of James the younger and of Joses, and Salome, the mother of Zebedee's sons. In Galilee these women had followed Jesus and cared for his needs. Many other women who had come up with him from Galilee to Jerusalem were also there.

Now it was the day of Preparation, and the next day was to be a special Sabbath. Because the Jews did not want the bodies left on the crosses during the Sabbath, they asked Pilate to have the legs broken and the bodies taken down. The soldiers therefore came and broke the legs of the first man who had been crucified with Jesus, and then those of the other. But when they came to Jesus and found that he was already dead, they did not break his legs. Instead, one of the soldiers pierced Jesus' side with a spear, bringing a sudden flow of blood and water. These things happened so that the scripture would be fulfilled: "Not one of his bones will be broken,"[e] and, as another scripture says, "They will look on the one they have pierced."[f] MATTHEW 27:45-56; MARK 15:33-41; LUKE 23:44-49; JOHN 19:28-34, 36-37

"It is finished."

FROM OSWALD CHAMBERS

≫ When we tell God that we want at all costs to be identified with the death of Jesus Christ, at that instant a supernatural identification with His death takes place, and we know with a knowledge that passes knowledge that our "old man" is crucified with Christ, and we prove it forever after by the amazing ease with which the supernatural life of God in us enables us to do His will. That is why the bedrock of Christianity is personal, passionate devotion to the Lord Jesus. PH 164

≫ When we speak of the blood of Jesus Christ cleansing us from all sin, we do not mean the physical blood shed on Calvary, but the whole life of the Son of God which was poured out to redeem the world. All the perfections of the essential nature of God were in that blood, and all the holiest attainments of mankind as well. It was the life of the perfection of deity that was poured out on Calvary, " . . . the church of God, which He purchased with His own blood" (Acts 20:28). We are apt to look upon the blood of Jesus Christ as a magic-working power instead of its being the very life of the Son of God poured forth for men. The whole meaning of our being identified with the death of Jesus is that His blood may flow through our mortal bodies. PH 162

ൟ That Christ is the substitute for me and therefore I go scot-free, is never taught in the New Testament. If I say that Christ suffered instead of me, I knock the bottom board out of His sacrifice. *Christ died in the stead of me.* I, a guilty sinner, can never get right with God; it is impossible. I can only be brought into union with God by identification with the One who died in my stead. No sinner can get right with God on any other ground than the ground that Christ died, *in his stead,* not *instead of him.* NKW 125

ൟ We are made acceptable to God only by relying on the eternal Spirit who was incarnated absolutely in Jesus Christ. The Spirit in us will never allow us to forget that the death of Jesus was the death of God incarnate. "God was in Christ reconciling the world unto Himself" (2 Cor. 5:19). PS 19

ൟ The death of Jesus is the only entrance into the life He lived. We cannot get into His life by admiring Him, or by saying what a beautiful life His was, so pure and holy. To dwell only on His life would drive us to despair. We enter into His life by means of His death. Until the Holy Spirit has had His way with us spiritually, the death of Jesus Christ is an insignificant thing, and we are amazed that the New Testament should make so much of it. PR 79

---

a. Some manuscripts [of Matthew 27:46] *Eli, Eli*
b. Psalm 22:1
c. Some manuscripts [of Mark 15:39] do not have *heard his cry and*
d. Or *a son*
e. Exodus 12:46; Numbers 9:12; Psalm 34:20
f. Zechariah 12:10

95

THE BURIAL OF JESUS

N ow there was a rich man from the Judean town of Arimathea, named Joseph, a good and upright man who was himself waiting for the kingdom of God. Joseph had become a disciple of Jesus, but secretly because he feared the Jews. A prominent member of the Council, *he* had not consented to their decision and action.

It was Preparation Day (that is, the day before the Sabbath). So as evening approached, Joseph of Arimathea went boldly to Pilate and asked for Jesus' body. Pilate was surprised to hear that he was already dead. Summoning the centurion, he asked him if Jesus had already died. When he learned from the centurion that it was so, Pilate ordered that the body be given to Joseph. So Joseph bought some linen cloth.

With Pilate's permission, Joseph came, took down the body *and* wrapped it in the linen cloth. He was accompanied by Nicodemus, the man who earlier had visited Jesus at night. Nicodemus brought a mixture of myrrh and aloes, about seventy-five pounds.[a] Taking Jesus' body, the two of them wrapped it, with the spices, in strips of clean linen cloth. This was in accordance with Jewish burial customs.

At the place where Jesus was crucified, there was a garden, and in the garden a new tomb, *Joseph's* own new tomb that he had cut out of the rock. The Sabbath was about to begin, and since the tomb was nearby, they took Jesus' body and laid it there, *where* no one had ever been laid. Then *they* rolled a big stone against the entrance of the tomb and went away.

The women who had come with Jesus from Galilee followed Joseph and saw the tomb and how his body was laid in it. Mary Magdalene and the other Mary, the mother of Joses, were sitting there opposite the tomb. Then they went home and prepared spices and perfumes. But they rested on the Sabbath in obedience to the commandment. MATTHEW 27:57-61; MARK 15:42-47; LUKE 23:50-56; JOHN 19:38-42

THE GUARD AT THE TOMB

The next day, the one after Preparation Day, the chief priests and the Pharisees went to Pilate. "Sir," they said, "we remember that while he was still alive that deceiver said, 'After three days I will rise again.' So give the order for the tomb to be made secure until the third day. Otherwise, his disciples may come and steal the body and tell the people that he has been raised from the dead. This last deception will be worse than the first."

"Take a guard," Pilate answered. "Go, make the tomb as secure as you know how." So they went and made the tomb secure by putting a seal on the stone and posting the guard. MATTHEW 27:62-66

"They took Jesus' body
and laid it there."

FROM OSWALD CHAMBERS

   The death of Jesus was not a satisfaction paid to the justice of God—a hideous statement which the Bible nowhere makes. The death of Jesus was an exact revelation of the justice of God. When we read of the sacrifice of Jesus Christ, it is the sacrifice of God also. "God was in Christ reconciling the world unto Himself" (2 Cor. 5:19). BSG 78

   The only one who can reckon he is "dead indeed unto sin" is the one who has been through identification with the death of Jesus. When he has been through that moral transaction, he will find he is enabled to live according to it; but if I try the "reckoning" business without having gone through identification with the death of Jesus, I shall find myself deceived; there is no reality. When I can say, "I have been crucified with Christ," a new page of consciousness opens before me; I find there are new powers in me. I am able now to fulfill the commands of God, able to do what I never could do before; I am free from the old bondage, the old limitations, and the gateway to this new life is the death of Jesus. GW 86

❧ The death of Jesus Christ is the performance in history of the very mind of God. There is no room for looking on Jesus Christ as a martyr; His death was not something that happened to Him which might have been prevented: His death was the very reason why He came. MUH 326

❧ By the death of the Son of Man upon the cross, the door is opened for any individual to go straight into the presence of God; and by the resurrection our Lord can impart to us His own life. PR 111

❧ When once we see that the New Testament emphasizes Jesus Christ's death, not His life, that it is by virtue of His death we enter into His life, then we find that His teaching is for the life He puts in. SA 40

---

a. Greek *a hundred litrai* (about 34 kilograms)

96

THE RESURRECTION

hen the Sabbath was over, Mary Magdalene, Mary the mother of James, and Salome bought spices so that they might go to anoint Jesus' body. Very early in the morning on the first day of the week, while it was still dark, the women took the spices they had prepared and went to the tomb.

There was a violent earthquake, for an angel of the Lord came down from heaven and, going to the tomb, rolled back the stone and sat on it. His appearance was like lightning, and his clothes were white as snow. The guards were so afraid of him that they shook and became like dead men.

Just after sunrise, *the women* were on their way to the tomb and they asked each other, "Who will roll the stone away from the entrance of the tomb?" But when they looked up, they saw that the stone, which was very large, had been rolled away from the tomb entrance. When they entered the tomb, they did not find the body of the Lord Jesus. While they were wondering about this, suddenly two men in clothes that gleamed like lightning stood beside them, *one,* a young man dressed in a white robe sitting on the right side. They were alarmed. In their fright the women bowed down with their faces to the ground.

But the men said to the women, "Do not be afraid, for I know that you are looking for Jesus the Nazarene, who was crucified. Why do you look for the living among the dead? He is not here; he has risen, just as he said. Come and see the place where they laid him. Remember how he told you, while he was still with you in Galilee: 'The Son of Man must be delivered into the hands of sinful men, be crucified and on the third day be raised again.' " Then they remembered his words. "But go quickly, tell his disciples and Peter: 'He has risen from the dead and is going ahead of you into Galilee. There you will see him, just as he told you.' Now I have told you."

Trembling and bewildered, the women went out and fled from the tomb. They said nothing to anyone, because they were afraid, yet filled with joy, and ran to tell his disciples.

Mary Magdalene came running to Simon Peter and the other disciple, the one Jesus loved, and said, "They have taken the Lord out of the tomb, and we don't know where they have put him!"

When *the women* came back from the tomb, they told all these things to the Eleven and to all the others. It was Mary Magdalene, Joanna, Mary the mother of James, and the others with them who told this to the apostles. But they did not believe the women, because their words seemed to them like nonsense.

Peter and the other disciple, however, got up and started for the tomb. Both were running, but the other disciple outran Peter and reached the tomb first. He bent over and looked in at the strips of linen lying there but did not go in. Then Simon Peter, who was behind him, arrived and went into the tomb. Bending over, he saw the strips of linen lying there by themselves, as well as the burial cloth that had been around Jesus' head. The cloth was folded up by itself, separate from the linen. He went away, wondering to himself what had happened. Finally the other disciple, who had reached the tomb first, also went inside. He saw and believed. (They still did not understand from Scripture that Jesus had to rise from the dead.) MATTHEW 28:1-8; MARK 16:1-8; LUKE 24:1-12; JOHN 20:1-9

"He is not here; he has risen,
just as he said."

FROM OSWALD CHAMBERS

> ❧ Our Lord rose to an absolutely new life, to a life He did not live before He was incarnate; He rose to a life that had never been before. There had been resurrections before the resurrection of Jesus Christ, but they were all resuscitations to the same kind of life as heretofore. Jesus Christ rose to a totally new life, and to a totally different relationship to men and women. PR 113

᙮ We have to receive the Holy Spirit and let Him bring us to the place where we are so identified with the death of Jesus that it is "no longer I, but Christ that liveth in me" (see Gal. 2:20); and then go on to build up a character on the basis of Jesus Christ's disposition. The Christian life is drawn from first to last, and all in between, from the resurrection life of the Lord Jesus. SHL 18

᙮ By His resurrection, Jesus Christ has power to impart to us the Holy Spirit, which means a totally new life. The Holy Ghost is the deity in proceeding power, who applies the Atonement of the Son of God in our experience. BP 37

᙮ "All my fresh springs are in Thee" (see Ps. 87:7). Notice how God will wither up every other spring you have. He will wither up your natural virtues, He will break up confidence in your natural powers, He will wither up your confidence in brain and spirit and body, until you learn by practical experience that you have no right to draw your life from any source other than the tremendous reservoir of the resurrection life of Jesus Christ. BP 41

᙮ The resurrection of Jesus Christ grants Him the right to give His own destiny to any human being—viz., to make us the sons and daughters of God. His resurrection means that we are raised to His risen life, not to our old life. "Like as Christ was raised up from the dead by the glory of the Father, even so we also should walk in newness of life . . . we shall be also in the likeness of His resurrection" (Rom. 6:4-5). PR 114

᙮ Our Lord died and was buried and He rose again, and this is the declaration of the Resurrection in all its incredibleness. Any question that arises in connection with the Resurrection arises in the minds of those who do not accept the necessity of being born from above. PR 110

᙮ The resurrection of Jesus Christ has given Him the right, the authority, to impart the life of God to us, and our experimental life must be constructed on the basis of His life. PR 115

97

JESUS APPEARS TO MARY MAGDALENE AND OTHER WOMEN

Then the disciples went back to their homes, but Mary stood outside the tomb crying. As she wept, she bent over to look into the tomb and saw two angels in white, seated where Jesus' body had been, one at the head and the other at the foot.

They asked her, "Woman, why are you crying?"

"They have taken my Lord away," she said, "and I don't know where they have put him." At this, she turned around and saw Jesus standing there, but she did not realize that it was Jesus.

"Woman," he said, "why are you crying? Who is it you are looking for?"

Thinking he was the gardener, she said, "Sir, if you have carried him away, tell me where you have put him, and I will get him."

Jesus said to her, "Mary."

She turned toward him and cried out in Aramaic, "Rabboni!" (which means Teacher).

Jesus said, "Do not hold on to me, for I have not yet returned to the Father. Go instead to my brothers and tell them, 'I am returning to my Father and your Father, to my God and your God.' "

[a][Thus when Jesus rose early on the first day of the week, he appeared first to Mary Magdalene, out of whom he had driven seven demons.] She went to [those who had been with him and who were mourning and weeping] with the news: "I have seen the Lord!" And she told them that he had said these things to her. [When they heard that Jesus was alive, and that she had seen him, they did not believe it.]

Suddenly Jesus met *the other women*. "Greetings," he said. They came to him, clasped his feet and worshiped him. Then

Jesus said to them, "Do not be afraid. Go and tell my brothers to go to Galilee; there they will see me." MATTHEW 28:9-10; MARK 16:9-11; JOHN 20:10-18

THE GUARDS' REPORT

While the women were on their way, some of the guards went into the city and reported to the chief priests everything that had happened. When the chief priests had met with the elders and devised a plan, they gave the soldiers a large sum of money, telling them, "You are to say, 'His disciples came during the night and stole him away while we were asleep.' If this report gets to the governor, we will satisfy him and keep you out of trouble." So the soldiers took the money and did as they were instructed. And this story has been widely circulated among the Jews to this very day. MATTHEW 28:11-15

> *"I am returning to my Father and your Father,*
> *to my God and your God."*

FROM OSWALD CHAMBERS

~ Our Lord's cross is the gateway into His life: His resurrection means that He has power now to convey His life to me. When I am born again from above, I receive from the risen Lord His very life.

Our Lord's resurrection destiny is to bring "many sons unto glory" (Heb. 2:10). The fulfilling of His destiny gives Him the right to make us sons and daughters of God. We are never in the relationship to God that the Son of God is in; but we are brought by the Son into the relation of sonship. When our Lord rose from the dead, He rose to an absolutely new life, to a life He did not live before He was incarnate. He rose to a life that had never been before; and His resurrection means for us that we are raised to His risen life, not to our old life. One day we shall have a body like unto His glorious body, but we can know now the efficacy of His resurrection and walk in newness of life. "I would know Him *in the power of His resurrection*" (see Phil. 3:10). MUH 99

~ The Ascension placed Jesus Christ back in the glory which He had with the Father before the world was. The Ascension, not the Resurrection, is the completion of the Transfiguration. BSG 56

❧ By His ascension our Lord raises Himself to glory. He becomes omnipotent, omniscient, and omnipresent. All the splendid power, so circumscribed in His earthly life, becomes omnipotence; all the wisdom and insight, so precious but so limited during His life on earth, becomes omniscience; all the unspeakable comfort of the presence of Jesus, so confined to a few in His earthly life, becomes omnipresence. He is with us all the days. BSG 59

---

a. The most reliable early manuscripts and other ancient witnesses do not have Mark 16:9-20 [the contents of which are placed in brackets hereinafter]

98

ON THE ROAD TO EMMAUS

A fterward that same day two of *Jesus' disciples* were [walking in the country], going to a village called Emmaus, about seven miles[a] from Jerusalem. They were talking with each other about everything that had happened. As they talked and discussed these things with each other, Jesus himself came up and walked along with them; but they were kept from recognizing him. [Jesus appeared in a different form to them.]

He asked them, "What are you discussing together as you walk along?"

They stood still, their faces downcast. One of them, named Cleopas, asked him, "Are you only a visitor to Jerusalem and do not know the things that have happened there in these days?"

"What things?" he asked.

"About Jesus of Nazareth," they replied. "He was a prophet, powerful in word and deed before God and all the people. The chief priests and our rulers handed him over to be sentenced to death, and they crucified him; but we had hoped that he was the one who was going to redeem Israel. And what is more, it is the third day since all this took place. In addition, some of our women amazed us. They went to the tomb early this morning but didn't find his body. They came and told us that they had seen a vision of angels, who said he was alive. Then some of our companions went to the tomb and found it just as the women had said, but him they did not see."

He said to them, "How foolish you are, and how slow of heart to believe all that the prophets have spoken! Did not the Christ have to suffer these things and then enter his glory?" And beginning with Moses and all the Prophets, he explained to them what was said in all the Scriptures concerning himself.

As they approached the village to which they were going, Jesus acted as if he were going farther. But they urged him strongly, "Stay with us, for it is nearly evening; the day is almost over." So he went in to stay with them.

When he was at the table with them, he took bread, gave thanks, broke it and began to give it to them. Then their eyes were opened and they recognized him, and he disappeared from their sight. They asked each other, "Were not our hearts burning within us while he talked with us on the road and opened the Scriptures to us?"

They got up and returned at once to Jerusalem. On the evening of that first day of the week, there they found the Eleven disciples and those with them, assembled together with the doors locked for fear of the Jews, and saying, "It is true! The Lord has risen and has appeared to Simon." Then the two reported what had happened on the way, and how Jesus was recognized by them when he broke the bread. [But the *disciples* did not believe them either.] MARK 16:12-13; LUKE 24:13-35; JOHN 20:19a

"How foolish you are, and slow of heart
to believe all that the prophets have spoken."

FROM OSWALD CHAMBERS

> Every fact that the disciples stated was right; but the inferences they drew from those facts were wrong. Anything that savors of dejection spiritually is always wrong. If depression and oppression visit me, I am to blame; God is not, nor is anyone else. Dejection springs from one of two sources—I have either satisfied a lust or I have not. Lust means—I must have it at once. Spiritual lust makes me demand an answer from God, instead of seeking God who gives the answer. What have I been trusting God would do? And today— the immediate present—is the third day, and He has not done it; therefore I imagine I am justified in being dejected and in blaming God. Whenever the insistence is on the point that God answers prayer, we are off the track. The meaning of prayer is that we get hold of God, not of the answer. It is impossible to be well physically and to be dejected. Dejection is a sign of sickness, and the same thing is true spiritually. Dejection spiritually is wrong, and we are always to blame for it.

We look for visions from heaven, for earthquakes and thunders of God's power (the fact that we are dejected proves that we do), and we never dream that all the time God is in the commonplace things and people around us. If we will do the duty that lies nearest, we shall see Him. One of the most amazing revelations of God comes when we learn that it is in the commonplace things that the deity of Jesus Christ is realized. MUH 38

    How did Jesus Christ deal with the foolishness of the two disciples on the road to Emmaus? This is the stupidity on another line: a stupidity of simple souls, honest and true, who had become blinded by their own grief and their own point of view.

Jesus said to them: "O fools, and slow of heart to believe all that the prophets have spoken!" (Luke 24:25) Here the word *fools* might be translated, "My little children, when will you believe what the prophets have written?" This is stupidity of a totally different order — a stupidity that Jesus deals with very pointedly, but very patiently. It is a stupidity that obliterates one's understanding of the Word of God because of personal grief, sorrow, or perplexity.

Is Jesus Christ saying to you, "My child, when will you believe what I say?" Is there a particular problem in your life that has made you become slow of heart to believe? Do not let the stupidity grow. Seek what the Word of God has to say about it.

Oh, there is such a need for people who will search the Bible and learn what God is saying to them! DDL 195

---

a. Greek *sixty stadia* (about 11 kilometers)

99

JESUS APPEARS TO THE DISCIPLES

While they were [eating] *and* still talking about this, Jesus himself came and stood among [the Eleven] and said to them, "Peace be with you!"

They were startled and frightened, thinking they saw a ghost. He said to them, "Why are you troubled, and why do doubts rise in your minds?" [He rebuked them for their lack of faith and their stubborn refusal to believe those who had seen him after he had risen.] "Look at my hands and my feet. It is I myself! Touch me and see; a ghost does not have flesh and bones, as you see I have."

When he had said this, he showed them his hands and feet and side. And while they still did not believe it because of joy and amazement, he asked them, "Do you have anything here to eat?" They gave him a piece of broiled fish, and he took it and ate it in their presence. So the disciples were overjoyed when they saw the Lord.

Again Jesus said, "Peace be with you! As the Father has sent me, I am sending you." And with that he breathed on them and said, "Receive the Holy Spirit. If you forgive anyone his sins, they are forgiven; if you do not forgive them, they are not forgiven."
MARK 16:14; LUKE 24:36-43; JOHN 20:19b-23

JESUS APPEARS TO THOMAS

Now Thomas (called Didymus), one of the Twelve, was not with the disciples when Jesus came. So the other disciples told him, "We have seen the Lord!"

But he said to them, "Unless I see the nail marks in his hands and put my finger where the nails were, and put my hand into his side, I will not believe it."

A week later his disciples were in the house again, and Thomas was with them. Though the doors were locked, Jesus came and stood among them and said, "Peace be with you!" Then he said to Thomas, "Put your finger here; see my hands. Reach out your hand and put it into my side. Stop doubting and believe."

Thomas said to him, "My Lord and my God!"

Then Jesus told him, "Because you have seen me, you have believed; blessed are those who have not seen and yet have believed." JOHN 20:24-29

> *"Blessed are those who have not seen*
> *and yet have believed."*

FROM OSWALD CHAMBERS

> ❧ Seeing is never believing: we interpret what we see in the light of what we believe. Faith is confidence in God before you see God emerging, therefore the nature of faith is that it must be tried. To say, "Oh, yes, I believe God will triumph," may be so much credence smeared over with religious phraseology; but when you are up against things it is quite another matter to say, "I believe God will win through." The trial of our faith gives us a good banking account in the heavenly places, and when the next trial comes our wealth there will tide us over. If we have confidence in God beyond the actual earthly horizons, we shall see the lie at the heart of the fear, and our faith will win through in every detail. Jesus said that men ought always to pray and not "cave in" — "Don't look at the immediate horizon and don't take the facts you see and say they are the reality; they are actuality; the reality lies behind with God." SHH 55

> ❧ Belief must be the *will* to believe. There must be a surrender of the will, not a surrender to persuasive power, a deliberate launching forth on God and on what He says until I am no longer confident in what I have done, I am confident only in God. The hindrance is that I will not trust God, but only my mental understanding. As far as feelings go, I must stake all blindly. I must *will* to believe, and this can never be done without a violent effort on my part to disassociate myself from my old ways of looking at things, and by putting myself right over on to Him. MUH 357

100

THE MIRACULOUS CATCH OF FISH

Afterward Jesus appeared again to his disciples, by the Sea of Tiberias.[a] It happened this way: Simon Peter, Thomas (called Didymus), Nathanael from Cana in Galilee, the sons of Zebedee, and two other disciples were together. "I'm going out to fish," Simon Peter told them, and they said, "We'll go with you." So they went out and got into the boat, but that night they caught nothing.

Early in the morning, Jesus stood on the shore, but the disciples did not realize that it was Jesus.

He called out to them, "Friends, haven't you any fish?"

"No," they answered.

He said, "Throw your net on the right side of the boat and you will find some." When they did, they were unable to haul the net in because of the large number of fish.

Then the disciple whom Jesus loved said to Peter, "It is the Lord!" As soon as Simon Peter heard him say, "It is the Lord," he wrapped his outer garment around him (for he had taken it off) and jumped into the water. The other disciples followed in the boat, towing the net full of fish, for they were not far from shore, about a hundred yards.[b] When they landed, they saw a fire of burning coals there with fish on it, and some bread.

Jesus said to them, "Bring some of the fish you have just caught."

Simon Peter climbed aboard and dragged the net ashore. It was full of large fish, 153, but even with so many the net was not torn. Jesus said to them, "Come and have breakfast." None of the disciples dared ask him, "Who are you?" They knew it was the Lord. Jesus came, took the bread and gave it to them, and did the same with the fish. This was now the third time Jesus appeared to his disciples after he was raised from the dead. JOHN 21:1-4

371

JESUS REINSTATES PETER

When they had finished eating, Jesus said to Simon Peter, "Simon son of John, do you truly love me more than these?"

"Yes, Lord," he said, "you know that I love you."

Jesus said, "Feed my lambs."

Again Jesus said, "Simon son of John, do you truly love me?"

He answered, "Yes, Lord, you know that I love you."

Jesus said, "Take care of my sheep."

The third time he said to him, "Simon son of John, do you love me?"

Peter was hurt because Jesus asked him the third time, "Do you love me?" He said, "Lord, you know all things; you know that I love you."

Jesus said, "Feed my sheep. I tell you the truth, when you were younger you dressed yourself and went where you wanted; but when you are old you will stretch out your hands, and someone else will dress you and lead you where you do not want to go." Jesus said this to indicate the kind of death by which Peter would glorify God. Then he said to him, "Follow me!"

Peter turned and saw that the disciple whom Jesus loved was following them. (This was the one who had leaned back against Jesus at the supper and had said, "Lord, who is going to betray you?") When Peter saw him, he asked, "Lord, what about him?"

Jesus answered, "If I want him to remain alive until I return, what is that to you? You must follow me." Because of this, the rumor spread among the brothers that this disciple would not die. But Jesus did not say that he would not die; he only said, "If I want him to remain alive until I return, what is that to you?"

JOHN 21:15-23

"Feed my lambs. . . .
Take care of my sheep. . . .
Follow me!"

FROM OSWALD CHAMBERS

❧ Jesus did not say—"Make converts to your way of thinking, but look after My sheep; see that they get nourished in the knowledge of Me." We count as service what we do in the way of Christian work; Jesus Christ calls service what we are to Him, not what we do for Him. Discipleship is based on devotion to Jesus Christ, not on adherence to a belief or a creed. "If any man come to Me and hate not . . . he cannot be My disciple" (Luke 14:26). There is no argument and no compulsion, but simply — "If you would be My disciple, you must be devoted to Me." A man touched by the Spirit of God suddenly says — "Now I see who Jesus is," and that is the source of devotion.

Today we have substituted credal belief for personal belief, and that is why so many are devoted to causes and so few devoted to Jesus Christ. MUH 171

❧ When our Lord commissioned Peter He did not tell him to go and save souls, but — "Feed My sheep; tend My lambs; guard My flock." We have to be careful lest we rebel against the commission to disciple men to Jesus and become energetic proselytizers to our own way of thinking — "but the shepherds fed themselves, and fed not My sheep" (Ezek. 34:8). When we stand before God will He say, "Well done, good and faithful servant"? (Matt. 25:21) or will He say, "You have not been a shepherd of My sheep; you have fed them for your own interest, exploited them for your own creed"? When a soul gets within sight of Jesus Christ, leave him alone. SHH 107

❧ Peter had boasted earlier of his love for Jesus — "Though all men shall be offended because of Thee, yet will I never be offended" (Matt. 26:33), but there is no brag left in him now — "Lord, Thou knowest all things; Thou knowest that I love Thee." "Feed My sheep." The discipline of Divine loyalty is not that I am true to a doctrine, but so true to Jesus that other people are nourished in the knowledge of Him. SHH 128

---

a. That is, Sea of Galilee
b. Greek *about two hundred cubits* (about 90 meters)

373

101

THE GREAT COMMISSION

Then the eleven disciples went to Galilee, to the mountain where Jesus had told them to go. He appeared to more than five hundred of the brothers at the same time. When they saw him, they worshiped him; but some doubted. Then Jesus came to them and said, "All authority in heaven and on earth has been given to me. Therefore go [into all the world and preach the good news to all creation.] Make disciples of all nations, baptizing them in^a the name of the Father and of the Son and of the Holy Spirit, and teaching them to obey everything I have commanded you. [Whoever believes and is baptized will be saved, but whoever does not believe will be condemned. And these signs will accompany those who believe: In my name they will drive out demons; they will speak in new tongues; they will pick up snakes with their hands; and when they drink deadly poison, it will not hurt them at all; they will place their hands on sick people, and they will get well.] And surely I am with you always, to the very end of the age."

MATTHEW 28:16-20; MARK 16:15-18; 1 CORINTHIANS 15:6a

THE PROMISE OF THE HOLY SPIRIT

Then he appeared to James, then to all the apostles *besides* the Twelve. He showed himself to the apostles he had chosen and gave many convincing proofs that he was alive. He appeared to them over a period of forty days and spoke about the kingdom of God. On one occasion, while he was eating with them, he said, "This is what I told you while I was still with you: Everything must be fulfilled that is written about me in the Law of Moses, the Prophets and the Psalms."

Then he opened their minds so they could understand the

Scriptures. He told them, "This is what is written: The Christ will suffer and rise from the dead on the third day, and repentance and forgiveness of sins will be preached in his name to all nations, beginning at Jerusalem. You are witnesses of these things. I am going to send you what my Father has promised; but stay in the city until you have been clothed with power from on high. Do not leave Jerusalem, but wait for the gift my Father promised, which you have heard me speak about. For John baptized with water, but in a few days you will be baptized with the Holy Spirit." LUKE 24:44-49; ACTS 1:2b-5; 1 CORINTHIANS 15:5b, 7

JESUS TAKEN UP INTO HEAVEN

So when they *last* met together, he led them out to the vicinity of Bethany. They asked him, "Lord, are you at this time going to restore the kingdom to Israel?"

He said to them: "It is not for you to know the times or dates the Father has set by his own authority. But you will receive power when the Holy Spirit comes on you; and you will be my witnesses in Jerusalem, and in all Judea and Samaria, and to the ends of the earth."

After [the Lord Jesus had] said this [to them], he lifted up his hands and blessed them. While he was blessing them, he left them and was taken up into heaven before their very eyes, and a cloud hid him from their sight. [He sat at the right hand of God.]

They were looking intently up into the sky as he was going, when suddenly two men dressed in white stood beside them. "Men of Galilee," they said, "why do you stand here looking into the sky? This same Jesus, who has been taken from you into heaven, will come back in the same way you have seen him go into heaven."

Then they worshiped him and returned from the hill called the Mount of Olives to Jerusalem with great joy. And they stayed continually at the temple, praising God. MARK 16:19; LUKE 24:50-53; ACTS 1:6-12a

THE SPIRIT COMES

When the day of Pentecost came, they were all together in one place. Suddenly a sound like the blowing of a violent wind came from heaven and filled the whole house where they were sitting. All of them were filled with the Holy Spirit. ACTS 2:1-2, 4a

THE GOSPEL IS PREACHED

[Then the disciples went out and preached everywhere, and the Lord worked with them and confirmed his word by the signs that accompanied it.]

Jesus did many other miraculous signs in the presence of his disciples, which are not recorded in this book. If every one of them were written down, even the whole world would not have room for the books that would be written. But these are written that you may[b] believe that Jesus is the Christ, the Son of God, and that by believing you may have life in his name. MARK 16:20; JOHN 20:30-31; 21:25

"You will receive power
when the Holy Spirit comes on you;
and you will be my witnesses."

FROM OSWALD CHAMBERS

❧ Thank God that the almighty power of Jesus Christ is for us. All power is vested in Him in heaven and on earth, and He says, "Lo, I am with you all the days." All the power of the deity of Christ is ours through His resurrection. HRL 117

❧ The basis of missionary appeals is the authority of Jesus Christ, not the needs of the heathen. We are apt to look upon our Lord as One who assists us in our enterprises for God. Our Lord puts Himself as the absolute sovereign supreme Lord over His disciples. He does not say the heathen will be lost if we do not go; He simply says— "Go ye therefore and teach all nations." Go on the revelation of My sovereignty; teach and preach out of a living experience of Me. MUH 288

❧ A missionary is one who is wedded to be the charter of his Lord and Master, he has not to proclaim his own point of view, but to proclaim the Lamb of God. It is easier to belong to a coterie which tells what Jesus Christ has done for me, easier to become a devotee to divine healing, or to a special type of sanctification, or to the baptism of the Holy Ghost. Paul did not say—"Woe is unto me, if I do not preach what Christ has done for me" but—"Woe is unto me, if I preach not the Gospel" (1 Cor. 9:16). This is the Gospel—"The Lamb of God, which taketh away the sin of the world!" (John 1:29) MUH 289

⮞ By His ascension our Lord raises Himself to glory, He becomes omnipotent, omniscient, and omnipresent. All the splendid power, so circumscribed in His earthly life, becomes omnipotence; all the wisdom and insight, so precious but so limited during His life on earth, becomes omniscience; all the unspeakable comfort of the presence of Jesus, so confined to a few in His earthly life, becomes omnipresence; He is with us all the days. SHH 189

⮞ God will never answer our prayer to be baptized by the Holy Ghost for any other reason than to be a witness for Jesus. "Ye shall receive power, after that the Holy Ghost is come upon you: and ye shall be witnesses unto Me." Not witnesses of what Jesus can do, that is an elementary witness, but "witnesses unto Me"—"You will be instead of Me, you will take everything that happens, praise or blame, persecution or commendation, as happening to Me." No one can stand that unless he is constrained by the majesty of the personal power of Jesus. AUG 31

---

a. Or *into;* see Acts 8:16; 19:5; Romans 6:3; 1 Corinthians 1:13; 10:2; and Galatians 3:27

b. Some manuscripts [of John 20:31] *may continue to*

ADVICE GIVEN BY OSWALD CHAMBERS AT AGE 23 TO A WOMAN WHO HAD ACCEPTED AN ASSIGNMENT TO TEACH A GIRLS' SUNDAY SCHOOL CLASS

Be yourself and not a Sunday School teacher, [and by that] I mean enter heartily into the lives of each of the girls. This class may be the means of most valuable training for future work as well as to the glory of Jesus Christ and the building up of character. Have in mind two foundation truths ever clear and prominent; let them be the foundation of all your teaching and winning and encouraging and sympathizing:

First, the fact of the imputed righteousness of Jesus Christ. Second, the fact that when a soul has had that righteousness not only imputed but imparted, then begins the true battle for the building of character, a battle in which only patient steadfast endurance unto the end can prevail.

Press home on their minds the readiness of Christ to help them; instill into them thoughts from the books you read; above all, show infinite patience with wrongdoers. Never simply say—"That was wrong," but teach them rather that wrongdoing is sometimes a way to right-doing. Don't for Christ's sake, be dogmatic; teach, in fact, as though you did not teach. Draw into your own heart all the weaknesses of your lassies; win them individually by patience. In the evolution of character patience is everything. God is infinitely patient with us, and we must have patience with ourselves and with the slowness of the growth of our spiritual life.

Another thing, do not prepare a lesson and simply go through with it, but ever be prepared to have your lesson broken into by questions. Take this class for Christ's sake, or don't touch it.
—From *Oswald Chambers: His Life and Work,* pp. 39–40, 1933.